THE COMPLETE BOOK OF
LIGHT-TACKLE FISHING

Mark Sosin

THE LYONS PRESS

BOOKS BY MARK SOSIN

ANGLERS' SAFETY AND FIRST AID
PRACTICAL FISHING KNOTS (with Lefty Kreh)
THROUGH THE FISH'S EYE (with John Clark)
PRACTICAL BLACK BASS FISHING (with Bill Dance)
THE BLAZED TRAIL
ANGLER'S BIBLE
ANGLER'S BIBLE (II)
PRACTICAL LIGHT-TACKLE FISHING

TO DAD

*with gratitude for showing me the world of fishing and taking the time to
teach me its ways*

Library of Congress Cataloging-in-Publication Data

Sosin, Mark.
    The complete book of light-tackle fishing / Mark Sosin.
        p. cm.
    Rev. ed. of: Practical light-tackle fishing / Mark Sosin.
    Includes bibliographical references.
        ISBN 1-58574-095-0 (pbk.)
            1. Fishing. I. Sosin, Mark. Practical light-tackle
            fishing. II. Title.
SH441 .S735 2000
799.1'2—dc21   00-036240

Contents

ACKNOWLEDGMENTS

No individual can ever claim sole credit for a book. This effort reflects a melting pot of thoughts and ideas gathered and gleaned from a multitude of others during countless hours spent fishing the world's waters. Trying to remember where each bit of information originated or how it got molded into its final form would be impossible, because the interchange among fishermen on theories, techniques, and methods is an ongoing process that adds a rewarding dimension to the sport.

I am deeply indebted to the untold number of anglers, scientists, fellow writers, guides, captains, lodge owners, and manufacturers who so willingly and graciously shared their knowledge and experiences. Many are close friends, many are mentioned in the text, but more are kindred souls whose lives touched mine ever so briefly on distant stream, quiet lake, remote beach, or among the rolling seas of the great oceans.

Special appreciation must be showered on Paul Johnson, one of the truly farsighted researchers of our time and a treasured friend, for providing much of the information on fishing lines. Bub Church, Dick Kondak, and Russ Wilson have been my fishing partners for years and they have earned my gratitude for so generously allowing me to benefit from their lifetimes of expertise. A full measure of thanks must be directed toward Lefty Kreh, one of the most skilled and learned anglers I know as well as a favorite companion on many trips, for always being willing to share his thinking on any fishing subject.

Frank Woolner, the erudite editor of *Salt Water Sportsman* and elder statesman of the writing fraternity, not only penned the foreword for which I am truly grateful, but he helped me to get started in fishing journalism and has coached and guided my efforts since that first day.

Soft-spoken and extremely modest, Nick Lyons is a talented editor, gifted writer, and sensitive fisherman who has a deep appreciation for the outdoors. Without his urgings and encouragement, this project may not have been completed and, for that, I offer heartfelt appreciation.

Finally, I must acknowledge my two sons, Peter and Lee, who are constant reminders to us all of the responsibilities we face in teaching the next generation the wondrous joys of light-tackle fishing.

MARK SOSIN

Preface to the 2000 Edition

Fishermen today take everything for granted. We live in an era of fast foods, ATM machines, satellite dishes that bring us a plethora of television options, and a computer-driven internet that takes communications and knowledge to new levels. People expect instant gratification and demand that others share every shortcut possible with them.

It wasn't always like that. A mere twenty years ago, life was different. There were no ATM machines, satellite dishes, personal computers, or an internet. Fishing tackle was relatively primitive by today's standards. Some of the tactics and techniques considered commonplace in the twenty-first century were either being developed or perfected a scant two decades ago.

This book reflects the findings and practices of a platoon of young turks who set out in both freshwater and salt to raise the bar higher and higher. Determination propelled them to explore new waters and accept the challenges of bigger fish on lighter gear. Some performed incredible feats and worked out methods that prove just as valid now as they did back then.

Progress is made by pushing the leaders ahead. Once a gap develops, others will rush forward to fill the void. That's exactly what has happened in fishing. Such feats as taking oversized northern pike on a fly or getting the elusive permit to eat an artificial suddenly are classified as commonplace. No species today can avoid pursuit by devotees of every type of tackle. Record book pages overflow with the names of those who have picked up the light-tackle gauntlet.

From a technical standpoint, this book remains just as vital, valid, and valuable as the day the material was first assembled. The habits and the habitat of most denizens of stream, river, pond, lake, estuary, and ocean haven't changed in eons of time. Given some minor adjustments and refinements, the techniques we used then mirror those that rank on the cutting edge right now.

The only somewhat dated section of this book focuses on rods and reels. In the last quarter century, rod-building materials have vaulted from basic glass construction to various types of graphite and composites; the new materials are lighter, stronger, and more versatile. Construction processes have also improved dramatically. Reels, too, reflect Space-Age materials and sophisticated designs. Newcomers can only imagine what it was like to wage war on big fish with gear that would be considered a bit primitive by modern standards. That helps to reinforce the notion that the strength of *Light-Tackle Fishing* lies in the solid instructional concepts rather than specific tackle recommendations.

Several experienced fishermen have reviewed this book recently and reported that it should still be required reading for anyone who appreciates the challenges and rewards of light-tackle fishing. I'm proud that it is being reprinted. After glancing at some of the pages, I think it's time to re-read it myself.

—Mark Sosin
Boca Raton, Florida
February 2000

Introduction
by Frank Woolner

Quite a few years ago a young man came to visit me: he had submitted an article to *Salt Water Sportsman*, the magazine I have edited for almost three decades, and he had decided to make outdoor writing a career. This may be commendable if you are willing to work hard and make little money at the outset, but my aspiring scribbler said something that made me bite the stem off a favored briar.

His name was Mark Sosin and the first story he submitted was accurate and nicely typed, yet unlikely to win a Pulitzer Prize.

The statement was hardly a wish to succeed. Mark said that he wanted to become "one of the best informed sport-fishing writers in the world."

Writing is a craft in itself, but outdoor writing rarely soars unless the scribbler has struggled through a long apprenticeship, traveled widely, learned precisely how to use firearms, fishing tackle, boats, and all of the other gear germane to the business. Usually, that takes considerable time.

It was obvious that Mark was well educated in a number of fields, and his father had taught him the rudiments of angling. Now he was dead-set on learning a rather exacting trade and fully intended to go for broke. I don't think he ever doubted that he would succeed.

Sosin had asked for criticism and I poured it on him. Each article he submitted was better than the last. Prior to 1946 there were only a few bonafide authorities, but it was then that the current crop of highly capable pundits began to cut their milk teeth. Today there are lots of them, and Sosin ranks high on the roster. He strives for personal excellence in craft.

I have fished with Sosin on several coasts and can testify that he knows what he is doing. True to his pledged word, Mark is now well-versed in all of

Mark Sosin with a fiercely dentured piranha from the Amazon Basin.

the angling disciplines, fresh water and salt, and he has exhibited remarkable tenacity in studying everything pertinent to the craft.

This study has not been armchair research: he has traveled all over the world to see for himself, so he is a fisherman as well as a fishing writer. Perhaps the exception to prove a rule, Sosin's early prediction wasn't far off target. He is one of the best, and that "best" is a select group. Be it known that he was a charter mover of Salt Water Fly Rodders of America and is now past president of the Outdoor Writers Association of America. One doesn't attain these honors without a good deal of recognized skill.

From the beginning, and perhaps mainly due to his father's love of angling for sport rather than the big kill, Mark seems to have been light-tackle oriented. While he sampled just about all of the various techniques "in training," that dedication to thin-string and featherweight gear is apparent in this book.

Practical Light-Tackle Fishing delights me for several reasons. First, it does not draw any sharp line between fresh and salt-water tackle, other than noting that each combination must be practical in its sometimes limited sphere of efficiency. The laws that govern tactics on small sweet-water trout are basically unchanged when the fisherman seeks a giant bluefin tuna or marlin. In either case one goes as light as is practical—without resorting to questionable stunt-fishing—and the only difference is a steady beefing-up of that gear which qualifies as light.

If this sounds a bit vague, look at it this way: an inland trout fisherman may go to a leader tippet testing less than one pound, and a fly so small that most people need glasses to tie it on. That's light—yet it can also be effective in the hands of a master.

At the other extreme, a marine angler who hunts giant tuna—fish that will scale anywher from five hundred pounds up to better than a thousand—takes a calculated risk when he employs fifty-pound-test Dacron. This is so because eighty is still considered light in many quarters and nobody apologizes for using 130-unlimited on half-ton animals of the sea. These are not forgiving fishes: if you are stupid enough to crank the drag up tight they will either drag you right over the transom or smash the heaviest of gear. Skippers don't double-bolt expensive, specialized fighting chairs to cockpit decks for eye appeal.

Therefore, as Mark has noted in several passages, all things are relative. That which he constantly drives home is the fact that light-tackle fishing is a supreme challenge, a game for the advanced angler. Here, there is no longer any appreciable margin for error. Everything has to be just right or—everything will go wrong! No if or maybe about this: it is precision work.

Initially, tackle must be the finest that modern technology has devised. Where reels are fitted with drags, said drags must be silk-smooth and easily adjusted during each stage of a battle with a great gamefish. One uses the best lines available and treats them with loving care. Knots and other connections, those you might shrug off as good-enough with heavier gear, are critical: they should be as close to the 100-percent factor as human intelligence can make them.

Margin for error, as one goes lighter, decreases rapidly. Sport fishing is never pure luck; it is always an art and a science. In light-tackle angling, success depends on highly sophisticated tools—*and* education. One cannot succeed without both.

It can be argued that a fisherman's skill is most important, and certainly this is the turning point of the game if gear is adequate. Unfortunately, a beginner is the poor soul who most often goes into combat with an impossible outfit. As he learns his trade, fine gear becomes an absolute necessity. He becomes an advanced angler.

As we move into the 1980s, so-called practical or even heavy fishing tackle will continue to harvest most gamefishes in sweet and salt. However, there is ever-increasing interest in the challenge of ultralight. Surely those of us who fish for fun must ultimately place sport far ahead of tournament wastage or meat on the table. A gauntlet has been thrown, and we will not bow our heads in defeat.

I certainly do not agree with everything that Mark Sosin has said in the pages that follow, but I cannot fault him because I am also midway on the yellow brick road—a mite confused, bemused, and searching for that proverbial pot of golden perfection at the end of the rainbow.

Light-tackle fishing is not new: it has been with us ever since Dame Juliana Berners and then Walton or Cotton (take your pick) espoused featherweight tackle. It is "new" in today's world only because it has progressed. There is greater science in it now, and yet we can expect rapid advancement in the art.

Mark provides known basics and he makes sense. He has been there—on the tinkling little trout streams, the big inland impoundments where black bass are being flummoxed by new techniques, on the air-clear ocean flats and the big, booming blue water of the sea.

We can "gabble and honk and hiss," but there is no substitute for experience on site.

1

Light-Tackle Fishing

The light-tackle approach to fishing is totally different from any other you might choose to take. It requires greater skill than other forms, offers a demanding challenge that can almost lead to obsession, and makes the sport much more fun for the participant. The beautiful aspect is that each angler can interpret it in terms of his own pleasure and desire. Since light tackle spans all phases of fishing from casting equipment to trolling and bottom-fishing gear, anyone can become involved regardless of where or how he fishes.

Everything is relative. There is no clearcut definition of what constitutes light tackle nor is there a universal description. The popular image centers around a short rod with the softness of a buggy whip that has seen years of service, delicate threadlike line that looks as if it were manufactured by local spiders, and a reel so tiny that it is masked by the hand that holds it. That's only one facet—and a minor one.

Light-tackle fishing is a carefully thought-out approach that centers around your own ability as an angler. The equipment must be light for *you* and it must also be lighter than standard for the situation. The guiding parameters are your skill, the species you seek, and the conditions under which you must fish. It is vital to accept this concept of relativity. If, for example, you must snake a largemouth out of an entanglement of lily pads or bully a snook from under a dock, it will take heavier gear than if you happen to tangle with the same fish in open water. A trout that rises to a fly on the edge of a current or a striped bass that crashes an imitation sand eel in a tide rip is much more of a problem than it would be if you had the luxury of quiet waters and ample room to fight the fish.

The light-tackle angler is not only in the minority, but his methods could inconvenience other fishermen under certain conditions. From the beginning, one must be aware of this and exhibit good sportsmanship at all times. If you are in a situation where playing a fish on featherweight gear would spoil the day for others, then respect their rights on the water and use an outfit that is heavier.

Fishing is not a static sport. You can help to mold each adventure by choosing the tackle and the method of fishing that brings you the greatest enjoyment. There is no right way and wrong way, nor do you have to follow the herd. The excitement of light tackle is a fantasy for many, when it could be a reality with a minor investment in time and equipment. One of the great dangers when you start light-tackle fishing is peer pressure. Others try to convince you to go lighter and lighter. The important factor is to start at a reasonable level and then progress from there once you feel competent. As you gain skill and improve techniques you may want to pursue tackle combinations that are lighter than those with which you started.

A fine line separates the upper limits of light-tackle fishing from stunt fishing. You should be aware of it. The stunt fisherman recognizes from the beginning that he is hopelessly undergunned for the species and the conditions, yet he persists in his quest. In many cases, he becomes obsessed by the desire to "pull it off" and make a spectacular catch. There is no doubt in his mind that he will have to go through countless hookups until he finally locates a fish that cooperates. In salt water, a number of anglers are doing this in an attempt to set records in the six-pound category. A handful of these specialists do have tremendous skill, but many who try are counting more heavily on luck than on ability.

Light tackle is much less forgiving than more conventional gear, but that's where the fun and challenge come in. Angler error can be costly and there isn't much of a margin for miscalculation when you are at the limits of the tackle. However, if you land your percentage of fish with the gear you have chosen, you are practicing light-tackle sport and you are not stunt fishing.

Many feel that the dolphin, which attacks baits and lures aggressively, is the perfect light-tackle fish.

When a fisherman decides to tangle with a twenty-pound steelhead in a raging western river on two-pound-test line and ultralight spinning, one might reasonably question the motives. The same outfit would make sense in gentler waters for palm-sized bluegills, but it must be labeled a stunt in wild waters for husky fish. Even fifty-pound-test line would seem as fragile as bakery string if it were tethered to the jaw of a marlin that weighed half a ton and looked like the younger brother of a freight car.

Light-tackle anglers have always been innovators and pace setters. They have to be. As pioneers, they have been forced to probe the frontiers and shrug off ridicule and laughter while working diligently to develop new light-tackle techniques. These fishermen have always had an unquenchable desire to conquer new angling pinnacles. Equipment has to be modified and methods have to be refined, but that is precisely the magnet that draws the dedicated angler into the inner circle. Someone is always tossing in bed at night wrestling with a way to catch a particular species or trying to come up with an innovative approach that will give him an edge.

Although they are primarily credited with developing the technique for taking sailfish on fly, the late Dr. Webster Robinson and Captain Lefty Reagan opened a much greater vista to the caster who craved big fish. Their contribution was the use of the hookless teaser to lure gamefish within casting distance. Teasing amberjack with live blue runners, and other forms of exciting fish, are merely offshoots and refinements of the basic concept offered by Web and Lefty. To these men goes the credit for enlarging the world of the light-tackle angler in a myriad of directions.

One could define light tackle as a way of life and who could argue. It gets in your blood and gnaws at your well-being like an itch that you just can't scratch. You find yourself planning the attack when you are away from the water and mentally reviewing experience after experience. There is never an end to it. When that 5X tippet parted on that trophy trout last fall, you were enveloped by total frustration. All winter, you recreated the scene in your mind and you know now that you should have used the current to your advantage instead of letting your quarry get too far away where you couldn't control it and had no hope of following.

Some light-tackle aficionados choose to specialize, limiting their pursuits to the fly rod with floating line or bait casting or trolling with six-pound-class tackle. They may decide to chase a single species or use a variety of gear against anything and everything that swims. Each individual must satisfy his own needs and desires, yet I choose to view light-tackle sport as a far more encompassing opportunity. To me, the accomplished and complete angler should be able to handle all three types of casting tackle—fly, spinning, and revolving spool—with equal aplomb, and be versed in trolling gear as well. There are few anglers who have taken the time to master the various types of tackle, but it is a rewarding sensation to be able to fish competently with any type of gear thrust in your hands or stored in the boat's rod racks.

Light-tackle fishing is often opportunity sport. There are periods when it makes sense for a variety of reasons to limit yourself to heavier gear. However, if lighter tackle is rigged and ready within arm's reach, it can be pressed into service instantly. If you are going to carry light tackle with you, take the time to rig it. Each outfit should be armed with the best possible bait or lure and placed strategically so that you can grab it in an instant. Hesitancy can cost you an opportunity.

As you hone your light-tackle skills, you will automatically become a better all-around angler. For one thing, you'll have a new awareness on the water that you probably haven't enjoyed in all the years you've been fishing. The qualified light-tackle addict is always thinking, always observing, and always working on solutions to self-imposed problems. He begins to reason and that, in itself, gives him an advantage over others. Knowing what to do and when to do it are important to success.

No book can cover all the situations you are likely to encounter, nor should it. If you have to remember what the book said, you'll never cut the mustard as a light-tackle specialist. The key is to understand the basic concepts and

Susan Sosin with an African pompano—a rare catch made even more meaningful on plug tackle.

then apply them. No matter how many variations you happen to find in the angling world, the same approaches apply. You only have to think about the situation and compare it to something you already know.

Those of us who make our living on the water and who must travel to remote areas of the world are forever faced with alien situations. There are species of fish we have never seen before and may never fish for again. We sometimes fall victim to conditions that are less than ideal, no matter how carefully we plan. Mother Nature can be depended upon to foul up the most carefully laid plans, yet those of us in this business must come back with results.

There are a few times when we fail miserably and crawl back home dejected and disappointed. Fortunately, these instances are in the minority and it is mostly because of mental attitude in the preparation and execution of the trip. If this book helps you to think that way, it will have served its purpose. As an example, no matter how much tackle one owns, there is always the question of what to take on the water. Even if you've never caught the fish you seek, you can figure the tackle out without much difficulty. And, when you find your quarry, you can come up with an effective technique.

The first time I fished for tucunare or peacock bass at El Dorado on Colombia's Vaupes River, a tributary of the mighty Amazon system, I was almost ready to admit defeat. Rains upcountry caused the river to rise higher and higher and the traditional methods that the guides touted failed to produce more than a token fish. Typical bass-fishing methods just weren't working and the local hotspots were as cold as an Eskimo's nose.

In desperation, we portaged in to a clearer lake and, with the aid of polarized sunglasses, I began to see an occasional fish lying in the grass. After casting to specific fish with moderate success, I suddenly heard a tremendous commotion along the opposite shore. A heron had been disturbed and squawked its fury at the surface activity below it. We went over to investigate and what I saw made me feel stupid.

Herds of tucunare were cruising the shallows foraging on baitfish. The baitfish were congregated in the newly flooded areas where they were feeding on insects that were being swept up by the rising water level. That's when the light-tackle technique of casting to specific fish paid dividends. With the polaroids, I could see the fish and it was easy to drop a fly or lure in front of them. The bass were aggressive and ready to strike anything that moved.

The same basic technique worked almost as far from the equator as one can get. This time, we were up in Greenland pursuing Arctic char in the crystalline lakes. No one in our group had polarized lenses and they would cast at random with mediocre success. With the glasses and knowing about presenting a lure in front of a fish, it was simple to spot cruising pods of char and cast to them. They could have been bonefish or any other species that one spot-casts to, but the techniques are the same and it is merely a matter of applying them.

Once you understand how to choose your tackle, use it, and then play a fish on it, you can journey to the corners of the globe and enjoy the sport with the knowledge that you will be successful. I have had the privilege of fishing with many of the top light-tackle fishermen in the world and all of them follow similar patterns. It doesn't really matter whether a person concentrates on

Northern pike are fine game on light tackle.

trout in a limestone stream, smallmouths in a deep, clear lake, or billfish on featherweight gear. The drives are almost identical and the approach to the problem hardly varies. All are students of the sport and exhibit a thirst for knowledge that can never be slaked.

The first step is to perfect the mechanical techniques. You must be able to handle your tackle well and without thinking. It has to be second nature to you and simply an extension of your own hands. Then, one must learn to fight a fish to the maximum that the gear can withstand. Again, these are basics. After that, the emphasis is on thinking light tackle and understanding the most effective methods. There are times when lighter gear is merely a substitution for the standard approach, but you will find plenty of situations where lighter lines mean more fish and the approach you take can help you to outfish those who adhere to tradition.

As you reflect on the concepts, ask yourself questions and try to come up with the answers. If a line parts when playing a fish, honestly try to appraise what went wrong. You may inadvertently have thumbed your quarry when you should have dropped the rod tip and let it go. Others may be catching trout and you're not. It may require detailed analysis to come up with the right reasons, but it's worth the effort. On some streams where the trout are skitterish, you could be wading too fast. That doesn't mean that you're not covering the prime lies, but by moving too quickly, you are creating a wake and this wake from your waders is spooking the fish before you ever cast to them. The point to remember is that you must constantly think about what you are doing and why. When something happens, there is a reason. If you

Sailfish are great for the light-tackle buff. They don't grow exceptionally large and will jump more when hooked on featherweight gear.

Don't ignore the carp! On four-pound or even six-pound test, they can be strong fighters.

Bluegills on popping bugs—or dries, wets, or nymphs—are great crowd pleasers.

can zero in on that reason, you will increase your knowledge and catch more fish in the process. The most common mistake of most anglers is to fish mechanically and not think about what they are doing or what is happening.

No matter how seriously you take light-tackle fishing, remember that it should be fun. Not every fish is a trophy and that also gives you an advantage. With lighter gear, even the smaller denizens are more meaningful and a pleasure to catch. If you match your tackle to the species, the situation, and your own skill, you'll add a new dimension to your fishing.

2

The Modern Rod

Light tackle does not leave the margin for error that is inherent in standard-sized gear. Knowing this, those who choose to accept the more meaningful challenge posed by lighter tackle soon become fanatics when assembling outfits; often they are unwilling to accept anything less than the best for a particular task.

Tackle is as critical as technique. A skilled fish handler, for example, is seriously handicapped if he struggles with a rod that just doesn't have the power to move the fish or to gain maximum performance out of the breaking strength of the line. In that respect, there is no such concept as "good enough." If you plan to boat or beach fish consistently with featherweight gear, it must be right for the assignment.

The rod is the heart of any light-tackle system and must be selected with extreme care to do a specific job. One has to understand from the beginning that there is no universal or all-purpose stick that can successfully perform under a wide variety of situations. On the other hand, a rod that is tailored to cast a certain weight lure and fight a fish effectively with a line of given breaking strength can be used on dozens of species in both fresh and salt water.

Every time you combine tackle, you should create a system designed to do a particular job. Rods and reels are never assembled at random nor are they purchased that way if you're serious about your sport. Equipment should always be added with a specific purpose and to fill an existing or anticipated need. All rods are a compromise at best, but the trick is to stack the deck in your favor by choosing rods for definite purposes.

The typical customer walks into a tackle shop with only a general concept of the rod he wants. Usually, the procedure is to browse among the racks of rods and systematically wave one rod after another in the air, passing judgment based on feel. Manufacturers are as well-versed in this method of selection as the fishermen and some readily admit that they build "store action" rods designed to feel good in an angler's hands when he fantasizes himself as one of the Three Musketeers and slices the air with a fiberglass rapier.

With the exception of selected flyrods, many commercially manufactured and mass-marketed rods leave something to be desired in their design. Since most users know little about the product and judge a rod by less than meaningful standards, merchandisers produce rods that *sell* well, not necessarily those that *fish* well. The ultimate consumer is usually delighted with his purchase and, since he has no basis for comparison, brags about his choice. The sad fact is that not every fisherman would recognize a top design if it were placed side by side with a "store action" model.

People tend to believe what they read on labels and rod builders hedge their bets by describing their products in rather nebulus terms. The engineers might be on target originally, but by the time the sales department finishes their analysis, the rod in question can perform anything short of a miracle. It is not uncommon to eyeball labels that proclaim a particular rod can comfortably handle monofilament from two-pound test up to twelve-pound test and casting weights from quarter-ounce to at least an ounce and a half. Other rods can easily be fished with lines ranging from twelve-pound test up to thirty-pound or even forty-pound test and cast lure or sinker weights from half an ounce to four ounces.

If these sound like exaggerations, they are intended to be to make a point. You're not going to find many rod builders who will realistically tell you that a given rod will only fish four-pound-test line. They reason that they might as well corral the guy who wants to fish with two-pound test and include the angler who prefers six-pound and even eight-pound test. Hence, the label suddenly reads from two-pound to eight-pound test.

Rods are effective only within a limited scope. Don't ever let anyone convince you that a rod can cover a broad spectrum, because it can't. You can always push a rod's limits in one direction or another, but when you do, you are sacrificing a bit of the maximum advantage. The optimum is to use a rod within the specific limits for which it was designed.

In choosing a rod, you must first consider three things: presenting a bait or lure to the fish, fighting your quarry, and the breaking strength of line or leader you prefer to use. The secret is to achieve the most meaningful compromise. It's not always easy to do and requires some serious thought.

Your own preference often has to be subordinated to one of the other two factors or both. If you must tangle with a big fish, then the area of compromise should be in trying to get the bait or lure to your quarry. When it is more

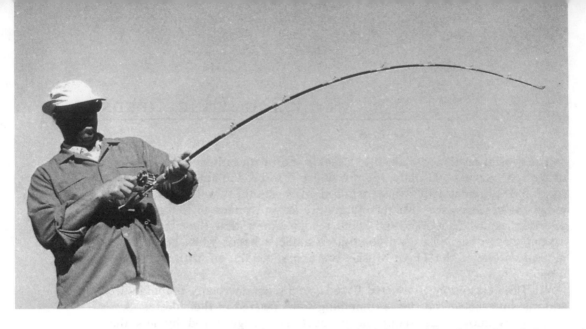

The short butt of a salt-water plug rod is designed for fighting a fish: it keeps the reel close to the angler's body and allows him to crank the handle with his elbow tucked in at his side.

important to present a lure of a given size or weight, then the fighting qualities of the rod are secondary.

Ultralight gear provides an extra measure of fun when tossing light lures to eastern trout or panfish in a quiet lake. It takes a delicate touch to handle two-pound-test line and even four-pound test doesn't leave a margin for mistakes. The same outfit, however, used in a glacially-fed torrent where the trout are big would be foolhardy. There is simply no way to turn the fish with gear that light and all you can do is hang on. A better decision would be to use slightly heavier line that would be a little more forgiving.

There are times when the decision must go the other way. Billy Westmoreland is a specialist in fishing deep, clear lakes, having had plenty of practice against the trophy smallmouth population in Tennessee's Dale Hollow Lake. In that part of the country, no one looks over his shoulder at a four-pounder and even a six-pound bronzeback doesn't make you a hero. Fishing with Billy is an education in getting trophy fish to strike. Over the years, he's had a few smallmouths up to the boat that would have broken the world's record and probably weighed more than a dozen pounds. Each time, the light line gave out just before he could slip a net under his hard-fighting opponent.

The obvious question is why Billy didn't go to heavier line instead of the four-pound test he insists upon using. It's all a matter of experience. Billy tried heavier lines, but he never got the big fish to strike, so he went back to the gossamer threads, reasoning that you can't land a fish that won't hit the lure. It takes a delicate touch to ease a big smallmouth out of cover and slug it out when the fish weighs more than the breaking strength of the line, but that's the way the game is played. Once you understand the rules, you can select the rod to do the job.

There are some who insist that you can't catch tarpon when they roll in the deeper channels, but my long-time friend Bob Stearns showed me years ago that a 66M18 Mirrolure (green back and silver sides) which is slightly more than three inches long can really do a job. That lure worked for us on tarpon in Africa as well as on this side of the Atlantic and the technique was the same. The problem, however, is that you need a seven-foot plug-casting rod and a smooth-performing revolving-spool reel with twelve-pound or fifteen-pound-test line to counterpunch that tarpon. After all, a hundred-pound tarpon is the rule rather than the exception in a lot of places and they are tough fish to bully out of deeper water.

The lure isn't particularly heavy and it won't flex the rod very much. It could be handled more easily on a spinning outfit, but spinning isn't as good a fighting tool as plug-casting tackle. The compromise comes in the casting technique. By letting enough leader hang down past the tip top of the rod, the effective weight of the lure is increased and casting is possible. A lighter line and matching rod would make casting a breeze, but unless the rod has the backbone to slug it out, you'll have a tiger by the tail with no effective way to end the tug of war.

Each situation must be considered independently and the rod selected accordingly. That's why it is often vital to have an assortment of rods available whenever you fish. Once, while Atlantic salmon fishing in Iceland, my ghillie and I spotted a healthy and husky salmon that had claimed a lie in a tiny patch of "dead water" between the roaring main current and a powerful back eddy.

Bait-casting outfits weren't designed for surf fishing or for big snook, but they can do the job if you pressure the fish from the moment it strikes.

From our vantage point on a cliff, not only was the fish visible, but the course of the river over a small waterfall and through a canyon made it evident that landing that fish was virtually impossible. The plan of attack dictated the tackle. It would take a bulky fly on a fast-sinking line to attract the salmon in the instant it had to make a decision; and the physical layout demanded tackle that could bully the fish. If that salmon could swim three feet to the main flow of water, the battle was over before it started.

Swapping my lighter flyrod for a model that comfortably handled a weight-forward 11 line, I circled the spot carefully and began to cast. It probably took ten minutes before the fly dropped on target (which was impossible to see from streamside) and the fish struck instantly. This was do-or-die fishing at its best. As I came back with the rod to strike the fish, my left hand clamped the line against the foregrip of the rod and I was determined not to let go, even if it meant breaking the eight-pound leader tippet.

For a moment or two, it was a matter of dropping and raising the rod tip, struggling to keep that great fish from getting underway. After stopping several surges, I managed to get the fish to change direction and enter the eddy. By the time I stripped line, the salmon was at my feet, brought closer by the swirling eddy; and it never did make the main current. Before the ghillie reached my side, the fish had been tailed and released; I estimated its weight at about thirteen pounds. The same salmon under a different set of circumstances would have been perfect for a lighter rod, smaller fly, and matching leader tippet, but I doubt if the fish could have been stopped with anything less than I was using—where it had chosen to take up residence.

If you must make a decision on whether lure presentation or fighting the fish is more important, the edge should go to the latter. In the case of the salmon, both aspects were important. When you happen upon such exceptions as heavyweight smallmouths in very deep and clear water, you may be forced to go lighter than you ordinarily would. However, if you can get the lure to a tough-fighting fish with tackle matched to the chore, you have a better chance of success.

SELECTING THE ROD

You already know that there is no single, all-purpose rod, so the selection should be based on specific need. If you are going to use very light lines, the rod must be particularly soft to act as a shock absorber or cushion. This is absolutely necessary with one, two, or four-pound-test lines. That's why properly designed ultralight spinning and spin-casting outfits are whippy and flex all the way to the butt. If they were stiff, you would break the line on the strike and wouldn't be able to maintain pressure on the fish. Another advantage of the soft tapered rod is that it can cast very, very light lures because it is soft enough for the lure weight to flex.

The trend has been to make these rods under five feet in length. Aesthetically, a short rod with a miniature reel makes an attractive outfit and garners the attention of most anglers. In many cases, it would be better to make the

Bjorn Bjornson, one of Iceland's great salmon anglers, still prefers the two-handed rod. With it, he can keep the line out of the water more easily and achieve a more natural presentation.

rods between five and six feet, because it is easier to fish with a longer rod than a shorter one. A five-and-one-half-foot ultralight rod facilitates casting and it also helps to keep the line high and out of trouble in certain situations.

Rodmakers do not want to set the trend or establish the rules. They are in business to make a profit and their philosophy is to give the angler what he wants whether it is right, wrong, or mediocre for the application. Few fishermen ever complain and those who reach the manufacturers' ears are usually specialists. You would think that the rodmakers would listen to experts, but they don't, arguing that the general public does not want what the expert considers good. There is certainly an element of truth in that; yet the leaders in the field know tackle better than most.

With ultralight gear in the four-pound or six-pound range, longer rods make sense when you are fishing open water. Sometimes, I will go to a rod that is six feet or six and one-half feet if I want to cast farther and have more leverage in fighting the fish. In those situations, where tight casts under brush piles or other obstructions are necessary, the short rod might get the nod, especially from the confines of a crowded boat.

As you move up in the breaking strength of lines or leader tippets, the rules change slightly. Six-pound test can be particularly troublesome because it is heavy enough to challenge big fish, yet it is still relatively fragile and there is little cushion for error. Salt-water fly fishermen have learned that with a six-pound tippet, they have to use a rod that would balance with an 8-weight or 9-weight fly line. If the rod is more powerful than that, it doesn't have the needed shock-absorber effect and broken tippets will become a way of life. Even if you seek a fish over a hundred pounds, you are still limited to the same rod because of the need to baby that six-pound tippet. If someone shows you a husky fly rod and tells you he catches big fish on it with a six-pound tippet, you have a right to be suspicious.

When the International Game Fish Association came up with its new six-pound category, many anglers had the desire to get their name in the record books, but were at a loss to find the rods that would be effective. Obviously, it would take a certain softness to cushion the line on the strike, yet one needed backbone and power to fight one of the husky blue-water denizens. Soft rods that were short might weather the strike, but they had insufficient lifting power to beat the fish. The longer your quarry is in the water, the poorer your chances become of ever landing it.

The trend today is toward rods built on the type of blanks originally used for live-bait fishing on the West Coast. They have greater length and a soft tip for tossing a small natural bait, but enough reserve power in the butt to battle a big fish. Any rod transfers the power toward the butt and it is there that the reserve must be adequate. The tip, of course, cannot collapse or lifting power will be diminished.

A great deal depends on where a blank is cut. The same basic blank can produce several rods of different actions simply by cutting it closer to butt, tip, or somewhere in the middle. This technique is used by custom builders to create some of the finest light-tackle sticks. Some fishermen believe that a personally tailored rod is much, much more expensive than a mass-produced version. It would be easier for all of us if I could list specific rods from major manufacturers and tell you they do a job. Some are super rods, but many fall short of the mark if you want to join the ranks of the light-tackle specialist.

Refinements in glass blanks and a new type of fiberglass have reduced their weight and added strength. A seven-foot rod can be amazingly light, yet tailored for a fish as big as you might want to catch. If you do pick a custom rod builder to make rods for you, make certain he understands what you are trying to achieve with the rod. These specialists can frequently offer sound advice on the choice of the blank and the final construction of the rod. Some are so good at their trade that you can describe a rod over the telephone and they will build a better rod than you imagined before you dialed.

Most rods for lines between eight-pound test and fifteen-pound test range from six to seven feet in length. One can no longer label a rod for fresh water or salt. Instead, it should be built to handle a line weight and the emphasis should either be on casting quality or on its ability to fight a fish. You can then fish that rod anywhere in the world and for any species of fish—*if* you use the line for which it was designed and let the fish you seek dictate either a fighting rod or casting tool.

Although spinning is still much more popular, the workhorse outfit both

Joel Arrington smiles after whipping a cobia on plug tackle off North Carolina. Mate Bill Basemore handled the gaff.

inland and along the coasts for the serious light-tackle devotee is the bait-casting or plug-casting outfit. Bass fishermen prefer a shorter version with a pistol-grip handle that is between five and six feet in length. The offset handle makes one-hand operation easier and the shorter rod works well in tight quarters. Here, too, there are personal preferences and variations. With lighter lures, you must have a slightly softer tip and this could mean a little longer rod. For some reason, most folks insist that a light rod be short, but that, in itself, is a fallacy. Action is the key and a softer rod that is longer can often cast better. When you are making precision casts around brush piles, in flooded timber, or in spots where you need a low trajectory, the shorter rod is an advantage because you can flip the lure under the umbrellalike limbs with less effort than it would take to handle a longer rod. You can also backhand the lure and keep the angle low. Longer rods are better for distance casting and for open-water situations.

Marine anglers created a fish-fighting tool in their version of a plug rod. Seven feet is the standard length and the butt is short with the blank running right through it. Veterans at this sport prefer a butt that doesn't exceed twelve inches including the foregrip, which is only an inch and a half in length. The shorter butt keeps the reel close to one's body and makes it easier to pump a big fish. Armed with fifteen-pound-test line, this is a tough outfit that can whip a sailfish, tarpon, or anything else you might want to cast to. Basically, these rods are fighting sticks and the uninitiated have difficulty understanding just how much punishment the plug rod can dish out.

A few years ago, fresh-water bass fishermen discovered what the light-tackle salt-water troops have known for a generation, and the so-called "worm rod" was born. This rod action was stiffer than the usual fresh-water rod and the argument advanced was that it was needed to work a worm in brush and set the hook when a largemouth sucked in the colorful plastic offering. The truth is simply that fishermen discovered a more effective fishing tool for certain situations and stiffer rods began to gain acceptance.

The prevalent idea is that a rod must be soft and whippy to be considered light. So many fishermen brag about their "light" rods and how much fun they are that one hesitates commenting or doing more than nodding in agreement. It would be heresy to point out to these dedicated anglers that their selection of a rod puts them at a considerable disadvantage for the line they are using. Few seem able to equate light lines with properly tapered rods that are strong and have a controlled flex.

Lifting power in a rod is important. It's another way of defining the reserve strength, backbone, guts, or whatever term you prefer to use. With fifteen-pound test, twelve-pound test, and even lighter stuff at times, you want all the lifting power you can get. If the tip collapses, the battle is lopsided in favor of the fish. It's surprising how stiff the blank can be and yet cushion a relatively light line.

In fighting a fish, Sosin's Law says, "Wherever the head of the fish goes, the tail is certain to follow." If you're going to move that head, you must have lifting power in the rod to lift the fish. If you have any doubts about how strong ten-pound-test or fifteen-pound-test line can be, rig up a rod and tie the line to a doorknob. Lean back on the rod and try to break the line. If the rod breaks first, don't bother writing.

There's a growing breed of largemouth fishermen who prefer spinning over bait casting because they feel they can work a lure better; this is particularly true of those who fish crankbaits. The most popular rods are six and a half or seven feet in length and they are basically stiff. Reels have high-speed retrieve ratios. With an outfit like this, the bass fishermen can move the bait better, gain leverage in setting the hook, and handle the fish better once it is on.

OTHER CONSIDERATIONS

Specialty situations demand tackle that meets a different set of requirements. The steelhead fisherman, for example, needs a very light rod that can toss an egg cluster delicately and have a sensitive tip that will enable him to monitor the progress of bait or lure. Steelies are husky critters and can be tough in fast-moving water. That means that the rod must be able to pressure the fish and have reserve power in the butt to absorb the transfer of power.

A steelhead rod is usually eight feet to nine feet in length and there are spinning models as well as those made for bait-casting reels. The added length makes it easier to cast a soft bait and, by holding the rod tip high, the angler can guide the progress of his offering downstream. For river trolling, the same rod can be held to the side of the boat and it will help to spread the lures as the skiff works back and forth across the current.

Flipping a live shrimp in front of a cruising bonefish or permit presents a

George Maki, a great steelhead guide, holds a typical product of his skill.

similar problem. The bait is very light, yet the fish are strong and it takes a good rod to whip them. Again, it's a matter of matching the rod to the situation. Veteran light-tackle guides often make special rods from fly-rod blanks for this type of fishing, but cut just a bit off the tip of the blank. There is still enough softness in the longer rod to ease a shrimp in front of a cruising fish, yet a fly rod has ample backbone to carry the fight once the fish is hooked. A stiff rod makes it virtually impossible to present the bait without casting it off.

Over the reefs, those fishermen who enjoy the challenge of working a deep jig and wrestling some unseen denizen out of perhaps 180 feet of water have another set of requirements. They will use a seven or seven-and-a-half-foot plug rod. When it comes to spinning tackle, the choice will be an eight-footer at the outside and perhaps seven-and-a-half feet on the short end. One reason for the longer rods is that there is stretch in monofilament line and when the rod is snapped upward to move the heavy jig, most of the force is absorbed by the stretch in the line. Without a longer rod, the fisherman would barely be moving the lure.

These jigging rods have very short butts that look totally out of place to anyone who has never used that type of tackle. You can imagine the reaction to an eight-foot spinning rod with a twelve-inch or fifteen-inch butt. Some viewers feel that the rod builder ran out of cork or just didn't know what he was doing, but the rod is a tool for fighting big fish in deep water. You want the reel close to your body so that you don't have to reach for the handle of the reel. That can make a big difference when you are sweating and trying to lift a fish out of 120 feet of water.

Muskie fishermen take the opposite approach and opt for a short, stout, bait-casting rod with an extended butt that enables them to put two hands on it. Usually, they are casting large plugs or a big bait and need both hands to heave it out. When they retrieve close to the boat, they want a rod that is short enough so that they can maneuver the lure in a figure 8. Many strikes occur right at that moment and it makes sense to keep the lure in the water at boatside. If it weren't for that aspect, the longer, salt-water plug rod would still be a better deal for this type of fishing.

The caster who enjoys working topwater lures makes other demands on rod builders. He needs a rod with a relatively stiff tip so that when he whips the rod back and forth to manipulate the lure, the plug will move rather than the rod tip collapsing. This is particularly important when working a stick-bait where you want to "walk the dog" and create a flip-flop action from side to side.

The typical surf rod has always been a mammoth creation designed for maximum casting distance and the ability to handle a great deal of weight. Even if you're not built like a gorilla, a rod of this type and length is imperative along some stretches of coastline to keep the line above the wave tops when fishing natural bait. The light-tackle angler, however, often takes advantage of other aspects of surf fishing. With a shorter rod and lighter lines, he probes the areas around jetties and he looks for stretches of beachfront where a slough runs close to the sand. By working pockets and cuts, he has eliminated the need for a longer rod and he often does better when he couples his knowledge with tidal stages. This type of fishing demands shorter casts, but the bait or lure must appear natural. At times, weakfish and sea trout move in the breakers and anglers fish for them with light spinning or plug-casting gear.

Gulf Coast fishermen favor the popping rod, a lightweight stick designed to move a popping cork for sea trout and redfish. These rods have fairly long butts and they are geared for the angler who wades the shallow estuaries in search of fish. Many of the commercially available versions of these rods have particularly soft tips. A slightly stiffer tip would make more sense both from the standpoint of popping the cork and also in setting the hook or fighting the fish.

Trolling rods sometimes confuse anglers also, and lead them to make a poor choice. Shorter rods are certainly better fighting tools if you don't have to worry about light lines and other considerations and that's why the standard models are relatively short. No matter where you troll, the rod must have enough backbone to drag the size baits and lures you will be using and still have the reserve power to set the hook. If the rod lurches forward when you are simply dragging bait, it leaves something to be desired.

The odds are that wherever you choose to troll, you will seldom catch a fish over a hundred pounds. The exceptions might be marlin, swordfish, some Pacific sails, tuna, and sharks. However, for most fishing, a rod that handles thirty-pound-test line is certainly adequate and it is light enough to have some fun. You can, if you prefer, drop down to twenty-pound class or even twelve-pound class.

There is a tendency among rod builders and particularly those who market nationally to overrate a trolling rod. That is, they will label a twenty-pound rod as a thirty-pound and so on. Custom makers offer you the option of two or three models within a given class depending on the size of the baits to be used and the species you expect to catch. Since line is the factor that determines the lightness of the tackle, it makes sense to use a slightly heavier trolling rod if there are options.

Lately, heavy-duty spinning tackle is being pressed into service for offshore trolling, especially for sailfish and white marlin. Spinning was never designed for this type of work, but specialized rods have now been created with gimbal butts to handle twenty-pound-test line. By securing a short piece of soft wire such as copper balao wire around the top of the reel seat, a trigger is fashioned that enables the reel to be put in freespool with the bail open. This achieves the same dropback as a conventional reel and either live or dead baits can be trolled.

The typical conventional trolling rod features roller guides, a machined reelseat, a fiberglass or aluminum butt, and a chrome-over-brass or stainless-steel gimbal all mounted on a glass blank. Even in lighter models, the rods are extremely heavy and tiresome to hold, especially when you are belly-up to the transom trying to persuade some blue-water heavyweight to come your way. It's true they are rugged and can take a lot of abuse, but it is questionable whether you really need this in rods for lines up through thirty-pound test.

My own needs forced me to look for another solution that may be of interest to you. Much of my work involves traveling around the world and fishing different locations. I wanted a rod that would be a good trolling stick, lightweight, and yet could be used to tease fish for casting tackle or even used as a casting rod in an emergency.

With the help of master rod designer John Emery of Miami, Florida, who built the rod to my specifications, we developed a rod that was seven-and-one-quarter feet long, had aluminum oxide guides instead of roller guides, was center-ferruled with glass-to-glass ferruling, and the blank ran right through the rod into the nylon gimbal. Cork was used for the grips and the reel seat was heavy-gauge annodized aluminum. The blank has a strong tip and fast taper, transferring the pressure into the butt where a tremendous lifting force is produced. It can bully a fish and it's a feather to hold. When it's not used for trolling, I can liveline a bait with it or perform a dozen other tasks. The ferruling enables me to pack it easily, the rod is versatile, and it's a pleasure to fish.

Whether you prefer to buy a rod ready-made or have someone fashion one for you, it's important to know what to look for in a well-built rod. Choosing the wrong rod is not only frustrating, but it can lead to lost fish. Remember from the beginning that even the trained eye can never be certain about a rod until it is put to the ultimate test on the water. With practice, you can get an idea of a rod's performance, but there is never a guarantee.

One of the easiest ways to make a selection is to fish with someone else's rod and then buy the same one or have the custom house duplicate it for you. That's not always possible and, if you're on your own in finding a rod, take your time. Fishermen have a tendency to wait until just prior to their one major trip of the year and then scurry around trying to find the right rod.

If possible, deal with tackle shops that will let you try the rod with a reel on it. That way, you can go outside and cast or rig up the rod and have someone play fish by pulling on the line.

The first step in checking out a rod is to get an overall impression of its quality. You are not concerned with rod action at this point, nor do you care about weight or how it feels. The primary consideration is to make sure the manufacturer used the best components, enough of them, and that he designed the rod with care and knowledge. Look at the stick very carefully. As a general rule, better rods have a minimum of five guides and a tip top. The only exceptions would be ultralight rods under five feet. These rods may have more guides, but if they have fewer than five, you should proceed cautiously. In fact, I would never buy a rod with four guides unless the blank was so fantastic that I planned to rewrap it before fishing. The reason is that there aren't enough guides to help the line follow the curvature of the blank when a fish has the rod doubled over. Fly rods will have a minimum of eight guides plus the tip top.

Underwraping a guide is not necessary, but when it is done, somebody took the time to add a step. Keep in mind that everything added to the rod, whether in materials or labor, translates into money. The finish on the wraps can be a key to the time spent in building the rod or the attention to details. That finish should coat the threads and become protective armor. If you can count every thread easily, the finish isn't very good. Quality rods are wrapped with fine thread. If the thread looks heavy, it's a labor-saving device.

Since you're going to be fishing with light lines, the guides you select are vital. Ceramics are among the most popular today with aluminum oxide widely used. There is also somewhat of a trend back toward top-quality stainless-steel guides, but nothing less than the best will do. A shock ring cushions the aluminum oxide to prevent it from breaking. Some ceramic guides will groove (in spite of claims to the contrary) and should be checked periodically. You can do this by rotating a Q-tip in the guide or pulling a nylon stocking through it. If there are any burrs, the stocking will hang up and so will the Q-tip.

Not all ceramic guides are the same. A good one will reduce line wear and serve you well. Hard chrome over stainless is another excellent combination, because the guides are particularly smooth and tough. Again, the guides you select should be chosen with care. They all look good when they are new, but the question is whether or not they will last.

Tungsten carbide is another material used in the manufacture of guides and it is extremely popular in some areas. However, tungsten carbide is a difficult material with which to work and if it isn't polished properly, it will fray a line in a matter of minutes. This material is susceptible to a crust forming around the ring if subjected to salt water and that can also be rough on the line. Because it is tough to groove, tungsten carbide is the first choice of wire-line trollers, but users of monofilament should approach these guides with extra caution, in spite of all the promotional material to the contrary.

All of these styles are made in fixed-foot models with a bridge or supporting member under them for strength. This is fine for standard rods, but with extremely light sticks, you may want to fish with a flexible foot guide that is made from twisted wire (usually stainless steel). These flexible foot guides follow the contour of the rod blank better when it is under pressure and they are lighter in weight. That makes a difference when you are using ultralight spinning. Flexible foot guides are not the primary choice of plug casters or fly fishermen. Makers of ceramic guides have been introducing extremely light-weight models (some with a single foot) for just such applications and many are ideal for the task.

The size of the guides and their placement are as important as style. Right after World War II, tackle innovator Bob McChristian, who is best known for his Seamaster Flyreels, produced a gathering guide (the first one in front of the reel) that had an opening slightly larger than a pinhole. The guide had two feet that raised it well above the rod blank. Bob's theory was that the height of the guide and its distance from the reel face were the critical aspects and not, as most people believed, the diameter of the ring. He could demonstrate his theory to your satisfaction with identical rods and then explain that the massive ring guides were a cop-out against accurate placement since they were extremely forgiving.

Paul Johnson, who is Director of Research for Berkley and Company and one of the most respected scientists in fishing-tackle research, reports that he ran a series of tests on the gathering or stripper guides on a number of rods. To eliminate the human factor in these experiments, Paul developed an automatic casting machine. By changing the size of the first guide and making all casts with the machine, he was able to determine that there was an optimum for each rod.

The size of the other guides and the tip top are significant. If you are going to tie leaders to your line, the knots are going to be enlarged and the guides must be wide enough to allow the knots to pass through without binding. It's frustrating to buy a rod and then find that a simple knot won't fit through the tip top or the first few guides. After a certain point along the blank, there is no need for the diameter of the guides to be any smaller in size. Sometimes, it is done to give the rod a more saleable appearance and a neater look, but the "improvement" is seldom functional.

Small guides on a fly rod can also be disastrous. You must have enough room for the line to pass easily through the guides and, if you are using the light wand against big fish, there should be ample space for the knot joining the backing to the fly line to pass through without bumping. If it even nicks a guide, it could part the line or break the leader, not to mention what happens to guides when a fast-moving line hangs up.

To provide you with some ballpark figures, the distance from the face of the reel to the first guide on ultralight spinning should be about twenty-two inches. You can figure twenty-five inches for medium spinning, thirty-four inches for the average surf rod about eight-and-a-half or nine-feet long, and seventeen inches to nineteen inches for a plug rod. The average distance from the fly reel to the stripper guide on a fly rod is about thirty inches.

Guide spacings should be progressively closer as you approach the tip top. The purpose is to guide the line when the rod is under pressure so that it does not touch the blank or fall behind it. An adequate number of guides will smooth out stress concentrations and follow the contour of the blank. You can test guide placement and number in a store very easily. Take a line and rig it through the guides (you don't even need a reel). Have one person pull down on the line as another holds the rod. Watch the curvature of the rod and the way the line follows it when the rod is under pressure. With a rod tailored for a conventional reel, the line may actually touch the blank or fall behind it. With spinning, there will be particularly sharp angles between guides if there is an inadequate number of guides or they are placed incorrectly.

Check the reel seat on the rod to make sure it is of top quality. It should be coated or otherwise protected against damage from corrosive elements. Annodizing or plating are two methods used to make metal impervious to salt or other corrosives. There are a few reel seats made from Cycolac and other plastics that don't require protection. It is now questionable how much value there is to a double-locking nut on a reel seat, but it does represent a touch of quality on the part of the manufacturer or at least his good intentions to add to the finished product.

The grade of cork used can be determined by studying it and comparing it to that on other rods. The finer the pores in the cork and the less they are filled, the better the grade. Specie cork is the name applied to the top quality. Other synthetic materials such as cellite, hypalon, and others are used for rod grips. Most are somewhat heavier than cork, but they are often more durable.

Handling a rod blank can be deceptive unless you have a great deal of experience. Without a tip top, for example, the action of the blank feels different than it will when the rod is completed. Weight distribution is another factor. Those blanks with fast tips and larger diameter butts often feel lighter than slower action shafts because the weight is concentrated near the point where the rod is held. Not until the blank is weighed will the angler believe the difference. In fact, some fishermen actually put lead in the butts of certain blanks to change the weight distribution and make them feel lighter.

Most rod blanks are smooth because a spirally wrapped blank was once associated with poor quality. That is no longer true, but the notion persists. Spiraling merely represents the cellophane tape used to bind the cloth fibers prior to the application of heat. Centerless grinding removes any trace of the cellophane and makes the blank smooth, but the operation is critical. Blanks with the spiral still on them are a bit stronger than the identical design that has been ground. If you have a choice and want a tougher rod or slightly stiffer one, take the spiralled version over the smooth. Otherwise, pick the smooth.

When cloth is wrapped around a mandril, the side where the cloth stops is called the spline. This is actually the stiffer side of the blank and guides should be located on the spline or opposite it. You can locate the spline in the tackle shop in a matter of seconds. Find a smooth floor (not carpeted) and spread your feet so that they are about eighteen inches apart. Put the rod butt in front of your left foot and hold the tip in the palm of your right hand. Use your left hand to push in on the rod about a foot below your right hand. As the rod deflects, it will snap one way or the other, coming to rest on the spline. You can actually feel the torque generated if you try to move it out of the spline position.

The time has now come to wave the rod around the store, but we're going to do it with specific purposes. If it's a casting rod, make an imaginary practice cast in front of you, flipping the tip sharply. Watch for the dampening action or how long it takes the rod to recover. The tip should vibrate, but the height and frequency of the vibrations should diminish rapidly and the rod should come to rest. A rod that continues to vibrate or moves from side to side with the evenness of a pendulum will be a poor casting tool and it is questionable whether it will transmit power effectively in fighting a fish.

Push the tip of the rod against the floor or ceiling and watch the bend that develops. Watch it closely. You are looking for flat spots and you also want to see how limber the rod is where it bends. Does it have a progressive taper that permits power to be transmitted evenly or is the rod limber and does the power snake its way along? If the tip is soft, you can't work a lure effectively and the rod won't be sensitive. You'll also have trouble setting the hook with a soft tip. The exception, of course, is a rod for very light lines where you need this forgiving feature.

Next, rig line through the rod and take a look at the curve as you apply pressure to the rod. Checking guide spacing is only part of the test. You want to follow the rod curvature foot by foot, looking for flat spots. Study the first quarter of the rod, starting at the tip. If it lays right out and the tip doesn't have any curve, it will contribute little to the rod other than length.

A rod designed as a fighting tool must have more reserve power than you might suspect. You need the backbone to lift the head of the fish and a good rod that is tailored for fifteen-pound-test line should be able to lift five pounds of dead weight off the floor with a foot of line extending past the tip top. This also applies for a big fly rod designed to tackle tarpon, amberjack, cobia, marlin, sharks, and anything else that grows big and unruly.

The handle of any rod should be tested for comfort. If you are buying a bait-casting stick, try various handles until you find the one that feels most comfortable. There are many interchangeable handles in addition to the one that comes on the rod.

Soft and spongy materials such as cellite are being used for grips. Some people like the synthetics and others find the softness fatiguing, especially when they cast all day. Be sure to run your own tests before agreeing to one material or another.

Cork has traditionally been the material used on the foregrip of fly rods, but there has been some use of synthetics as cork gets more difficult to obtain. My own preference is for cork because it is firmer and my hand doesn't tire as quickly when I hold it. The shape of a fly-rod grip is equally significant. The narrowest part of your hand as far as your grip is concerned is between your palm and pinky, yet that is exactly where you grip a fly rod. You're going to find that a tapered handle that gets narrower toward the reel seat on the fly rod is more comfortable than the famous cigar shape that has the narrow part forward toward the first guide.

When you're buying a fly rod, the most important test you can make is one to determine the natural frequency or recovery rate. Place the butt of the rod almost against your belt buckle with the shaft parallel to the floor at waist level. Hold the handle and snap the rod sharply either up and down or from side to side. Watch the tip and study its behavior. It will vibrate from side to side in decreasing swings until it stops.

A well-designed fly rod will vibrate no more than two or three times before smoothing out completely and coming to rest. If the rod tip continues to vibrate, pass it up because you'll never cast it properly. Each vibration causes shock waves in the line and these have to be removed during the casting process.

The height of the vibrations is critical. The first one should be the widest vibration and all subsequent ones should shorten very quickly. If a rod swings from side to side several times in a wide arc, you'll never cast it. The easiest way to learn about the recovery factor is to compare several fly rods. Within minutes, the whole effect will be evident. Then, try a glass rod in comparison with a well-engineered graphite rod.

You will also want to determine whether a fly rod has fast action, slow action, or a progressive taper. With the rod in the same position described above (butt at the belt buckle), swing it from side to side steadily and observe the spot where the tip appears to be hinged. That's the pivotal point on which the tip seems to swing. If it is near the tip top, you are holding a fast-action rod and if it flexes all the way down the shaft near the handle, the rod has a slow taper. A progressive taper bends somewhere in the middle. Both fast-action and slow-action rods can be more difficult to cast than a medium or progressive taper. In the first case, only the tip works and, in the second, the whole rod works back and forth.

Another way to make the same test is to hold the rod handle in front of you at eye level and let the tip rest on the floor. Use your thumb and forefinger to press the rod slightly and watch how the tip flattens out on the floor. If only the first three or four inches are flat, it is a progressive taper, but if the flat area exceeds six inches, look for another rod.

The longer and huskier fly rods often come with extension butts. Atlantic salmon fishermen sometime back in the dim recesses of history decided that a six-inch extension butt would be ideal, since it would hold the reel away from the body and make fighting the fish easier. The idea was on target, but the measurements were a bit off. A six-inch butt gets in the way and can be a handicap when fighting a fish bigger and tougher (with apologies) than the average salmon.

A rod must have plenty of reserve power to lift a fish out of deep water. This fly rod can raise five pounds of dead weight off the floor of the sea and still have something left.

The choice of most specialists is a two-inch butt. Instead of a removable version, it makes more sense to install it permanently and leave it there. When a heavyweight is streaking for the next county, you don't want to be fumbling in your pocket for an extension butt.

Rod color may seem totally unimportant except from an aesthetic point of view, but it can make a difference in some situations. White rods or those that are lightly or brightly colored may reflect light as you cast and could be seen easier by fish. This doesn't happen all the time, but in clear streams or on shallow flats, it may spook fish, because the movement through the air is more visible. As you hone your abilities in light-tackle fishing, you play the odds and eliminate as many negative factors as you can.

Whether you settle on a one-piece rod or a two-piece model is a matter of personal preference. There was a time when metal ferrules weakened a rod, but some of the glass-to-glass connections and especially those using a solid glass plug are exceptionally strong. If the rod you select is two-piece, by all means check the ferruling system and make sure it fits properly. The glass-plug type should have a slight separation between sections to take up the slack when the rod wears. There should also be a quarter-inch or so in the bottom of a metal ferrule. Once metal bottoms out, there is nothing you can do to make it fit. With glass, you can carefully sand off the bottom of the female section.

Many light-tackle anglers still prefer bamboo rods, and there is no doubt that, for special purposes, no material can compare with bamboo for "feel" and delicacy. Each bamboo rod, even those made by companies, has a quality all its own, and you should not buy a bamboo fly rod without first testing it. Be sure it fits your exact needs. A bamboo rod is a lifetime possession, something to cherish as well as use. Prices vary vastly, and a new bamboo rod made by an expert craftsman can cost up to $800 today; used rods by such vintage rodmakers as Dickerson, Gillum, Payne, and Garrison can cost even more.

Bamboo, for me, is best suited to fly rods, to the smaller rivers, and for fresh-water gamefish. There's no advantage to using bamboo in salt water; glass and graphite will do the job better, and give you an extra margin of safety when a truly large fish is hooked. And salt-water angling could well damage a delicate bamboo rod.

But on a smaller river, for trout or other smaller gamefish, bamboo can be a delight to use. Buy the best you can afford; they are a treasure to own.

GRAPHITE AND COMPOSITES

Graphite was the first major breakthrough in the direction of Space Age high-performance rod materials and testing is currently underway with other materials as well as composites. Understand from the beginning that all graphite rods are not the same, just as all glass rods are not the same. Some are better than others because of the amount and quality of the material used and others excel because the design is superior.

Sensitivity is the outstanding feature of graphite and this can be translated into more fish, because you have a better idea of what your bait or lure is doing at any given moment. Two of the best light-tackle anglers in the country decided to experiment when graphite was first unveiled. Fishing side by side, one used a glass rod and the other graphite. Both men were using the same lures and both were of relatively the same skill. At predetermined intervals, they switched rods. When the day was over, the conclusion was that the person using the graphite rod caught more fish than his partner and it didn't matter which angler had the graphite. This is not to say, of course, that graphite will make anyone a better fisherman, but it demonstrates the advantage of a more sensitive rod.

To understand this sensitivity, you must be familiar with the word "modulus" or modulus of elasticity. This refers to the stiffness of the material or its resistance to deflection. The stiffer the material, the better it transmits vibrations. Graphite is incredibly strong. On a specific weight basis (ounce for ounce), it is four times stronger than steel and twice as strong as fiberglass, but that is only true when the materials are compared at the same weight.

Graphite is about three times stiffer than fiberglass, so if a graphite rod is identical to a glass rod in taper, length, and design, it would have to have much thinner walls and a smaller outside diameter. The stiffness, however, makes it difficult to test a graphite rod in a tackle shop. Because it is lighter and stiffer, there just isn't sufficient weight to throw against the stiffness. That's why it feels so different than glass, which is much more responsive to testing. The only way to check a graphite rod is to rig it up and cast it. That goes for any type of casting tackle, whether fly, spinning, or plug.

The high cost of graphite rods coupled with reports of excessive breakage have kept many anglers peering through the windows at graphite, but afraid to own it. On the other hand, companies that know how to build graphite rods are achieving excellent results and breakage is minimal. A responsible outfit will certainly stand behind their products.

Any manufacturer who puts soft handles on graphite rods has a questionable engineering staff. The dampening effect of synthetics will destroy some of the sensitivity of the rod and that is precisely why one wants graphite in the first place. Put a casting plug on a graphite rod and drag it over the grass or a concrete driveway and you can feel this sensitivity.

Building a composite or a combination of glass and graphite is tricky business, because there are a number of variables. One of the major problems is that graphite fibers only elongate about 1 percent before they fail, while glass can stretch to 4 percent. If you have glass and graphite working side by side in a rod, the glass is only working at 25 percent of capacity when graphite is at maximum. The next few years will be characterized by experimentation and the marketing of various composites. In the final analysis, fishermen will have better rods, but the road to success will have its potholes.

When you cast a graphite rod or set a hook with it, you discover that it loads much more quickly than glass and it does so over a much shorter arc. Even in fighting a fish, the rod doesn't bend as much as a glass rod would, yet it is applying just as much power. In the beginning, you have to feel your way with graphite, because your body and mind are used to the stresses on a glass rod and the configuration is not the same.

Through the years, fishing rods have been overdesigned to incorporate an almost unrealistic safety factor. The amazing aspect is how much abuse a fishing rod can withstand. Short of a car door, there isn't much that will destroy it. Who among us has not used a rod as a probe to dig a snagged lure out of a submerged brush pile or hauled back in an attempt to pull a hook loose from a tree and tried to yank the tree roots out as well. Rods weren't meant to be wading staffs, depth gauges, push poles, boat hooks, or tree-pruning tools.

The trend now is toward high performance and this comes from correct design rather than building in a safety factor that is far too high. Light-tackle fishermen should be among the first to appreciate this approach. Nobody abuses a bamboo rod and yet many trophy fish have been taken on cane over the years. A fine watch can be carried anywhere and it will perform well, providing no one uses it as a hammer or door stop.

Cecil Jacobs, a specialist in Space Age materials for the 3M Company, points out that in order to gain sensitivity in a rod and develop a delicate action, you have to bring the stress level of the rod above 50 percent. If you are stressing the rod at only 50 percent when you reach the highest stress configuration, you are losing delicacy and sensitivity.

Glass stress levels are often as low as 40 percent, while graphite measures 60 to 70 percent. Engineers are not only working with a more sensitive material in graphite, but they are working the material at a higher stress level. There is less margin for error, but you can still roughhouse graphite within its limits, providing you don't try to duel a submerged tree stump to free a lure.

It is impossible using existing glass to design a glass rod at higher stress levels. There is a new glass now being used that does permit an increase, but not as much as with graphite. Stress levels between 60 and 70 percent now seem about the limit of practical sensitivity. The problem at this point is to educate the fisherman.

Although graphite can be made into any type of rod, some applications are more meaningful than others. The key situations are where a longer, lighter, or more delicate rod is required. The bass fisherman, for example, who wants to walk a worm over brush or feel the blades on a spinnerbait turn will marvel at the performance of correctly designed graphite. Ultralight rods will weigh less and be more sensitive if they are made from graphite. Surf rods can be made longer and lighter, opening the possibilities of casting even farther or working a stick that is effortless to cast.

Some of the greatest gains to date have been in fly fishing. Because of the stiffness of the material and its ability to store energy and unload it in a shorter arc, fly casters usually improve their distance with graphite. It appears to be inversely proportional to the skill of the caster. That is, the better casters will gain less than mediocre performers. The reason is simple. Timing and the ability to throw a tight loop are the keys to distance. Loop size is determined by the power stroke. The shorter the power stroke, the tighter the loop. It takes plenty of practice to learn to do this. Graphite, however, produces a shorter power stroke because of the nature of the material.

We talked earlier about checking fly rods for vibrations. Graphite has better dampening properties than glass and it reduces the standing waves and natural frequency better than glass. With the shorter power stroke and fewer disturbing fluctuations of the rod tip, you have to cast better. Graphite won't improve your technical skills, but it will help you to cast farther.

When you fly fish with graphite, you benefit from the sensivity of the tip, especially if you are fishing nymphs. For the first time, you begin to feel a trout pick up a nymph. Equally important, you set the hook faster with just a gentle flick of the wrist and you should hook more fish because of the speed with which the shock waves are transmitted to the tip.

As if this weren't enough, graphite has opened a new dimension of fly fishing. Many anglers in years past thought that it was fashionable to use short fly rods for trout, especially on Eastern streams where the waters were only forty or fifty feet wide. In practice, these rods were a serious handicap, although the anglers erroneously believed that they were taking a sporting approach. Anyone who was using a rod under seven-and-a-half feet (and probably eight feet) was fighting his tackle all the way.

With a longer fly rod, it's easier to roll cast and you can certainly handle the fly better. There is less line on the water and that means the possibility of drag is reduced. Regardless of material, you can strike quicker and more effectively with a longer rod and playing a fish is certainly easier.

The lighter weight of graphite has made it possible to design fly rods longer than was ever possible in the past. Picture the advantages of a nine-foot rod that can handle a 5 or even a 4-weight line or a ten-foot rod that will properly fish an 8-weight line. There are specific situations that are better handled with a rod over nine feet or nine-and-a-half feet, but the extra-long lengths are not the answer for every assignment.

Sometimes, long rods make sense for fishing in tight quarters rather than for distance casting. Not long ago, Lefty Kreh and I were in Pennsylvania fishing the *Caenis* hatch on Falling Springs. Noted fly tier Poul Jorgensen was with us and Poul supplied the imitations tied on number 24 hooks. The flies were so tiny that you couldn't see them on the surface of the water and could barely identify the materials when you held one in your hand. Trout were plainly visible everywhere and all the rod movement in the world couldn't distract them from their mission of gorging on the thousands of tiny flies floating downstream. It wasn't necessary to keep a low profile or mask your presence. The main problem was trying to figure out where your fly was in relation to the countless naturals gliding with the current. Even our 7X leader tippets were invisible to tiring eyes. The only valid method was to make a cast and gauge the drift. If there was a bulge near where you suspected your fly was at the moment, you tightened the line and hoped.

If we had nine-foot graphite rods or even longer ones, we could have maintained better control and achieved less drag on the flies. At that time, however, we only had shorter glass rods with us and we missed more fish than we should have.

3

Reels and Drag

There can be no compromise when it comes to the performance of a reel for light-tackle fishing. Settling for less than the best is as dangerous a practice from the standpoint of hooking and landing fish as purposely putting nicks in monofilament line. Experienced anglers tune each reel to perfection, take excellent care of them in the field, and hesitate lending one even to a long-time friend.

A good fishing reel is a well-engineered piece of machinery built with the precision of a fine watch. It is the pivotal point in a light-tackle system and not only reflects on casting accuracy and distance, but is the cornerstone of the fish-fighting system in your hands. One could easily speculate, however, that there isn't a pair of anglers in one thousand who attach proper significance to the selection and operation of a fishing reel. Most fishermen are content to listen to the advertising claims or marvel at the cosmetics of a reel without worrying about the mechanical parts hidden behind the side plates.

The serious light-tackle aficionado can be as finicky about performance as an overstuffed brown trout is about its diet. Impressive four-color ads in the popular magazines or statements that millions of a given model have been sold are not proof enough that the reel in question is a modern-day miracle. He reasons that anglers often have little idea of what they are buying and know even less about what to expect in performance.

Mass production results in substantial cost reductions and it has made thousands of products, including fishing reels, available to most of us at prices that we can afford. The word "lemon" has crept into our vocabulary in this context to explain quite simply what can go wrong with a mass-produced item at one extreme of the tolerances or another. The serious fisherman discovers that selecting a make and model is only the first step. The actual reel must be checked carefully to make certain it will perform as it was designed to do.

CHOOSING A REEL

There's a tendency among consumers to assume that once a product is marketed, it has been thoroughly tested by knowledgeable people and that it boasts the finest engineering. Unfortunately, the pressures of competition often force a company to play catch-up ball and they are more interested in getting a product on the shelves than in lengthy testing programs. Sometimes, the opposite is true. One company hurries to get to the marketplace first with a product and does not take the time to test it thoroughly. You'll discover to your disappointment that there is often a vast difference between laboratory tests and performance in the field.

Price should never be accepted as the sole test for quality. It may very well be an indicator, but there are enough examples of less expensive reels outperforming those that cost more to warrant further investigation. That's why the educated light-tackle angler approaches the purchase of a reel with "show-me" skepticism.

The first step in choosing any reel is to analyze your needs carefully. Regardless of how cautious you are in selecting the specific model, you can still make a mistake if you don't buy the reel that you need. The analysis should start with the type of fishing you intend to do and the rod or rods on which the reel will be used. If you plan to bass fish with a bait-casting reel, use twenty-pound-test line, screw the drag adjustment knob down to the stops, and tow-bar the bass out of cover with the rod, your primary concern is casting ease and not drag performance.

The angler who plans to use light lines for Chinook salmon or the salt-water enthusiast who is going to deep jig with that same bait-casting reel has a different set of requirements; drag is now crucially important. There is no reason, of course, why you can't have both features in the same reel, but your selection must certainly encompass the primary needs.

As you figure the principal uses of the reel, you must also consider the rod. An ultralight spinning rod is no place to clamp on a spinning mill that can hold three hundred yards of fifteen-pound-test line. The reel must be in tune with the rod and balance with it. You already know that the rod has been chosen to do a specific job, so it is now a matter of finding the reel that will hold an adequate supply of that line.

Consider line capacity carefully. The fresh-water angler will most likely be concentrating on species that are not noted for long, sustained runs. He can enjoy his sport with a reel that doesn't have extensive line capacity and not get in trouble. An outfit tailored for six-pound-test line may be used in fresh water for bass, trout, northern pike, walleye, catfish, and a dozen other species and it is doubtful that even the most aggressive fighter would not strip off fifty yards of line. Certainly a hundred yards would be the maximum you might expect in all but the most unusual fresh-water situations. Usually, the only time a fish takes a lot of line is in a river when it starts moving downstream and the angler isn't able to stop the critter or follow it.

Take the same six-pound outfit into salt water and you face a different challenge. Toss a jig or shrimp in front of a prowling bonefish on the shallow tropical flats and when that gray ghost slurps in your offering and streaks for safety, you'll watch a hundred yards peel off that reel in a blur, and probably closer to a hundred-fifty yards or more. Big-game fishermen who probe blue water with featherweight gear may spool upward of four hundred yards on a reel, since all that can be gone before they get the boat turned around.

Running out of line in the midst of a fight is almost inexcusable and demonstrates poor preparation, unless a larger than anticipated species happened to strike while you were fishing for something else. Fresh-water fishermen should invariably have at least a hundred yards of line on a reel and the salt-water sportsman would do well to use two hundred yards as a minimum and build from there.

Any reel you select should be able to withstand the corrosive elements of weather and certainly salt water. Since everyone interchanges tackle between fresh and salt water, there is no longer a valid reason to label a reel for a specific type of water. It doesn't cost any more to buy protection, even if you never expect to fish salt water. Simply make certain that internal or external parts will neither rust nor pit.

WHAT TO LOOK FOR IN A SPINNING REEL

Since spinning is by far the most popular method of fishing, let's use the reel as a guide in determining what to look for in the tackle shop. My own preferences have leaned toward open-faced spinning as opposed to spin casting, because it seems to be a superior and more functional system for many species and situations. With spin casting, the bell cover hides the line, so you cannot eyeball any problems before they cause grief. Line flow is restricted through the tiny opening in the cover. Line capacities are always much less than they are on open face and, as a rule, you would be hard-pressed to find an acceptable drag mechanism on most closed-face reels. A few exceptions do exist among ultralights, however, and these might be worth investigating.

The typical prospective purchaser will pick up a reel, look at the outside, crank the handle a few times, and tell the salesperson to put line on it as part of the sale. Most anglers have no idea what's inside a spinning reel or how it functions. It certainly doesn't hurt to look or at least check with friends who might have the same reel and learn how it has performed for them.

At this writing, the trend is toward fully skirted spools that drape back over the housing and prevent line from catching under the spool and dirt or debris from finding its way into the inner workings. In the future, other design wrinkles may be important and it pays to study several different models until you can determine the trend. There's usually a reason for manufacturers switching to a new design. The reason may not be valid, but you should be

Performance hinges on mainte-nance. After each trip, a reel should be cleaned and a demoisturizing spray applied to places where corro-sion might occur.

A reel should be washed off at the end of the day, but the water must be directed so that it washes parti-cles off the reel and not inside it.

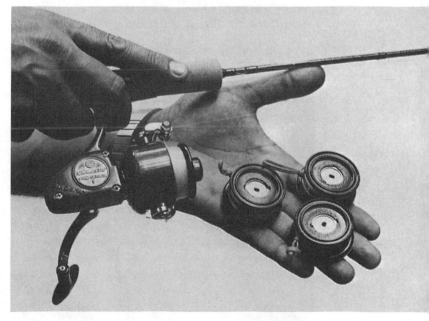

Serious light-tackle anglers are nev-er without extra spools of new line. It's much easier to change the spool than replace the line when you are on the water. Spare spools may have line of the same or different break-ing strength.

aware of it. Of course, that doesn't mean you have to toss all your old reels in the scrap heap and replace them. When you find a good reel, keep using it until someone can show you a better model that is far superior. Even though skirted spools are once again in vogue, I continue to use some reels that have performed well over the years even though they don't boast the latest features. You can count on those reels to perform and the drag systems are honed to a smoothness that the manufacturer never considered. Why change?

While you are examining the outside of the reel, look at the roller and bail assembly. A poorly designed roller that will not rotate under pressure can destroy monofilament line very quickly. The material from which the roller is made is another consideration. Tungsten carbide has been used on a number of reels in recent years because it is a very hard material and will not groove. The problem, however, is that it can be very abrasive if it is not polished to perfection and that is sometimes difficult to do. Hard chrome over stainless steel may be a more suitable type of roller.

Rollers are often wedge-shaped and taper down to a very narrow end. Line works down in the notch or groove and it is virtually impossible for the roller to turn under pressure. A buildup of dirt under the sleeve compounds the problem. You can get a clue whether or not a roller will turn by running a piece of line over it while exerting pressure on the line with your hands.

Bails have caused spinning enthusiasts more trouble over the years than all other things combined. Even the best bails are somewhat fragile, so it pays to ferret out the strongest you can find. Bail springs at one time were the curse of the light-tackle angler. They always seemed to fail at a critical time and more than one sport found himself trying to replace the spring in the field or threatening to destroy the reel on the spot.

The latest reels boast bails without springs that can be closed manually or

Newcomers tend to blame it on the line, but carbide rollers on spinning reels often fray monofilament. Rollers should be kept lubricated and free of dirt so that they can turn.

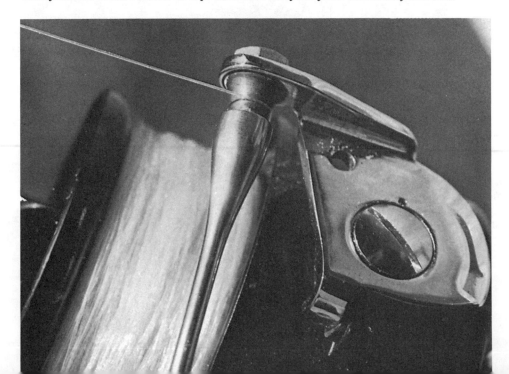

automatically via a trip lever. This is an important option in the newer reels and worth considering. If you travel a great deal, you may want to investigate models in which the bail folds alongside the housing. The bail springs in any reel that still has them should be examined closely. Test the bail by opening it half way and then letting it snap shut. There should be plenty of tension. At the same time you buy the reel, purchase an extra set of springs and carry them in your tackle box. If the day comes when you need them, you'll smile gleefully.

Automatic bails that pop open at the touch of a lever are somewhat questionable for the serious angler. The more mechanical gadgets you have, the greater the chance of a malfunction in the field—and it could be costly. Manual pickup rollers, however, have probably been underplayed over the years. Most are very good because they are larger than the standard rollers and they will turn under pressure. If you've tried these and have had trouble getting the line back behind the roller (which must also be done manually), all you have to do is pick the line up on your finger and turn the handle an instant before the lure hits the water. Once you get used to the technique, it is automatic and can be performed time and time again.

In fishing for permit with a live crab, the technique is to cast in front of the fish and swim the bait naturally until the permit charges it. Then, drop the rod tip, open the bail or remove the line from behind the roller, and let the fish move off with your offering. Then, engage the reel, wait for the line to come tight, and strike the fish. It's simple enough, except when you are using a reel with manual pickup. As the fish moves off, there is no way you are going to get the line back on the roller without cutting a neat and painful groove in your finger.

That is the main disadvantage of fishing bait with a manual pickup and it applies to many more situations than permit. The manuals are fine for artificial lures, but somewhat questionable whenever it is necessary to freespool line.

Many of the latest spinning reels offer the owner the option of a left or right-hand retrieve by doing nothing more than switching the handle from one side to the other. If you're naturally right-handed, you should be reeling with your left hand and vice versa. The handle length and shape should also be considered. On small reels, the knob is frequently fashioned so that you can squeeze it between the thumb and first finger of the hand with which you reel. Engineers spend a lot of time figuring out shapes for this grip and you should make certain it is comfortable for your hand before you buy the reel. Larger reels generally feature a torpedo or rectangular shape and some of the massive spinning mills may even have doorknob handles. The larger ones are designed to slip between the middle finger and ring finger in the same manner that you grip a rod with a spinning reel mounted on it.

Cosmetics and appearance are particularly important to a reel manufacturer. His goal is to attract you to his product and then have you pick it up and try it with the eventual result of selling it to you. All of us can be motivated by appearance. Sometimes, however, appearance can work negatively. If you saw a tiny handle on a large spinning reel, it would look out of place and wouldn't give the feeling of power and massiveness that a bulky handle with a big knob would create. If the knob is comfortable in your hand, that's no problem, but a long handle can be.

You are much more efficient in reeling if you spin your wrist instead of cranking your arm. In fact, you gain retrieve speed in the sense that you can spin your wrist much faster than you can turn it. When you are working a lure cast after cast or trying to recover line as you pump a hard-fighting fish, a shorter arm on the spinning reel gives you an advantage. Manufacturers, for whatever reason they choose, are not about to buck tradition and start offering the option of a shorter handle. Usually, you have to modify your own or have someone else do it for you, if you want a shorter handle. If the reels aren't too far apart in general size, the threads will usually be the same and you can adapt the handle from the smaller reel on the larger one. It's a trick worth knowing and remembering.

Not every dealer and particularly not the discount houses are willing to let you remove the side plate to inspect the inner workings of the reel, but it's worth the time if you can get permission to do so. Unless you are a machinist or have a working knowledge of metals, you may not be able to detect anything, but it's worth a glance. Try to get a general impression of how the parts mesh together, how simple the working mechanism is (there's usually less to go wrong with a basic design), and if the reel maker is trying to take such shortcuts as slipping plastic parts where metal should be. The plastic might be adequate, but at least you can question its presence.

THE DRAG SYSTEM

More fish are lost on light gear because of an improperly functioning or poorly designed drag system than for any other reason. The prospective light-tackle angler who buys a reel without thoroughly testing the drag may be stacking the deck against himself. On a spinning reel, the drag should be physically located as close to the spool as possible because this is one way of moving toward smoothness. If you must work through a gear train to apply drag, you suffer from variations in gears and teeth.

Instead of thinking of drag as a brake, consider it to be a *resistance to rotation*. A brake brings a moving object to a stop. When you are fighting a fish, you don't want the spool to lock up and stop yielding line or you'll break the line. You merely want resistance created that will slow the spool down or force the fish to overcome a predetermined pressure before it can take line.

In discussing drag with senior engineer Gary Oberg and design engineer Bob McMickle of Berkley and Company, I learned that drag performance on spinning reels is directly related to the machining of the spool. These experts point out that if the hole through the spool that accepts the shaft or axle is not perpendicular to the drag surface, you will have an erratic drag. That's a good reason in itself to try an individual reel before you buy. In those companies where precision is ignored instead of worshipped, manufacturers often create a "floating spool" that will offer large enough tolerances to counter poor construction. It's one way of skirting precision.

All good drag systems in spinning according to these engineers are spring-loaded. That means there is a spring in series with the drag that exerts continuous pressure. The springs allow much better resolution and also provide a cushioning effect in taking up variations.

A retaining ring holds most drag systems in the face of spinning reel spools. The drag adjustment knob exerts pressure to the system and also holds the spool on the axle. Almost everybody takes the sequence of washers in the drag system for granted and few anglers ever remove the retaining ring to check. It's worth the effort. You are looking for the amount of surface area (number of washers and size) and effective drag, but equally important, you want to make sure there is a hard washer and then a soft and then a hard washer and so on. Hard washers are alternately keyed to spool and shaft. As a general rule, the more stages a drag has (hard and soft washers), the better it will perform, assuming, of course, that materials are correctly chosen.

Even if you cannot remove the drag system and inspect it, there are a number of tests you can make and these should be performed regardless of any other inspections. Start by checking the drag in a light condition. Put a spool of line on the reel, rig the line over the roller, and let about eighteen inches extend. Set the drag so that the weight of the reel is sufficient to make the reel barely lower itself. You'll have to play with the drag adjustment knob to do this, but that's easy to accomplish. Nobody fishes with a drag setting that light, but it's a good starting point for testing. If the reel lowers itself in jerks or unevenly, you can assume that the drag is erratic and that there are flaws in construction.

A good reel has a full range of drag adjustments and you can feel them as you continue to turn the knob. Avoid a reel that will go from barely any drag to full drag in about a half turn of the drag adjustment knob. The fine settings are very important when you are trying to establish a precise amount of drag.

Drags on spinning reels should be removed and inspected periodically. Washers should be lubricated and replaced when necessary.

Drag on a reel should be set with a scale so that you know the exact amount. Always measure it on a straight pull from the reel.

After you complete the test of lowering the reel by its own weight, mark the setting of the drag adjustment knob and start turning it clockwise until the reel is fully locked up. Make these adjustments slowly, pulling the line after each change to determine that the drag is getting progressively stronger and that it doesn't happen suddenly at one point. From the setting where the reel lowered itself, it should take one full turn (360 degrees) to reach maximum drag. This is a minimum and it can be to your advantage if it takes more, providing, of course, the drag increases progressively and not all at once.

Now back off on the drag knob a bit and yank on the line. You are trying to detect variations in starting drag. It takes more effort to start the spool turning than to keep it turning. Some reels have a considerable differential, which could be trouble on the water in a tight situation. If there is a youngster around who will take the line and run with it, encourage him to do so while you monitor the reel. The rod tip should tip toward the child and remain there as line comes off the reel. If the rod tip bounces up and down, the drag is anything but smooth.

As you crank the line back on the spool, make certain the line does not pile up on the front or back lip of the spool. Line buildup means that the spool must be realigned with shim washers. When the spool is pushed too far out (say from too many drag washers), line piles up on the back. If you don't push the spool out far enough, line piles up on the front.

Most reels are too loose rather than too tight and shim washers under the rotating head may make a difference. You can check this by holding the rotating head and turning the handle. Excessive looseness will be obvious. Before adding any washers, however, remember that you don't want the line to pile forward on the spool and you must test each addition first.

THE BAIT-CASTING REEL

There has been a rebirth in the popularity of the bait-casting reel (or the plug reel, as it is known by the salt-water crew) because anglers are beginning to recognize that it's fun to fish, easier to obtain casting accuracy, and a much more competent fighting tool than a spinning reel. Choosing the right size for your needs follows the same basic procedure outlined for a spinning reel, except that you will be looking at a different type of construction and drag system.

Bait-casting reels come in a variety of sizes, but there are three major categories. For heavy fresh-water fishing such as muskies and a number of salt-water assignments, the preferred size will hold approximately two hundred fifty yards of fifteen-pound-test line. Medium-size reels can spool about two hundred yards of twelve or fifteen-pound test, while the smaller reels are tailored for lighter lines and even less capacity. Some anglers still enjoy using reels that are antiques and boast direct drive with no drag for such assignments as river smallmouth fishing, trout, and other species that don't tax the equipment.

The major problem in using light lines with bait-casting reels centers around the tolerances between the reel frame and the flange of the spool. Frequently, light line will slip behind the spool, forcing you to take the reel apart to release it. Usually, the line becomes nicked or frayed back there, so you then have to rerig the outfit and that takes more time. If you intend to use very light line, check the tolerances before you buy the reel.

Analyze the fishing you plan to do and select the reel that will give you the proper line capacity. For bass fishing, the narrower spool models are easier to cast and, even with a centrifugal brake to prevent backlashes (or overruns, if you prefer), it does make a difference. Everyone's hand size differs and many of us have our own ideas of what feels comfortable. Don't take any chances. Put the reel on the rod and cup it as if you were retrieving line. One style may feel more comfortable as you go through the motions of fishing.

The centrifugal brake, located on the left sideplate of the reel, adjusts spool tension and determines how freely it will turn. A wide range of adjustments can be important, because you will need the variations for different lures and wind conditions. Rig up the rod and hang a lure or casting plug on the end. With the reel in freespool, turn the centrifugal brake adjustment knob clockwise until the descent of the lure is stopped. Try casting at this setting and you should find that you don't have to thumb the reel at all once the cast is made and it still won't backlash. Now run a series of tests by backing off the adjustment knob and you will be able to move the spool from side to side. Remember that tightening the brake eliminates the lateral play, but it also sacrifices casting distance for backlash control. The better reels come with spare parts that include different-size centrifugal weights so that you can increase the dampening action or decrease it depending on the situation and your skill.

Follow the same series of drag tests with bait casting as you did with spinning. Within the last couple of years, manufacturers of bait-casting reels have made significant improvements in their drag systems and most stock reels have relatively smooth drags. Back in the middle 1960s and earlier, some of us started to modify the drags on the more popular bait-casting reels because the factory versions were literally unfishable on species that ran more than a dozen yards.

The parts of a bait-casting reel are exposed in this cutaway model. Note that when the star wheel is tightened, this pushes a spring against the drag plate. The drag is located inside the main gear.

Larger power handles make it easier to fight a big fish on a bait-casting reel. They also help when you need a fast retrieve. Handles are available for most of the popular reels and can be installed quickly.

If you intend to fight big fish with a bait-casting reel, it must have a smooth drag. This model has two large drag washers and two pressure plates, creating a multi-stage effect.

In fact, Lefty Kreh, Norman Jansik, Gordon Young, and I worked on the modification that has been the forerunner of the present drag systems and eventually offered it to a major reel manufacturer. That reel maker rejected the idea after agreeing that it was far superior to the system in their reels. Others, however, exhibited a bit more vision and did not hesitate to copy the principle. They are somewhat surprised today to learn how long their "revolutionary new system" has been around.

When you examine a bait-casting reel, study the design of the level-wind mechanism and its construction. Knowledgeable anglers prefer level winds that do not disengage when the cast is made. They reason that unless the level wind and the line move together, the line will cut across at an angle while fighting a fish and this could cause it to fray or break. It's not worth the risk.

THE FLY REEL

With the exception of the husky, specially designed fly reels for salmon and the larger salt-water species, the question of drag is academic. Most fly reels are merely storage cylinders around which a fly line and perhaps a little backing for safety are wrapped. The concern of selective anglers is for a lightweight reel that will not add an undue burden to the rod. Other features of importance are the design from the standpoint of line tangling around a projection when the cast is made, a good click mechanism that will prevent an overrun in the event a bigger fish than expected is hooked and takes line, and quality components that wear well.

Some fishermen prefer a flange on the spool or a method of exerting finger pressure to brake the reel when necessary. The typical fly-rod fish seldom demands this form of attention, but it could be critical if a trophy-sized critter inhales fly or popping bug.

Salmon and the tough combatants of salt water, fish that may easily weigh more than twenty pounds and more likely would pull the needle on the scale to seventy-five pounds, place a significant challenge in front of the handful of anglers who pursue them. Tarpon, sharks, billfish, amberjack, cobia, and even those big striped bass that are becoming commonplace in fresh water have all been landed on reels without a drag, but that's doing it the hard way. A smooth drag not only increases one's chances, but the pride of ownership that comes from a handcrafted fly reel is often worth the price.

Bob McChristian's Seamaster and the FinNor were once the only two big-game fly reels available and they still rank among the best. The number of fish that have been taken on these legendary reels is staggering. In the past couple of years, several new entries are on the market including the John Emery fly reel, the Billy Pate reel, and the Hart reel. The Pflueger Supreme 578 is a mass-produced fly reel with some fine features at a lower cost than the hand-machined reels. It is excellent for the casual participant, but cannot compare to the more expensive models.

Salmon anglers have traditionally worshipped the Bogdan reel, but production has always been extremely limited. Stanley Bogdan is a master machinist

An impressive number of salt-water and salmon fly reels are on the market today. Among the things to look for are adequate line capacity and a smooth drag.

and his reels are magnificent, but the salt-water specialists always felt they had too many working parts and opted for Seamasters, FinNors, and others that are marvels in simplicity and boast a minimum of parts.

Salt-water fly fishermen demand drags that can take extreme punishment and still perform smoothly, because light leader tippets aren't very forgiving. Line capacity is equally vital. Even the standard models hold two hundred fifty yards of thirty-pound-test Dacron backing plus a WF-13-F fly line (you bet there's a number 13). The trend nods toward even more line capacity because all of these reels are single action (one revolution of the handle for one revolution of the spool) and the fly line itself takes up a lot of room. By increasing the basic reel size, the fly line on a percentage basis takes up less spool capacity and that means the *working* spool diameter is greater, enabling the user to recover line faster and more with every revolution.

In many salt-water situations, the fish is spotted before the fly is presented and mistakes are disastrous. If the fly line wraps around an external projection on the reel, it might destroy the cast or, if the fish does strike, it will pop the leader instantly. Even the handles are tapered so that line will fall off and everything possible is done to mask any projections that could catch or foul the line.

The big difference of opinion in choosing a reel centers on whether it is better to use a reel with a direct drive and without an anti-reverse or to fish with a reel that has an anti-reverse and not worry about the handle turning backward when line is pulled from the reel. The decision is not easy. A number of veteran anglers have been focusing on direct-drive reels of late. There is no anti-reverse on these mills. These experts reason that when they recover line in fighting a fish, they want to know that every time they turn the handle, line is coming in. With an anti-reverse reel (which has the advantage of protecting your knuckles from being laid open by a rap from the whirring handle), you are not always certain when you are recovering line. Others disagree and opt for the anti-reverse. Bob McChristian makes his Seamasters both ways and both types are superb.

With exceptionally light leader tippets and a correspondingly light drag setting, you should use a direct-drive reel without an anti-reverse. On a very low setting, the anti-reverse will cause problems and you might not be able to recover line because the drag will slip before you generate enough pressure to keep the spool revolving. With direct drive, you know that the spool turns when you rotate the handle.

The super-deluxe reels for the serious salmon or salt-water fly fisherman range in price from about $150 to over $300. All of the reels are well made and you won't suffer with any of them.

TROLLING AND CONVENTIONAL REELS

Although a smooth drag still ranks as the primary consideration in selecting any reel, the bigger reels make it easier for engineers to design superior systems simply because there is much more room inside the sideplates. When trolling for salmon in the Great Lakes or along the Pacific Coast, line capacity isn't quite as critical as it is for marine gamefishing where each species is noted for hard strikes and long runs. Drag performance, however, still makes a difference.

For particularly large fish, the design of the drag is only one aspect. Materials used can make the difference, because heat buildup can be intense and, if it isn't dissipated, it will glaze the washers and cause erratic performance. All of us have known cases where someone pours cold water on a reel to reduce this heat buildup.

The same tests outlined in the section on spinning apply to conventional reels as well and it is worth the effort to try an individual reel before buying it. The more sophisticated versions of trolling reels for offshore fishing feature a drag lever instead of a star wheel. The main advantage of the lever is that drag adjustments from free spool to lock drag can be made by simply pushing the lever forward. Again, test the range of the lever at each setting. You should be able to apply a progressive amount of drag, rather than the drag appearing all at once. If you are going to move from free spool to strike drag, there should be some form of drag limiter that keeps you from pushing the lever too far forward and breaking off the fish.

New reels are being produced for the rapidly growing sport of six-pound and twelve-pound-test fishing. Be sure to check any reel used for six pound to make certain the line won't slip behind the spool flange and the reel frame. Adequate line capacity is important with light lines and equally significant with heavier gear if the fish are exceptionally large. In fact, some reel models are made with narrow spool and wide spool to offer the angler a line capacity option.

Many of the offshore reels are still designated by the "O" system or ocean numbers. The way to remember the sizes is to start with thirty-pound class, which matches to a 4/0 reel. As the line size increase, the reel size moves up. A 6/0 is right for fifty-pound, a 9/0 for eighty-pound, and a 2½ or 3/0 should be attached to a twenty-pound rod.

On the West Coast, anglers prefer reels such as the Penn Senators up to perhaps the 4/0 size and several of the smaller Penn conventional casting reels to toss live bait to cruising gamefish. The problem is that the predators are heavyweights and it takes stout tackle to whip them from the decks of the long-range party boats that make the distant run to the hot fishing grounds.

Carl W. Newell (940 Allen Avenue, Glendale, California 91201) makes adapter kits for several Penn reels that provide cast aluminum spools along with specially designed reel support posts and reel feet. The wider posts brace the reel and take any wobble out of it, enabling the user to cast a lighter bait with relatively heavy line. The clamp-type reel foot keeps the reel from shifting on the rod. Reel manufacturers are beginning to copy Newell's ideas and incorporate them in their reels. Newell has also developed his own series of light-tackle reels, which are excellent.

Wire-line trollers both in fresh water and salt find it is much better to use relatively narrow-spool reels for wire because they help prevent overruns and keep the wire from shifting if pressure is eased. There's also something to be said for narrow-spool reels in certain types of offshore fishing such as white marlin, but you don't see many of them in service. Some reel designers talk about using fly reel frames for special lightweight offshore reels for very light line classes and perhaps they will be on the market soon.

GEAR RATIOS

Gear ratios are a measurement of how many times the spool revolves for each complete revolution of the handle. Fly reels, as you already know, are usually one to one, meaning that the spool rotates only once when the handle makes a full rotation. A few are of the multiplying variety with a two to one retrieve, but these are the exceptions. For fresh-water assignments, the reel isn't very important and in salt water, tradition limits the choice of most anglers to one to one.

Spinning takes the opposite approach and the latest reels feature retrieve ratios up to five to one. Providing the gears in the reel are strong enough to withstand this pressure, the faster ratio makes sense in both fighting a fish and in working a lure. Most of the well-known brands will stand up to tough fishing conditions and this can be an asset.

High-speed performance also characterizes the newer bait-casting reels. Since the smaller spools on these reels don't recover much line for one turn of the handle, the increased ratio is important both in fighting a fish and in trying to buzz a bait across the surface. Because of the smaller spool diameter on bait casting, some bass fishermen prefer spinning for working crankbaits and buzzbaits so that they can move the lure faster and with less effort.

Specialists often own fast and slow-retrieve reels and switch them depending on the assignment. For some lures, they prefer the slower retrieve ratio and for others they will opt for the high-speed mills. A few reels on the market have a fast retrieve when working a lure, but drop back when fighting a fish. This may seem logical at first, but it would probably be better to choose a compromise reel with a moderate retrieve.

The higher the gear ratio, the more force produced on the main gear and the greater the drag required to brake it. From a design standpoint, that's not much of a problem with the smaller and lighter reels, but it can become critical on very large reels. There's just too much torque and too much force needed. A lower retrieve ratio helps to solve this problem and that's why you won't find husky big-game reels with a four to one or five to one ratio. Some of the largest reels drop as low as two to one and there are some old monsters around that were made with a one to one gear ratio.

MAKING YOUR DRAG WORK BETTER

Those anglers smitten with the light-tackle big-fish syndrome become fanatics in fine tuning a drag. One can sit on the sidelines and chuckle over the attention to detail, but until that fisherman has been in the arena and slugged it out with an adversary that is particularly big and strong, it's impossible to appreciate the value of a silken drag. Once the desire to fish with a smooth drag gets in your blood, it demonstrates that you understand how critical it can be. An erratic drag will always trouble you, because you know it can lead to disappointment and disaster. Even when you fight a trout or bass, it's much better to rely on a drag that flows rather than hold your breath while line jerks off the reel spool.

If you want to test a drag, take a full spool of line, rig it through the rod, tie the end to the bumper of a car or to a drum on a lathe, and strip that line off at about twenty miles per hour with the drag set for striking. The rod tip should dip once, recover, and point directly at the source of the pull while you maintain pressure on the rod. If that tip bounces up and down like a jumping bean, you're in trouble. Run the test three times in succession with the same line and there's a good chance the drag will bind and break the line. The reason you need to develop the line speed is to create heat buildup. Drags perform one way when the washers are hot and under pressure and another when they are cold. If the heat becomes excessive, you're going to have problems.

Various drag materials find their way into fishing reels; before analyzing each one, let's take a moment to talk a little more about heat and its effects. When a fish runs, there is a tremendous heat buildup and this, among many other things, changes the coefficient of friction. The rate at which line comes off the reel determines the approximate amount of heat generated at a particular setting. If line is being stripped fast, the total amount of mechanical energy converted to heat occurs quickly and temperatures inside the reel soar.

That's why the rate at which a drag can cool itself through heat dissipation among its own washers, the reel handle, sideplates, and so forth is very important. A big fish that peels off a lot of line against a heavy drag creates tremendous heat inside the reel and this can be particularly damaging. Rubber in some drag washers can become gooey and oiled leather can almost fry. Teflon can withstand tremendously high temperatures because it was never a liquid but a powder and the only thing it will do is go back to a powder.

Once you damage a washer under extreme heat, the drag becomes undependable. You may be able to pull line off the reel and the drag feels smooth, but when you subject it to heat again, the same erratic performance will occur every time. A good material has the ability to cope with heat and change very little over a wide temperature range from an ambient starting condition to a serious temperature rise of several hundred degrees. You can insert washers made from fifteen different materials in a well-designed drag system and they would all seem smooth at first. Put a load on the reel as you would in fighting a fish, crank it off on a lathe or with an automobile, and each material will produce different results.

Drag allows line to slip from the reel at predetermined tensions. The ideal, of course, produces a relatively uniform slippage rate over a wide range of tension settings. Students of drag discover early that it takes more pressure to overcome friction and start a spool spinning than it does to keep the spool rotating once it begins to move. Known as starting drag, this initial drag force is controlled by static friction that is a function of the system. Running drag often ranges well below starting drag, but, again, the lower the differential, the better it is for fishing. How fast the fish runs and how the system responds further complicates the problem.

Not all fish are sprinters. Even some of the fastest species sometimes move off steadily rather than streaking at burst speed. To counter this form of movement, a high-performance running drag is vital at slow speeds. On the other hand, fast runs are commonplace and that's when some materials produce crises. A few change their characteristics at high speed and produce an increasing amount of friction rather than the same amount or less. Slow-running drags that bind and catch can cost fish and so can poorly engineered high-speed drags.

Light-tackle anglers lean toward softer drag washer materials such as leather, felt, Teflon, Delrin, asbestos, cork, brake-lining material, and others. Remember that the soft washers are alternated with hard metal ones and that a multi-stage drag (those with several hard and soft washers) is usually smoother than a single-stage drag. The exceptions are in fly reels or big reels where there is ample room to install a massive single-stage drag.

In spinning, the metal washers are keyed to the axle or shaft and the spool, while in bait-casting reels, the keying is done inside the drive gear and to the shaft. By holding the hard washers in position through keying, the soft washers actually float and can slip on either side, because each soft washer is independent of the system.

Remember that the better systems use a spring system to apply pressure that produces a linear progression of adjustments over a wide range. The idea works fine until you reach the point where the spring bottoms out. Then there is a direct hook-up to the screw thread and you can lock the reel in a fraction of a turn. That is exactly what happens when someone keeps tightening a drag and suddenly breaks the line. Usually, the spring has bottomed out and the reel actually locks with barely any additional turning of the adjustment knob.

Soft washers also act as springs because they have their own degree of resiliency. This changes the spring constant of the hard spring in the system. If, for example, there is an imperfection in a drag washer or a high spot, it applies pressure as the washer walks around. When the high spot matches with unevenness in another washer, the drag becomes erratic. With a soft material, if one washer is wavy, the material is usually soft enough to absorb the high spot without changing the torque and without varying the load at any given spot significantly. This smooths out the total effect of the drag.

When the soft drag washer material is lubricated, you are changing the coefficient of friction. This, in turn, allows you to apply more pressure. As you add more pressure, you flatten the components and get much better contact on the washers all around. You are actually forcing some parts that might wobble not to wobble and this helps to eliminate chatter and unevenness.

Oiled leather is a favorite material among light-tackle specialists for modifying drags, but this material demands attention. Washers must be changed reasonably often, kept well-lubricated with oil, and one must remove any pressure at the end of the day by backing off the star wheel or drag adjustment knob. Leather will cold flow, which means it will deform under pressure. The same pressure will also squeeze the oil out.

A combination of top-grade machine oil and Never-Seez (a high-temperature lubricant) applied on leather does about the best job of anything. You can obtain Never-Seez at plumbing supply houses or by writing to Never-Seez Compound Corporation, Broadview, Illinois 60153. There are different grades of leather and, if you are installing your own washers, it pays to use the best and select it yourself. Chrome-tanned cowhide does a good job.

For cutting your own washers, you will either need an adjustable gasket cutter or a set of punches in the more common sizes. Take the existing washers out of the reel, trace them on the leather, felt, Teflon, or Delrin, and cut out the material. It might sound ridiculous to make your own washers, but it isn't difficult and the results can be monumental.

The same combination of light oil and Never-Seez works on felt washers, which, by the way, is another excellent material. There are many grades of felt and it pays to buy the best you can find. Until recently, the recommended treatment for cork washers was Neatsfoot compound, but some specialists are now switching to #0025 Special Lubricant with Teflon, marketed by Roy Dean Products Company, 23440 Kean, Dearborn, Michigan. You can buy it by mail from J. Lee Cuddy Associates, 8255 N.E. Second Avenue, Miami, Florida 33138.

With the exception of leather, felt, or cork, the common opinion is to avoid getting any lubrication on the drag washers. Gary Oberg, an engineer specializing in the design of drags, believes just the opposite. The first thing he does to smooth out a drag is to take some light grease such as Lubriplate or #0025 Lubricant, put a little on his fingers, and try to spread it as evenly as possible so that a thin film coats the washer.

Teflon washers are sometimes included with a new reel or available as an option. Teflon is really an anti-friction material and it cold flows. More important, it can really increase the amount of drag when a fish is running at high speed and this can be particularly dangerous when coupled with reduced spool diameter. It has been hailed as a cureall by many and it does work in some cases, particularly where you aren't going to apply much drag pressure.

To get the same drag loads with Teflon as you would with oiled leather, you would have to increase the spring system or crank the existing one way down. When you do that, you start to apply loads to the system that were never intended. The result is that the threads can be stripped and you can deform or damage other parts of the reel. Delrin works very much like Teflon, but it does not cold flow.

Changing drag washers or lubricating them is about all one can do to most reels to improve performance. If a mill doesn't work better after those efforts, it's probably better to look for a new one. There are times, however, when you may have to go to extremes as some of us did with a popular bait-casting reel that cast well, had adequate line capacity, but concealed a drag system that had to be an embarrassment to the engineers who designed it.

Our only alternative was to rebuild the whole drag the best way we could with a minimum of effort. That meant having someone mill out a shoulder in the center of the drive gear and remove a click spring that had no business being in the reel. This increased the amount of room for drag washers considerably. The second step was to create a new drag pressure plate to replace the finger type that worked the click spring as well as put pressure on the drag. If you fought a fish with that modified reel and compared it to a brand new model out of the box, you would not believe the difference.

LAPPING IN THE GEARS

Boyd Pfeiffer, a well-known tackle tinkerer, outdoor writer, and good friend, passed along a tip about lapping in the gears on bait-casting reels that is worth repeating. It is his feeling and that of others that part of the problem of backlashes while casting can be traced to minute spurs and uneven surfaces on the machined parts of the reel. These cause the mechanism to bind and jerk momentarily and that's all it takes.

To polish the reel, you must take it apart and pack the sideplates and the level-wind mechanism with a fifty-fifty mixture of grease and toothpaste. Boyd has researched the subject and believes that Pearl Drops toothpaste is one of the most abrasive and hence one of the best for the project. The grease serves to suspend the toothpaste.

It takes from eight to twenty hours to polish the gears and that's a lot of turning by hand. The hardier anglers sit in front of the television and turn the handles the manual way, but if you can locate a motor that turns at about 100 rpm's—such as the one that comes in a youngster's building set—it will do the job. Boyd says that the easiest way to rig it is to remove the handle and use a small piece of rubber tubing as a universal joint.

Periodically, you're going to have to repack the mixture to the worm gears and pawl to make sure they are coated. When the polishing is finished, take the reel apart, clean it with soap and water to remove the toothpaste, and use a degreasing agent to remove the grease. Then, reapply a thin coat of lubricant and you should have the casting reel of your dreams.

4

Lines, Leaders, and Knots

There is no such thing as a second chance. If the thin web of line that spans the distance between angler and quarry fails, the fish has earned its freedom and another story about the one that got away is born. The line is the critical link and it is the hub of light-tackle fishing.

When you think about it, the deciding factor as to what constitutes light tackle centers on the breaking strength of the line. No matter what the rod and reel look like, if the line will self-destruct at six pounds or ten pounds or thirty pounds, that is where the measurement will be taken. Only the line gives us a basis for comparison and the key to the relativity of what might be light for a situation and what we would consider average or heavy.

An erratic drag might be frustrating and a rod with the wrong taper may prove a handicap, but poor quality or weakened line is a total disaster. Especially when dealing with light tackle, there is barely a margin for error and a less-than-perfect line tilts the odds strongly in favor of the fish. Successful aficionados seldom overlook a detail in stacking the deck in their favor.

Ironically, most fishermen know less about fishing lines than all other tackle items combined. Stand in any tackle shop and you'll hear the customers speak authoritatively about gear ratios of reels or the fact that the reel seat on a given rod may be annodized aluminum. Their knowledge of lines, however, diminishes abruptly after they read the breaking strength on the label. In fact, few will even ask for line by brand name and fewer will specify a premium line. To their untrained eyes, all fishing line is basically the same. This error can be fatal.

Serious light-tackle anglers are more concerned about their line than the rest of the tackle. They may not know all the reasons that cause line failure, but they do recognize that it happens more often than most of us suspect. Psychologically, these fishermen have reasoned that changing lines frequently is the cheapest insurance they can buy and that is precisely what they do. It is not uncommon, for example, for the dedicated angler to throw a line away after a single day's outing in which he fished under difficult conditions and tried to subdue big fish on light line. There are a handful of fishermen who may discard a line after a single fish and, when we investigate a little more about what can happen to a line, it may make sense to you, too.

If you learn nothing more from this book than what can happen to a fishing line through "normal" usage, you will come out ahead and probably land more fish in the weeks and months ahead than you would have. Anyone who ignores the line on his reels or makes any assumptions not based on fact, plays a dangerous game of roulette. Unless you know you can depend on the line, there is no way you can play the light-tackle game consistently and win. That line will get you almost every time.

MONOFILAMENT BASICS

Nothing can be more costly than false economy. Anglers, for some unknown reason, assume that the line on their reels will remain in peak condition forever or at least until there isn't enough left on the reel spool to reach the water. Milking another month or season out of the mono on a reel seems to be a popular pastime and there are those foolish enough to challenge laboratory tests of leaving line on reels for several years. The quickest way to recognize a competent fisherman is by looking at his reels. If the line boasts newness and the spools are filled to capacity, you can bet he takes his sport seriously.

With normal usage, monofilament is tailored for an average life of one year. Anything beyond that means that the product is being abused and you are pushing it past its effective limits. Therefore, even the most casual angler should change line once every twelve months. That, of course, merely signals the starting point. If you fish under difficult conditions or pursue your sport above typical usage, you must change more frequently.

The myth about testing lines that has lasted for years centers around the overhand knot. Experts tell us to tie one in the line and break the line. If the knot seems to part rather easily, the line should be changed. Paul Johnson, Director of Research for Berkley and Company and one of the most knowledgeable people in the world on monofilament, disagrees. To begin with, nobody uses an overhand knot in the middle of the line while fishing, so it probably isn't a good measure of anything. It would be more meaningful if you were to tie a knot that you did use constantly and test that, but Paul recommends another approach.

The first step is to look at the surface of the line. If it appears dull instead of bright and shiny, your suspicions should be aroused. The surface of the line gets attacked initially by heat, light, abrasion, or a combination of these

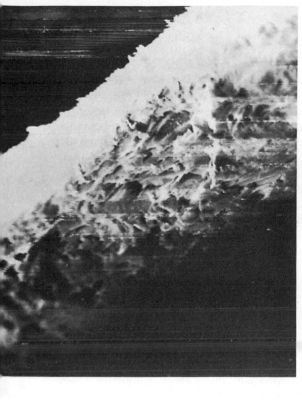

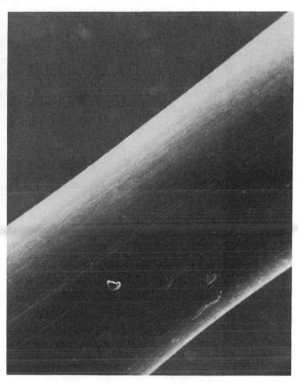

Scanning electron photomicrograph of economy-grade ten-pound-test nylon monofilament that has been heavily fished under abrasive conditions. Berkley and Company photo

Scanning electron micrograph of Trilene XL unused nylon monofilament line. Berkley and Company photo

factors and begins to turn dull. Frequently, powder shows on the surface and it gets on your hands. This powder could be a monomer bleed inside the line or it could represent abrasion. Perhaps ultraviolet light is breaking down the molecules.

All of us want to run a line through our fingers to tell if there is abrasion or if it is rough. The problem with that approach is that oils from the skin transfer to the line, helping to lubricate the line's surface and make it look shiny. Johnson suggests you run the line between your lips or over your upper lip. Fingers on most men are too calloused for any degree of sensitivity, but lips are perfect. Any roughness or abrasion warrants closer inspection under a glass or you can save time by replacing the line.

Testing line by breaking it can also be meaningful, provided you use a long enough length and exert a steady pull. If you snap a short length apart like you would when trying to break a piece of string, you're introducing other factors and not getting a true measurement of break strength. Weak spots will show up much better over a ten-foot length than they will if you pull ten inches apart by hand. Wrap the line around a railing or doorknob or something else and pull steadily until it breaks. If you have some of the original line on the storage spool, you can break this for a comparison. Without the comparison or a scale, it's difficult to tell anything. You may feel great today compared to yesterday, but then yesterday you were in the hospital. Everything is relative.

Heat and light destroy monofilament. No one can tell for certain how line was stored in the tackle shop, but it should be kept in a cool, dark place and not where the ultraviolet rays of the sun or fluorescent lights can reach it. Temperatures as low as 100 degrees can weaken monofilament and higher temperatures are much worse. Just leaving a reel in the back seat of your car on a hot summer day can be a problem and the trunk of the car can be torture. You don't have to leave a reel in the trunk for a month to monitor perceivable changes in properties. Heat encourages the molecules to relax and the line starts losing strength.

PREMIUM LINES

The greatest argument for the use of premium quality monofilament fishing line lies in the tighter standards to which the line is manufactured. There are no bargains in lines; you get exactly what you pay for. Premium lines require a more sophisticated manufacturing process and closer quality control. These increased costs are reflected in the retail price of the line.

If you were to take a spool of ten-pound-test economy monofilament and a spool of ten-pound-test premium line and run a simple comparison of break tests in a hundred samples, the results would be startling. Remember each of the one hundred samples is from the same spool of line, yet in the economy grade, the variations would be as much as plus or minus two pounds. That means that it might vary from ten to fourteen pounds dry strength. The premium line would be made to a tolerance of plus or minus one-half pound.

There's more to the story. Chemists call the class of compounds from which nylon is made *polyamides*. They soon discovered that there were a number of mixtures or blends that could be made and each had different properties. The simplest was to take one type called a homopolymer and make line. Homo, of course, means one, so a homopolymer is one polymer. Type 6 ranks as the most common homopolymer and it has become the basis for most economy lines. The problem with homopolymers, however, is that the blend of properties must be a serious compromise. As you change one factor, other dependent properties change as well.

It didn't take chemists long to conclude that if they could blend a couple of polymers together in the manufacturing process, they could make better fishing line. By splicing two different compounds together, such as Type 6 nylon and Type 11, they developed the copolymer which is the second class of lines. Type 6 has the characteristics of being stiff and somewhat wiry, but by adding Type 11, the end product is a much more flexible fishing line with higher tensile strength.

Someone discovered not very long ago that there is a surprising similarity between the creation of steel alloys and nylon technology. At the moment, scientists are working feverishly to advance the state of the art through the creation of nylon alloys that would produce properties never believed possible in monofilament. You may want to make the mental comparison between cold rolled steel and the stainless steel alloys we have today. The same approach is possible with nylon, yet researchers don't understand how the alloy works. In fact, there are no textbooks on the subject. Some lines made from nylon alloys are being marketed right now and they are among the top premium lines available. Through this technology, we can look toward major breakthroughs that will bring us lines of tomorrow.

TENSILE STRENGTH AND OTHER PROPERTIES

Scientists needed a common denominator to compare various nylon monofilaments and also to measure monofilament against braided lines, wire, or anything else. They finally agreed that tensile strength offered the logical solution. Expressed in pounds per square inch (psi), tensile strength is nothing more than the break strength of the line in pounds divided by the cross sectional area in inches.

Memories have a habit of playing tricks on us. Old timers fondly recall the early monofilaments, insisting they were stronger than the modern lines. The truth is that the lines they referred to had a tensile strength no higher than 50,000 psi. Today, the typical fisherman has been trained and educated to expect a tensile strength of 90,000 to 100,000 psi in a fishing line and would reject the early nylons as being too weak. None of us actually measure tensile strength, but experience and use help us to sense it.

We could, however, set up our own testing system by using a scale and a micrometer. All you need is the break strength in pounds measured on the scale (or read on the label) and the diameter of the line. Divide the diameter into the break strength and you have a relative measurement. It would tend to be on the low side if compared to actual tensile strength because the break strength on the label is lower than the actual break strength.

Presently, premium quality monofilament fishing lines have a tensile strength about 100,000 psi. Polymer chemists talk theoretically of lines that would test at 500,000 psi or roughly five times greater than we have today. Realistically, our chances of seeing lines of 500,000 psi in this century are remote. A more accurate estimate would be lines in the 150,000 psi range and possibly 200,000 psi by the year 2000.

If one could increase tensile strength by even 50 percent, to 150,000 psi, the benefits would be dramatic. Line diameter would be reduced, knot strength would become significantly higher, and the line would have different fish-fighting characteristics than the lines we now have. The hook-setting qualities would not be the same, castability would be demonstratively better, and margin for error would be greater.

Assuming one only wanted to increase tensile strength, research efforts should be expended in that area. There are twenty-three properties in a fishing line, however, and singling out only one of these would be as unharmonious as a piano player concentrating on his thumb and ignoring the other fingers on his hand.

The trick obviously becomes balancing these twenty-three properties. When you think about it, not all fishing is the same, which translates into the fact that different types of line may be needed for various fishing situations. With the bright horizons of nylon alloys, this approach may not only be possible, but it is increasingly practical. After all, to take one line and dwell on only a couple of properties, saying that it represents the ultimate in fishing line may not make sense. Fishing rods are tailored for specific applications, yet we expect one line in various breaking strengths to meet every need.

The wave of the future appears to be specially tailored lines for casting, trolling, abrasion resistance, and perhaps the time will come when a manufacturer will create a line for the light-tackle enthusiast who wants to challenge big fish on featherweight gear.

CASTABILITY

The common belief is that limp lines cast better than stiff ones. If that were true, Dacron would probably do a better job on spinning outfits than monofilament. Researchers are adamant in telling us that the predominant influence on castability is diameter rather than limpness.

The smaller the diameter of the line, the farther it casts and the more accurately it will present the bait or lure to a target. Tournament casters recognized this quite some time ago and those who tried for distance used particularly light lines with the finest diameters.

If we could achieve monofilament with a tensile strength of 200,000 psi, fourteen-pound-test or seventeen-pound-test line might have the diameter of ten-pound test as we know it today. Remember that even though the tensile strength is doubled, the diameter is not halved because tensile strength does not increase directly proportional to the diameter.

ABRASION RESISTANCE

Another misconception among anglers is that hard-type monofilament has greater abrasion resistance than soft monofilament. The laboratory troops smile knowingly and factually state that abrasion resistance is directly related to the surface of the material and what is happening at that surface.

Regardless of what the bulk of the nylon might be, if the surface is vulnerable to nicks, scratches, cuts, and scrapes, stress concentration points are created. When you are fighting a fish or stressing the line in any way, concentrations of force occur at these points and the monofilament breaks. If you look at nylon as a viscoelastic material or, in layman's terms, a frozen liquid, you might find an interesting parallel in the kitchen of your home. When company comes, your wife will use her best glassware, but after dinner, she won't put the glasses in the dishwasher. Instead, she'll wash them one at a time, refusing even to soak two at a time in the sink. Experience has taught

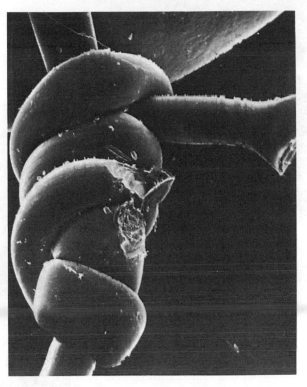

Improved clinch knot in ten-pound-test monofilament with knot accidentally damaged by clipper when mono tail was trimmed. Berkley and Company photo

her that if two glasses rub together, they might nick and scratch each other. The slightest stress at the point of the nick or scratch will cause it to spread and the glass will break.

Veteran fishermen are alert to the problems of abrasion and check their line when they land each fish or quite frequently when fishing around rocks, pilings, or other obstructions that could fray a line. Usually, they will cut off the abraded section periodically and retie the lure or terminal gear.

What the majority of fishermen don't recognize is how drastically the tensile strength of the line can be reduced by introducing an abrasion mark or a nick in the surface. Even a fine nick that is barely discernible to the eye or barely perceptible to the touch can cut down the break strength of the line by more than 50 percent. Nick the surface of the line as little as 1/1000 of an inch or less than the thickness of a human hair and you have introduced a focal point for stress.

The first thought a fisherman has when a fish breaks off is to blame the line. In a way he's right, but not for his usual reason. The part of the line that broke was definitely weakened, but there is nothing wrong with the rest of the line down on the reel spool. Failure occurred because of lack of skill on the fisherman's part in either recognizing the abrasion and cutting off the frayed line or in simply leaving the line on the reel too long.

A thousand things can abrade line. Many are underwater, but some are in a fisherman's hands all the time. A faulty line guide could be a problem or there might be a burr on the opening in the bell cover of a spincast reel. Some spinning reels feature carbide line guides that are almost guaranteed to abrade a line instantly. Fishermen must learn to look beyond the obvious. Of course

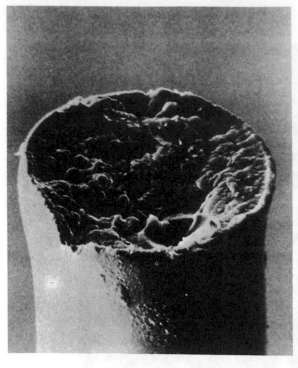

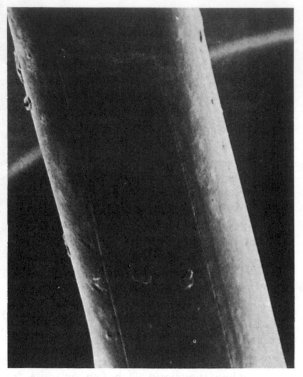

Wet nylon monofilament broken under tension; this shows the effects of absorbed water. Berkley and Company photo

Unused nylon monofilament damaged by a rough comb during processing. Berkley and Company photo

the line is frayed, but did you ask yourself why? That's when you should start checking back. Drag a nylon stocking through the guides and if it hangs up, you'll probably find a nick or groove. Consider where you were fishing and take a long, hard look at the roller on the spinning reel. Sometimes, you can find the reason and eliminate it.

LABELING LAWS

If a container of milk is labeled to contain one pint, it must have sixteen fluid ounces. It could have thirty ounces, but it cannot contain one drop under sixteen. No one is permitted to shortchange the consumer willfully. Selling fishing lines is no different.

When monofilament gets wet and absorbs water, it becomes weaker. Most copolymers in use today will absorb 5 percent water and a few might even approach 10 percent. Tests show that fully saturated monofilament is anywhere from 10 percent to 30 percent weaker than dry monofilament.

Knowing that the wet test is less than the dry test and fully comprehending the labeling laws in the United States, manufacturers aren't about to take a chance. They are going to make certain that even if you leave the line in a bucket of water for a month, it will still test ten pounds (usually slightly over) if the label touts it as ten-pound test. In case you decide to do some practice casting on a desert and the line dries out, you can be certain that it will test well above ten pounds.

Recognizing this is vital if you intend to enter record fish or participate in tournaments where breaking strength may be tested. Certain lines are advertised as "tournament lines" and the implication is that they will not break *over* what the label says. It sounds great until you start thinking about it. Even premium lines have a degree of variance in the same spool. We noted earlier that it could be plus or minus one-half pound for ten-pound test. The other part of the problem, however, is the difference between wet test and dry test. If you took the extremes, there has to be a considerable cushion for the line to meet all conditions. It would be perfect if ten-pound-test tournament line broke at 9.5 pounds, but it doesn't work that way.

In effect, the angler may be using seven-pound-test or eight-pound-test line when the label says it won't break over ten pounds. You can do your own interpolating for the various breaking strengths and manufacturers, but keep in mind that no one is going to take a chance on violating the labeling laws if they are reputable and buying line from someone who isn't reputable is pure folly. It's possible, of course, to buy your own force gauge or push-pull gauge and test the line yourself. Many tournament anglers do this until they hit upon the make that is best for their needs.

COLOR

Monofilament fishing lines can be made in a rainbow of colors that will harmonize aesthetically with any tackle combination. The only aspect worth considering, however, is what happens to color in an outdoor and underwater environment. Most of us who have ever pushed our heads under the surface of the water know that colors do not appear the same as they do in the air. Understanding what happens to colors will prejudice one's choice of lines.

When a red line goes underwater, it turns brown to the eye and then black. Yellow line may appear white beneath the surface, but blue line will retain its blue color. The primary exception to the shift in colors seems to be fluorescent lines. Even at great depths, fluorescent lines tend to look the same as they do in the air. Technical people claim it happens because the nature and physics of fluorescents have the capacity to utilize available light underwater and convert it, continuing to make the color the same. As an example, shocking yellow above water will become pale white underwater, but bright fluorescent yellow retains that color at depths far greater than one would expect to see yellow. No one can accurately say what effect this will have on fish, but you should be aware of the phenomenon.

Not all high-visibility lines are fluorescent. Some are produced through a process called optical brightening. A series of tests run at Rainbow Springs, Florida, and reported in the August 1975 issue of *Sports Afield* demonstrated that optically brightened monofilament was less visible at depths below fifteen feet than fluorescent lines and also had a chameleon effect, especially when viewing the lines from the bottom toward the surface. All lines are somewhat visible underwater.

Under certain situations and particularly in bass fishing, the ability and convenience of being able to watch the line is an important asset. Bassmasters can tell when a fish picks up a plastic worm or inhales a jig and rind by noting the telltale tug on the line . . . a tug that cannot be felt but can be seen.

Not all colorants are incorporated in a fishing line the same way. The least expensive and simplest method is to dip the monofilament in a dye that will penetrate a few thousandths of an inch into the surface. Scientists refer to this type of coloration as fugitive, because it leaches out quickly and is highly susceptible to attack by ultraviolet light. Sometimes, special chemicals are introduced in the solution to help establish the dye in the monofilament. Although these chemicals make it easier for the dye to penetrate the monofilament, they also weaken the line. Few fishermen realize that economy lines are frequently weaker because of these dyes, which don't last very long, anyway.

Premium lines have the pigment incorporated into the mass of nylon at the time the line is being made. Such lines not only resist fading and ultraviolet attacks, but this process apparently does not adversely affect the nylon. That's just another argument in favor of premium quality lines.

FACTS YOU DIDN'T KNOW

They didn't have hard facts to substantiate their theories, but leading light-tackle anglers were definitely on target when they discarded a monofilament line after a hard-fought battle with a particularly big and difficult fish. Researchers today explain the phenomenon in terms of stress (the break strength of the line measured in pounds) and strain (which is nothing more than stretch or elongation). The relationship of these two factors are shown in graph form as a stress/strain curve. It's an impressive way of demonstrating what happens to the various types of line.

Anybody who has ever used monofilament knows from experience that as you first begin to pull on the line, all the force or stress is used to stretch the line. Graphically, the curve of monofilament starts with a gentle slope until full elongation has been achieved and then it starts to climb rather steeply. This initial area represents the hook-setting region. Monofilament cannot compare with braided lines for hook-setting qualities, because the first amount of force stretches the mono instead of driving the hook. With braided lines, just the opposite is true. Remember that the total elongation of mono ranges from 20 percent to 30 percent, while braided Dacron only stretches 10 percent.

On the other hand, in fighting a fish, the early elongation of monofilament makes the line forgiving and gives the angler a safety cushion until he can get the system working. Dacron doesn't have much of a builtin shock absorber.

Once the initial stretch has been achieved, there is an immediate transfer of stress to the line. The more force you exert on it, the more it continues to strain. When you relax this tension, the line recovers and goes back to zero. These are the *elastic limits* of the line and they can be shown graphically under the curve. As long as you don't exceed these limits in fighting a fish, there will be no damage to the line.

If you exceed the elastic limits, you enter a zone of permanent deformation. The molecules in the line are being stretched and they are being displaced. *You have weakened the line and there is no way that it can return to its original condition.*

When you are fighting a fish and the line breaks or your rig hooks in the bottom and you have to break it off, you must go to the full break strength of the line and you have exceeded the elastic limits. The entire length of line from the reel to the fish or obstruction has been weakened and it should be discarded. That length of line is no longer as strong as the material deeper on the reel spool.

On a long-running fish, all of us consider ourselves fortunate if the line breaks close to our quarry, but we are actually deluding ourselves. The line may still appear shiny and new. It may be smooth and show no signs of abrasion, but it has been weakened once the elastic limits are exceeded. This can be demonstrated in the laboratory very simply. Most line tests are run on an Instron machine, a sophisticated piece of equipment that will strain a line at a predetermined rate. If you started to stretch the line and then shut the machine off before the line reached its elastic limits, the dial would return to zero. If you performed the same experiment, but allowed the line to exceed its elastic limits before shutting the machine off, the dial would not return to zero but somewhere above it.

How much a line has been weakened depends on the brand, because we are really measuring fatigue strength, one of the twenty-three properties. In fact, if you continued to fatigue the line, it would get weaker and weaker. The bottom fisherman who seems to catch more real estate than fish or the angler who has a tendency to lose a lot of fish should probably stock up on bulk spools of line. With a strong, fast-running fish that smokes line off the reel and breaks off, the problem is compounded, because there is no way of telling where in that long length of line the weakspots have been set up, but they are there.

When we talk about fighting fish in a later chapter, you'll realize that the successful light-tackle specialist learns to apply maximum pressure without breaking the line. Frequently, this pressure exceeds the elastic limits, but it stays just under the break strength. That's a good argument for discarding the line after the battle. In fact, since the line is fatiguing each time you exceed the elastic limits, long battles can be disastrous if you continue to maintain the same amount of pressure.

IMPACT STRENGTH

Exceeding the elastic limits with a steady pull is one way to break a line, but impact is another and it can occur more frequently on the fishing scene than most of us suspect. When the gal in the neighborhood bakery ties string around a cake box, she breaks the string by letting a U fall between her two hands and then snapping her two hands apart quickly. This method ignores the breaking strength of the line and focuses on its impact resistance or ability to withstand shock.

You can take a 4 x 8 sheet of heavy plateglass, place it on a table so that part of the glass extends over the edge, and leave it there for a month. When you finally lift the glass, you'll discover that it actually started to flow and the plate is no longer flat. The molecules in the glass were trying to accommodate the stress. If, however, you attempted to bend the glass by hand, it would shatter. In this exaggerated instance, the strain rate was too great.

Strain rate is the term used to define how fast you are applying load and it is expressed as a percentage. To find strain rate, you simply divide the length of the sample into the theoretical amount of stretch or elongation that would take place in one minute (assuming the line did not break). The standard test in a laboratory on an Instron machine is to stretch a ten-inch line sample at the rate of ten inches per minute. The strain rate in this case is 100 percent, or ten divided by ten.

Life on the water is a bit more complicated than in the sterile atmosphere of a laboratory. A steelhead or salmon reportedly can swim at a burst speed of fourteen miles per hour, or 1,232 feet per minute. If you made an eighty-foot cast and hooked one of those torpedos that happened to run directly away from you, the strain rate would be 1232 divided by 80, or 1540 percent per minute. That can be a lot more taxing on your tackle than the cozy test of ten inches per minute.

Some of us shouted into the darkness of night for years about the effect of impact on lines and on knots. Scientists tell us that impact isn't involved in most fishing situations and they may be right, but when impact *is* a factor, it can cause major problems. Consider what happens, for example, when a bass strikes a surface lure and dives for cover. It may be moving at a speed in excess of 1,000 feet per minute, while you are swinging the rod sharply from the horizontal to the vertical trying to set the hook. The strain rate is tremendous and the impact certainly a consideration.

What do you suspect happens when a northern pike slams a spoon just as you have finished the figure 8 around the boat and are about to lift the lure from the water? In fighting a fish, you can expect a sudden surge near the boat, yet if the drag locks or you don't react instantly, that old impact problem is going to haunt you.

Since monofilament usually stretches between 20 and 30 percent of its length, let's compromise at 25 percent. Going back to our steelhead or salmon example, we can figure that the monofilament will stretch about twenty feet (25 percent of our eighty-foot cast). With a fish that is moving at 1,232 feet per minute, it only takes about one second for it to stretch the line and break it. (Twenty feet divided by 1,232 feet per minute equals .0162 minutes. Multiply .0162 by 60 to convert to seconds and the answer is .97 seconds.) That doesn't give an angler much reaction time to compensate for the impact.

The shorter the length of line involved, the more significant the effect of impact on it will be. When a fish dives away from the net, the line is short and there isn't much area to absorb the shock. If the fish suddenly spurts away a hundred feet from the boat, there is much more cushion. Stretch in monofilament helps to absorb this impact.

When someone rates the breaking strength of a knot, the tests were run on an Instron machine at the rate of ten inches per minute. That's fine when a fish is running and the drag is yielding line. What it fails to explain, however, is the effect that impact has on certain knots. As an example, when the Spider Hitch was introduced as a substitute for the more complex Bimini Twist, a few of us had our suspicions. My good friend and associate, Lefty Kreh, with whom I have explored the world of knots, went into the laboratory and watched a series of tests. He asked the technician if the machine could be made to run any faster and, when the answer was affirmative, insisted that they do so. Suddenly, the Spider Hitch began breaking below the unknotted line strength. Apparently, under impact, the knot crushed internally and collapsed. In my judgment and in Lefty's there is still no substitute for the Bimini Twist. The Spider Hitch will do an excellent job until impact enters the picture. That's a totally different ballgame.

KNOT TYING

Choosing the right knot for the line you are using is usually overlooked, but it is a vital factor. Certain knots work miraculously in lighter lines, but there is no way to tighten them adequately in heavier breaking strengths. Other knots will hold securely in larger diameter lines and fail miserably in gossamer threads. You'll also discover that knots for monofilament may not hold in braided lines and vice versa. When you are tying two different materials together, knots can really be a problem. Don't be fooled by appearances of strength.

Recently, a new factor has been introduced known technically as statistical reproducibility. That's an impressive phrase to indicate that certain knots can be tied well almost every time and by anyone, while other knots sometimes don't work on every attempt. The knots you should favor are those that you can tie well the majority of tries.

Take the time to learn a few knots and make them work for you. If you are ever in doubt about a knot, it is better for it to break in your hands than on a fish. When you have finished a knot, you should have confidence in its ability. Equally important, recognize that knots in monofilament seem to slip just before they break, so pull up all knots as tightly as you can, using pliers, if necessary, on heavier tag ends. When you trim that tag end, leave just a little tail so that it doesn't slip through when the knot is stressed. Don't attempt to burn this tag end or you may damage the knot from the heat generated by match or lighter.

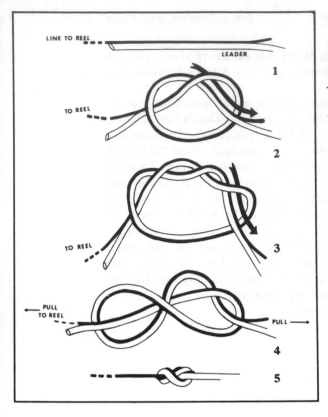

Surgeon's Knot

A remarkably quick and strong knot for joining two lines of similar or dissimilar diameters, the Surgeon's Knot works best when the heavier line is no more than five times the breaking strength of the lighter line. This knot may be simple to tie, but it's effective and you should know it.

1. The longer length of line should go from left to right (if you are a right-handed tier) and the shorter length from right to left. Allow several inches on each tag end to tie the knot.

2. Holding both lines together, make a simple overhand knot. Remember that both strands of line must be worked together.

3. The tag end of the longer line is lying against the standing part of the shorter line. Hold them together and pass them through the overhand knot a second time, making a double overhand knot.

4. To tighten the knot, grasp the two lines on one side of the knot with your left hand and the two lines on the other side with your right hand. Be sure to keep the pairs of lines together. Now draw them uniformly and steadily apart until the knot is tight.

5. Trim the tag ends close to the knot and it's completed.

Snelling a Hook

Snelling provides an effective way of tying a leader to a hook. It is used primarily for bait fishing, because there isn't enough room behind the eye of a hook on a fly or lure.

1. Starting from the bend in the hook, insert the tag end of the leader through the hook eye so that it extends one to two inches beyond. Hold the leader against the shank of the hook and make a loop in the standing part so that the other end points back toward the bend of the hook. Slip this under your thumb and forefinger holding the first strand.

2. Hold the leader against the shank of the hook with your left hand. With your right hand, start wrapping the right arc of the loop around the hook shank and tag end of the leader. You must work from the eye of the hook toward the bend of the hook. Seven or eight turns are adequate. As you take each turn, you must hold it under the thumb and forefinger of your left hand.

3. Be sure to hold the turns firmly with your left hand. Grasp the tag end extending beyond the hook eye and pull it slowly away from the hook eye. The knot will form under your fingers. When you have pulled the tag end reasonably tight and the loops are secure against the shank of the hook, hold the other end (lying near the bend of the hook) with pliers and pull on the long end. Slide the knot against the eye of the hook and trim the tag end.

Steelhead Variation

Steelheaders often loop yarn or egg sacs under a short length of monofilament in front of the hook eye. A snell can be used for this if it is tightened along the shank of the hook and not seated against the eye.

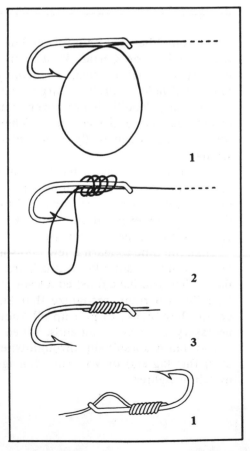

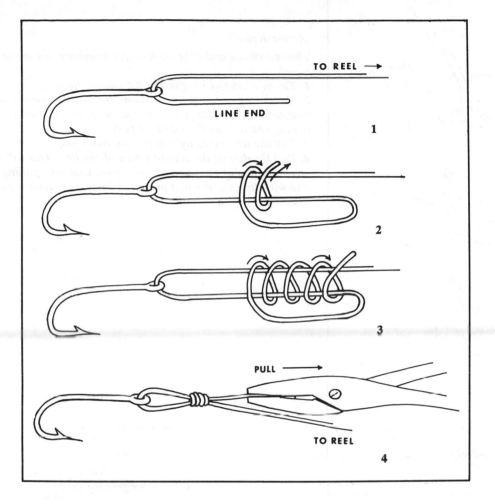

Duncan Loop or Uni-Knot

There are many uses for the Duncan Loop or Uni-knot, including a loop connection for a lure and a method for joining two lines together of the same or different materials. To join lines, you must make two knots and slide them together so that they are back to back.

1. The tag end of the line must be passed through the eye of the hook or, in the case of joining lines, held against the standing part of the second line.

2. Bend the tag end of the line or leader back toward the first loop, forming a second loop that hangs below the top two strands of line. Hold the top two strands together and pass the tag end repeatedly through the hanging loop several times, working from left to right or away from the first loop.

3. After five or six turns, tighten the knot by pulling steadily on the tag end. The wraps will "turn over" as you tighten. When the knot is reasonably tight, slide it down to where you want it.

4. When the loop is in position, use pliers to pull on the tag end and fully tighten it. If you are joining two lines, do the final tightening close to the second knot and then slide the two together so that they jam against each other.

All knot drawings by Barbara Lewis.

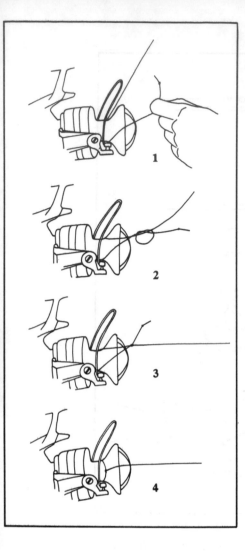

Arbor Knot

This is a simple and effective knot for attaching line to the arbor of a reel.

1. Tie an overhand knot in the tag end of the line.

2. Slip the tag end of the line around the arbor of the reel and hold it against the standing part. Now tie a second overhand knot with the tag end around the standing part.

3. Pull the tag end to tighten the overhand knot.

4. Pull steadily on the standing part of the line. This will slide the second overhand knot against the arbor. Continue pulling and the line will slip until the first overhand knot seats against the second one.

Speedy Nail Knot

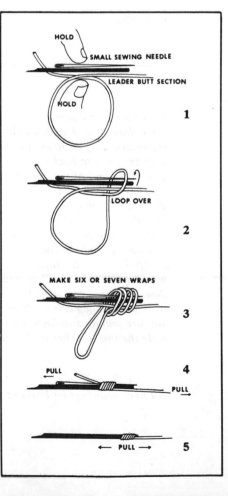

A Nail Knot is the same as a snell and can be tied quickly using the same technique. All you need is a needle or other small shaft as a stiffener. It's fast and you'll tie a perfect Nail Knot each time.

1. Lay a small sewing needle along the tag end of a fly line with the point of the needle toward the leader. Hold the fly line against the needle and lay the butt section of the leader in the opposite direction, with its tag end pointing toward the fly line. Now make a loop in the leader and hold the needle, fly line, and looped leader under the thumb and forefinger of your left hand.

2. With your other hand, grasp the leg of the loop closer to the tag end of the fly line and start wrapping it around fly line, needle, and leader. You will be working toward the standing part of the fly line.

3. You will have to hold the wraps tightly under your fingers or they will twist and come loose. After you have made six or seven wraps, pull the butt section of the leader away from the fly line. The hanging loop will pass through the loops of the Nail Knot as you tighten.

4. Pull both ends of the leader material until the loops are seated against the needle. Then slide the needle out and pull again.

5. When you have completely tightened the Nail Knot, test it by pulling on the standing part of the fly line and the standing part of the leader. Then trim the tag end of the leader, coat the knot with rubber-based cement for added strength, and you are finished.

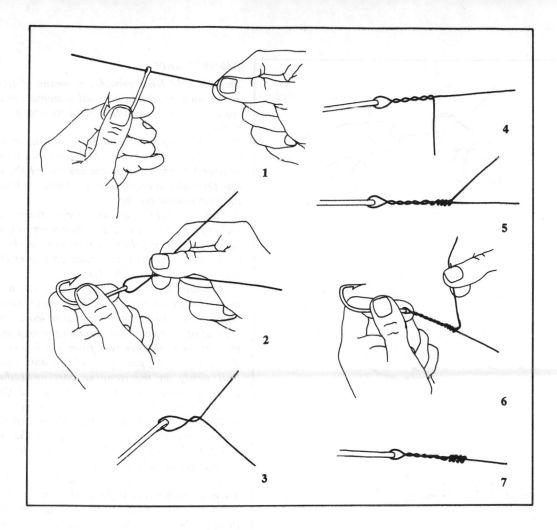

Haywire Twist

The Haywire Twist is the safest and best method of making a loop in the end of single-strand wire or for attaching it to hook or swivel.

1. Insert the tag end of the wire through the eye of the hook or swivel.

2. The tag end is then bent back across the standing part, forming a small loop. If you just wanted to make a loop, this is how you would start.

3. Hold the loop firmly just in front of the point where the tag end crosses the standing part. You may have to use pliers. Grasp the tag end and standing part of the wire between thumb and finger of your stronger hand so that they form a right angle with each other. Rotate your hand, holding the two wires a half turn or 180 degrees, while you hold the loop in place. This will create a twist.

4. Continue twisting one half turn at a time until you have several twists in the wire. Then, bend the tag end so that it is at right angles with the standing part.

5. Now wrap the tag end around the standing part in a barrel twist so that each strand lays against the previous one.

6. Wire should never be cut, because it leaves a burr that could cause serious injury. Instead, bend the tag end to form a handle and twist it back and forth until the wire breaks at the barrel twist.

7. The finished twist is neat, strong, and has no burrs.

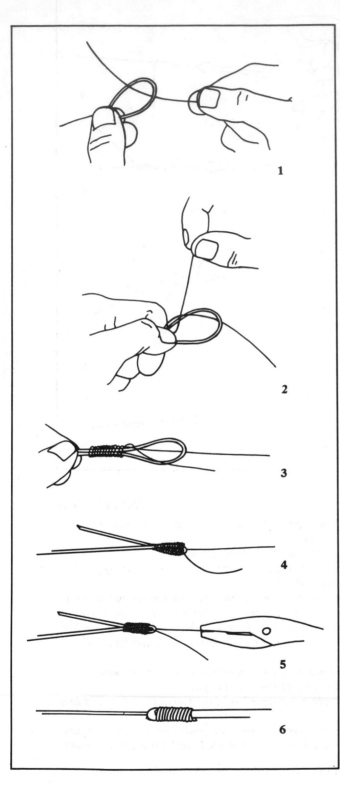

Albright Knot

The Albright Knot provides a means of tying together lines of greatly unequal diameters or different materials. It is usually used to attach a shock tippet.

1. Form a loop in the end of the heavier monofilament and hold it between the thumb and forefinger of your left hand. Insert the tag end of the second line through the loop, passing it from the bottom of the loop toward the top.

2. Slide the lighter line under your thumb several inches from the tag end and then start to wrap the tag end back around the loop toward the closed end of the loop. The first turn must cross over itself so that you can change direction.

3. Although fewer turns will hold it, ten to twelve seems about average. After you have made this number of turns toward the closed loop, push the tag end of the lighter line through the loop so that it exits in the same direction *from which it enters.*

4. The tightening process should be done carefully. Pull slowly on the standing part until the coils begin to tighten. Then tug on the tag end. Go back to the standing part, and so forth. With your thumb and forefinger, help slide the coils toward the end of the loop so that they will jam against the tag end.

5. When the knot is firmly seated, use pliers to pull the tag end as tight as possible.

6. Trim the tag end and the knot is finished. There's another way to finish this knot that is even more effective. Instead of pushing the tag end through the loop in the same direction from which it entered, push it through the opposite *direction.* Pull the knot tight, just as you would normally do. With the tag end, take a two-turn Nail Knot around the standing part of the lighter line. This will prevent the tag end from slipping and keep the knot from cocking to one side.

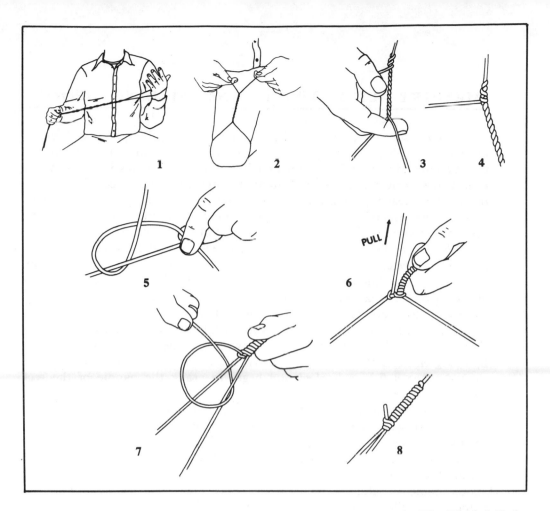

The Bimini Twist

Unquestionably the most valuable knot in a light-tackle angler's arsenal, the Bimini Twist creates a double line that has strength equal to or greater than the unknotted single strand. It's not as difficult to tie as you might suspect and, with reasonable practice, it can be tied in less than thirty seconds.

1. Always allow plenty of line to tie this knot. Start with about six feet and double it over. Hold the tag end against the standing part with your left hand. Slip the back of your right hand in the loop and twist the line at least twenty times.

2. You cannot release the pressure maintained on the line with both hands or the twists will unravel. Take the loop in your right hand and drop it over your knee. Then shift your grip so that the tag end is in one hand and the standing part in the other. Note that when you separate tag end and standing part, each forms a 45-degree angle with the twists. Together they form a right angle. This is critical. If the lines exceed this right angle, you cannot feed the line properly.

3. Move the standing part of the line toward a vertical position in line with the twists. At the same time, ease the tag end downward until it is at almost right angles with the twists. You have maintained the 90-degree angle from Step 2. You can either pull upward on the standing part or slip a finger in the V of the loop. At the same time, start to feed the tag end.

4. The first wrap of the tag end around the standing part crosses itself so that you can continue wrapping toward the loop. Each succeeding turn lies against the previous one.

5. When you have wrapped the tag end completely over the twists and it is at the V of the loop, hold the junction of the lines with thumb and forefinger.

6. Make a half hitch with the tag end around one of the standing legs of the loop and pull it tight so that it seats in the V where the loop comes together. At this point, you can slip the loop off your knee.

7. The final phase is to make a four or five-turn Clinch Knot around both standing legs of the loop and tease it back against the half hitch you just made. This will lock the knot.

8. Trim the tag end and you have a 100-percent knot.

MEMORY, LINE TWIST, AND FILLING SPOOLS

When you squeeze a sponge and release the pressure, the sponge will return to its original shape. Scientists refer to this as memory; monofilament has it too. You already know that if you stretch mono within its elastic limits, it will return to its original shape the instant the pressure is removed. What most people don't realize is that the force generated by monofilament as it tries to return to its original shape can be significant. In fact, metal reel spools (and certainly plastic ones) are sometimes bent out of shape by this force.

With a strong fish on the other end, the line is elongated and packed on the reel in the stretched attitude. Then, when the tension is eased, the damage occurs. After landing a big fish, take the time to let out a long length of line and then reel it back using normal tension. That will allow the line to return to its basic form and it will save a reel spool in the process.

A bait or lure that revolves in the water will twist monofilament line unless there is a properly functioning swivel between the line and the terminal gear. Spinning enthusiasts often experience twist for another reason. They become excited when a fish is hooked and begin to crank the handle of the reel without recovering any line. The drag continues to slip and every time the bail rotates, one twist is put in the line. When you consider that some reels today have a five-to-one retrieve, you are generating five twists every time you turn the handle once.

The only way to remove the twist is to cut off all the terminal tackle and stream the line behind a moving boat. After a short period of time, the twist should come out and the line will be usable once again. If the twist won't come out, you'll just have to replace the line.

Reel spools should be filled carefully and kept at capacity at all times. Trying to cast a spinning reel that is half full can be frustrating and both distance and accuracy will suffer. A reel should be filled within one-eighth to one-quarter of an inch of the spool lip. Conventional reels should also be filled to capacity, but not above the spool flanges.

You'll also find that it is difficult (if not impossible) to adjust the drag setting properly on a reel that is only half filled with line. There is much more latitude when the reel is full.

Without any consideration of spool diameter or reel size, some anglers will load any break strength monofilament on a reel. There are ground rules worth thinking about. With spinning, for example, casting anything heavier than twenty-pound test is a neat trick if you want to be accurate and achieve distance. At the other extreme, ultralight reels should never carry more than four-pound-test line and a spinning reel with a two-inch spool should never be loaded with more than ten-pound test. If the line is too heavy for the spool diameter, the line will be coiled tightly and memory will set in. Those tight coils will be a nuisance and hamper your fishing.

There are dozens of theories about how to hold the bulk spool of line in relation to the reel. You can get inexpensive line winders for spinning that mount on the reel or in which you place the reel spool and wind line directly. If you don't use these options, put a pencil through the bulk spool of line, have someone hold it and apply reasonable tension on the rim of the spool, and just crank it on. Trying to untwist monofilament by taking it off one end of a bulk spool doesn't really work because of the differences in diameter between the spinning spool and the bulk container.

If you take your light tackle sport seriously, you will probably decide to buy bulk spools of line and do your own changing. You'll find you can remove old line in a hurry if you push a quarter-inch bolt through an empty line spool and insert the end of the bolt in an electric drill. It's a lot faster than trying to do the job by hand.

BRAIDED LINES

Most of the attention so far has been given to monofilament line, which is a single filament extruded from nylon and then oriented. There's a reason. The majority of fishermen use monofilament in a wide range of applications and yet little is known about this synthetic line. A braided line, as the name implies, is made from twisting or actually braiding fibers; Dacron is by far the most preferred material today.

You already know that braided Dacron will stretch only about 10 percent while monofilament may elongate up to 30 percent. That makes it easier to set a hook with Dacron because of better energy transmission and it also gives the angler an advantage in pumping a fish out of the depths or toward the boat. With monofilament, most of the rod movement takes out the stretch and little is left to pull the fish toward you. Dacron, obviously, would also be a prime choice in those situations where fish are close to obstructions and there isn't room to give the critter its head.

In a stress/strain diagram, Dacron shows a fast-climbing curve to denote that there is little elongation in the early stages. Just before Dacron breaks, however, the line stretches and the curve flattens out. Because it is relatively soft and limp, braided line packs more evenly on a spool. It's also important to know that there is little difference in the breaking strength of Dacron whether it is wet or dry or somewhere in between.

A growing number of anglers have been using braided lines for bait-casting assignments and particularly for certain types of bass fishing where a positive hook-setting and fish-playing action is required. Because it does not stretch extensively and then try to return to its original shape, braided Dacron has become the choice of fly fishermen for backing on fly reels. Nylon can spread a spool, but Dacron offers no threat.

The primary use of Dacron has been for offshore trolling and especially in the heavier breaking strengths from fifty-pound class up. The main reason lies in the lack of stretch. Trying to pump a giant fish is taxing work and it can be compounded when most of the effort merely fights the line instead of the fish. With Dacron, when you move the rod, you are pretty certain to be moving the fish.

Keep in mind that Dacron can be severely weakened if it is pinched or crushed. One must also remember that different knots are often required in

Dacron and that the knot strength seldom seems as good as it is in monofilament. The best connections are simple splices which can be made with a special wire or tool.

MONEL WIRE AND LEAD-CORE LINES

There are times when even the light-tackle angler must get an offering deep to catch fish. Downriggers are one approach and planers another, but the majority of fishermen opt for soft wire line or lead core. How much you spool on a reel depends upon where you fish. Along some parts of the waterfront, a hundred feet is considered adequate, while four-hundred-fifty feet is standard at other spots.

For most situations, a hundred yards of wire will more than suffice and it should be spooled over a core of braided line that will serve as backing and also cushion the wire. One would think that wire line is indestructible, but that's not necessarily the case with soft wire. The greatest danger is kinking. If a line isn't bent too sharply, it can be straightened by moving it back in the same direction. However, extremely sharp bends seriously weaken the line and straightening will not help. When that happens, one must splice the two ends together.

The strength of lead core is in the braid. The lead, itself, is much softer than Monel and will kink and break easily. Sunset Line and Twine of Petaluma, California, has just introduced lead core in four different weights. Obviously, the heavier lines will sink deeper.

Thirty or forty-pound-test Monel can be considered standard along the coast. At normal trolling speeds, experts figure that they achieve ten feet in depth for every hundred feet of line streamed astern. That may vary and some may find it a bit conservative, but it should prove pretty close. You can increase depth by adding trolling sinkers. Rough calculations indicate an additional depth of about five or six feet for every four ounces added.

Wire line is frustrating to handle and that's one reason some people prefer lead core. For one thing, it must be kept on the reel under tension all the time or it will balloon up and tangle. In streaming the line, specialists put the clicker on on the reel and pull the line from the tip of the rod. If there is an overrun, it will give you a pleasant interlude from fishing. When you recover line, you must be careful to spool it evenly so it doesn't pile on one side of the reel. If it does, it will soon tumble down and you have a mess on your hands.

Veterans mark wire line every fifty or seventy-five feet by wrapping colored tape around it, using dental floss, or painting the line with nail enamel.

WIRE LEADER

The best advice anyone can offer about wire leaders is to use them only when you have to. Monofilament makes a more sensible choice, because in the experience of some of the leading anglers, it seems to produce more strikes. Fish sometimes exhibit a shyness to wire, even though monofilament may have a larger diameter.

Critters with teeth are the most logical argument in favor of wire, but even then, you only need wire near the bait or lure and the rest of the leader can be monofilament. Top-ranked offshore fisherman Dick Kondak feels, however, that with skipbaits, a wire leader can enhance the action of the offering and make it perform better.

The Haywire Twist serves as the primary method for twisting wire around a hook, swivel, or simply making a loop. There are no substitutes. Abrasion is never a problem with wire, but kinking can be the culprit. If it should kink, you can not straighten it without weakening the wire. Chances are it will break if you even try to restore it. There is nothing you can do but throw the wire away and start over.

You'll hear plenty of arguments along the waterfront whether it is better to use bright stainless wire or the coffee-colored variety. Some say that the bright wire is actually less visible underwater, but the colored wire apparently is the number-one choice.

Many anglers prefer to use braided wire for short leaders. This is particularly popular in fresh water for pike and muskies and equally accepted in salt water. When measured against the single strand, braided wire is slightly larger in diameter and even more so when it is plastic coated. The big advantage of the braid and particularly the nylon-coated material is its flexibility and resistance to kinking. It will, however, curl and when that happens, replacement is the answer.

Muskie and pike fishermen insist on coated-wire leaders, yet some of us who fish for a variety of species feel that these specialists might be overlooking a better way. Even against sharp dentures, heavy monofilament can be pretty tough material and it won't be chopped in half as easily as one might suspect. It would be worth a try to use sixty-pound mono as a shock leader for pike and maybe a bit heavier for muskies if one were worried. Chances are you would get more strikes with the mono and you wouldn't lose many fish if you changed the leader frequently. If you were still concerned about the teeth on a muskie, a very short length of coffee-colored single-strand wire would solve the problem and the rest of the leader could be monofilament. For some reason, that length of nylon-coated leader may rob you of a great many strikes.

FLY LINES

The sophistication built into fly lines today stands in stark contrast to the horsehair lines of Izaak Walton's day and the silk fly lines that followed. Although single-filament fly lines are available, most of the modern lines are made by applying a plastic coating to a braided core. By varying the amount of coating and where it is placed, an assortment of tapers and different line weights can be created. The specific gravity of the plastic can be varied to make a line either float or sink.

Fly lines can be categorized either as floating or sinking. Floating lines are by far the more popular and certainly the easiest to fish and cast. The world of the fly-rodder has been expanded recently with the introduction of new sinking lines that enable him to reach depths previously believed to be beyond the reach of that tackle. High-density lines were once considered the ultimate in sinking tapers, but they have since been surpassed by ultra-high-density or super-high-density lines. Some of these contain lead in the coating and sink much faster than any other manufactured fly lines.

Actually, these super-fast sinkers were forced upon line makers. The West Coast steelheaders and salt-water anglers perfected the art of fishing with lead-core fly lines that they made themselves from a spool of lead-core trolling line. Men such as Bill Schaadt, Frank Bertaina, and Dan Blanton did much to popularize lead cores and spread the word. Lead cores, of course, will kink and they are anything but easy to cast, requiring a specialized technique. Line-makers felt that putting a castable coating over a line that would sink almost as fast as lead core would gain part of the market back. These lines certainly are an improvement and worth your time to investigate.

As I mentioned in the section under wire lines, Sunset Line and Twine Company now manufactures lead core in four different weights. This break-through was in response to pleas from those of us who discovered a new world with the lead. On the West Coast, pioneers carefully removed the lead from the standard braid and substituted heavier fuse wire in its place to create special lines that would plummet like a rock. Some of those lines were so heavy that they would drag bottom even if you opened the floodgates on a dam or they would take a fly to the coral heads on a reef a hundred feet below the surface.

Lead-core lines now come in at least four different densities. Level fly line makes an ideal backing unless you need maximum depth or distance, in which case Amnesia shooting line is best.

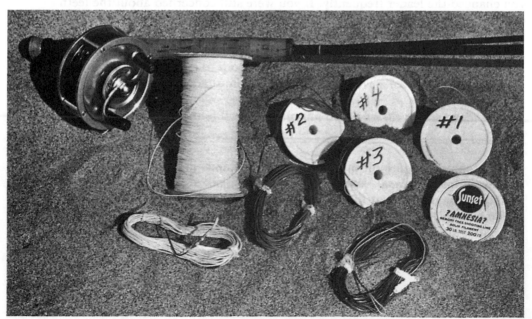

Braided Dacron should be used for fly-reel backing because it stretches very little under pressure. Monofilament can spread a reel spool if wound back with a fish on the other end.

Level fly lines are the most basic, boasting a uniform diameter from one end to the other. They are slightly less expensive than the double taper, which has a uniform diameter through most of its length, but tapers to a narrower diameter at either end, enabling the user to reverse the line if he so desires. Fly fishermen sometimes prefer the double taper when roll casting or for particularly delicate presentations.

Most knowledgeable fly fishermen prefer the weight-forward fly line and many are beginning to use this taper for even the most delicate situations. On a weight-forward line, there is a short front taper, heavy belly section, short back taper, and the rest is small-diameter running line. In most cases, the weight of the line is concentrated in the first thirty feet, which is referred to as the *head* of the line. With this design, you can achieve a faster and longer presentation. The heavy head section shoots forward and pulls the lighter running line with it.

To gain even more distance, steelhead and salmon fishermen on the West Coast began to attach monofilament running line to the head section and the single taper or shooting head was born. Now shooting heads are manufactured commercially and are available in a variety of line weights.

No one in this century did more to improve and standardize fly lines than the late Myron Gregory, a long-time tournament caster and master fisherman as well as a close friend. Myron must be credited with urging the American Fishing Tackle Manufacturers Association (AFTMA) to adopt a set of fly-line standards that he designed. We have a simplified system today thanks to Myron Gregory.

The AFTMA code identifies a level fly line with the code letter L; double taper, DT, weight forward, WF, and single taper or shooting taper, ST. If the line floats, the letter F is used as a suffix and if it sinks, you'll find the letter S after the number. The prefix number tells you the type of fly line and the suffix identifies it as floating or sinking.

The average fly caster holds about thirty feet of line in the air past the tip top of the rod when he casts. This arbitrary length was adopted for purposes of standardization and a number code assigned to various weight ranges. The weight is expressed in grains and 437.5 grains equal one ounce. Most lines made today range in size from 4 through 12, but 3's have been made and the salt-water troops often lean toward 13-weight lines. The following table sets the AFTMA standards:

LINE NUMBER	WEIGHT (IN GRAINS)	TOLERANCE RANGE (IN GRAINS)
1	60	54-60
2	80	74-86
3	100	94-106
4	120	114-126
5	140	134-146
6	160	152-168
7	185	177-193
8	210	202-218
9	240	230-250
10	280	270-290
11	330	318-342
12	380	368-392

5

Fishing with Natural Baits

There's an important difference between waiting for something to happen and making it happen. Bait fishing tends to breed a passive attitude, because most anglers erroneously believe that they merely have to cast their bread (or any other bait) upon the water and wait for the imminent results. Anywhere you pursue the sport, you'll see rods resting in forked sticks or angling skyward from gunwale holders aboard boats. The click mechanisms on the reels are engaged so that they will sound the alarm when something picks up the bait. With that philosophy, it's no wonder most folks have difficulty catching fish.

The serious bait fisherman is aggressive. Purists may shuffle him to some lesser category on the hierarchy of angling accomplishments, but these self-appointed jurists know little of the skill involved in fishing bait. It can definitely be classified as an art and there are no shortcuts for mastering it.

Understand from the beginning that concentration and attention to details lead to victory. If you choose to sit back and relax while suspending bait beneath a float or tethering it along the bottom, no one can fault you for your decision, but you must recognize that you are not utilizing your maximum potential. Catching fish demands work. It's not much easier with bait than with artificial lures. Successful anglers vary their technique constantly and rarely remain glued to a single method. If you honestly believe there is only one way to fish a particular bait or tempt a certain species, you have to come out second best. The problem focuses on finding the approach that will produce fish right now.

Fish must feed if they are to survive. Nature equips each species to search for its food in a certain way and to prefer certain offerings over others. Hunger, at times, may cause a fish to vary its diet considerably or abandon its natural caution. Competition from schoolmates may temporarily remove inborn wariness and result in a fish being more aggressive than it normally would. Under many situations, however, fish can be finicky feeders. If you can manage to take a share of those fish that are extremely selective, you'll automatically do very well with those that aren't.

To catch fish on bait, you must get your bait where your quarry can hear it, smell it, or see it. The most appetizing morsel in the world won't do a bit of good if its presence is unknown. Fish feed either by probing for food or by waiting in one spot and letting the food come to them. Bass in a lake might take up station around a submerged log or along a dropoff and wait in ambush. Pike and muskies will use the cover of a weedbed or the shadows of a rocky outcropping to conceal themselves. Trout in a stream not only seek safety and cover but they must also find a lie where the force of the water is broken by some object; yet they must be close enough to the flow to dart out and snag a passing goodie.

In salt water, the fish are on the prowl much more than they are in lakes or streams. Tides play a vital role in their existence and their body rhythms are tuned to this cycle. Salt-water angling looks much easier than fresh-water sport to those who have never tried it, but figuring out where fish might be on a stage of the tide isn't always the easiest thing to do.

Being creatures of habit, fish expect things to happen a certain way. Almost everyone knows that fish invariably face into the flow of water because it is easier for them to maintain their equilibrium and because that's the direction from which food will come. You can chase a sixteen-inch trout from the comfort of its favorite rock with a two-inch minnow, simply by dragging the minnow upstream behind the predator. Most gamefish are not used to being attacked by their prey and they will usually retreat hastily to figure out what happened.

If you expect that trout to eat the minnow or anything else, it should drift downstream as naturally as possible, following the path of the current. If it passes through the window or area that the trout watches for food, you can bet that the fish eyeballed the offering.

The more you know about the fish you seek and the way that species feeds, the easier it is to choose the right bait and present it effectively. Too many anglers are content to fish at random and let a bait dangle somewhere, hoping eternally that a fish will find it. Frequently, the careless angler lets the bait get buried in the grass or camouflaged on the bottom where it is tough to spot. A bait must be in the productive zone and effectively visible, yet it cannot present a stark contrast that might alert the fish.

Within given tolerances, light tackle will produce more fish with natural bait than heavier gear in most situations. The key reason is feel. You can monitor the progress of the bait better with lighter gear and it also tends to act more naturally in the water.

To become an effective light-tackle angler with bait, you must understand the concept of fishing it and develop a feel that no writer can put into words. That feel comes with experience and it oozes confidence once you master it. You learn it through total concentration and by applying a variety of techniques. Specific examples may help, but you must go beyond that and comprehend the theory. Only then can you apply it wherever you fish and for any species that swims.

In my earliest recollections, my father described this feel as "keeping in touch" with your bait. You had to know what your bait was doing every second it was in the water. If you weren't positive and you had the slightest doubt, he insisted that you reel in and start over again. As a boy, I can well recall the frustrations of drifting a worm into a lair that was certain to hold a trout and, after several minutes, withdrawing a bare hook. I suspect that a large percentage of the trout in that stream grew chubby on the worms that I fed them from our garden. More experienced fishermen, however, could hook trout constantly on a worm. The problem, of course, was that I failed to know what was happening to my worm. It's a tough lesson to learn.

During those early years of trout fishing, Dad and I also chummed grass shrimp along the coast for striped bass and tide-running weakfish, an art that is all but lost today. The trick was to drift a pair of tiny shrimp back in the chum slick at the same rate as the tide was flowing. If you were too slow, the bait would rise above the fish and if you were too fast, your bait would descend to the depths where a scavenger ingested it. Again, it meant developing a feel and keeping in touch with your bait.

The sinker-bouncer has the same problems. There may be some isolated instances where you want the bait to lie in one spot, but that's not the aggressive brand of fishing that one must develop. With the right weight of sinkers in relation to the line, the bait will move along the bottom. Your task is to make certain the sinker is on the bottom at all times and this takes a delicate touch. Sometimes you have to lift the sinker and let it bounce to convince yourself it's in position, but eventually you develop the needed feel and you know what's happening. That's when the fish seem to be biting better and better everytime you go out.

There are subtleties. Learning to watch the line can hone your senses and make you more effective. If you are drifting a cluster of eggs down a steelhead stream, you can often tell if the pencil lead has hung up by watching the attitude of the line. If you have trouble visually, by lifting the rod tip slightly, you can usually see if there is enough pressure on the line to convince you it is in direct contact with the lead. Otherwise, your weight is hung up and you had better get it free.

When you are fishing a live bait with no weights attached, the trick is to give the offering enough freedom to roam, but you still have to monitor what's happening. By watching the line and trying to feel through the rod at the same time, you gain an edge. There's no excuse for not knowing when the live bait has found an underwater haven to hide from the predator you hope will find it. Many of us who fish salt water have seen anglers ignore the antics of a crab and that perfect live bait crash dives for the bottom, burrowing into the sand and out of the way of danger.

Being impatient may not be the worst trait for bait fishing. If something doesn't happen rather quickly, reel in, check the bait, and try it again. Repeat the procedure over and over and over until you do score. Nothing is more frustrating to me than to discover a bare hook and then wonder how long I've been marking time.

The words of my father echo in my ears to this day and I shall never forget them as long as I fish. To him, nothing matches the importance of *keeping in touch with your bait*. Within that sentence lies at least 75 percent of all you need to know to catch fish on bait. Developing that touch takes years, but you can get the basics down quickly.

CHOOSING THE BAIT

Fish are opportunists, but each species has its own primary diet. The preference for various foods changes with availability and every fish will specialize in its feeding patterns from time to time, gaining an advantage by feeding on a single type of prey. Any tackle shop or marina operator can quickly tell you the most popular baits in the area you are about to fish.

The initial approach should be to match the most common baits that your quarry will be feeding on at a given time of year. Smallmouth bass, for example, may be feasting on crayfish and that would be the logical choice over minnows if you can get them. After a heavy rain, worms might be the answer to a trout's prayer, because the runoff should carry plenty of garden hackle into the stream and the fish will be looking for this type of food.

If more than one type of bait can be obtained, it makes sense to stock a variety. After all, bait ranks among the lowest expenditures for fishing, yet it is vital to success. If you insist on taking shortcuts, be prepared to suffer the consequences in terms of fish caught. You may end up not using some of the bait, but it's comforting to have the selection if the fish develop a case of lockjaw.

The other approach leans toward baits that may be foreign to the fish or not among their usual diet. Russ Wilson, a fishing companion and one of the most knowledgeable East Coast anglers I know, always seems to come up with variations on the theme. Through experimentation, Russ discovered that pickerel in a nearby pond responded better to killies, a popular salt-water baitfish, than they did to minnows. The killie is a hardy bait that will stay alive a long time and can take rough treatment. Pickerel crave them like a kid salivates over the thought of an ice-cream sundae.

One of the biggest mysteries in salt water centers around the effectiveness of the eel for offshore fishing. White marlin will charge an eel with ardor, yet no one, including teams of researchers, has ever been able to find an eel in the stomach of a blue-water fish. Those same eels, by the way, will tease snook in Florida waters, even though they are a staple of the striped bass fraternity. One day soon, the fresh-water striper addicts will start fishing rigged eels in lakes and impoundments.

Size of the bait you select can be very important. There are a few ground rules worth remembering. Start by trying to approximate the size of the natural bait in the waters you fish. If that doesn't work, try a slightly larger bait. Scientists have learned that even fish that are sated can sometimes be turned on again by a larger bait. One team of laboratory personnel found that given an option, a fish will take the largest bait it can swallow comfortably. From a fishing standpoint, that seems to support the theory of big baits, but there are times smaller baits are equally effective.

As a light-tackle fisherman, you should concentrate on choosing a bait that is large enough to attract the fish, but small enough for the fish to take easily. It's much simpler to get a hook into a fish when the bait doesn't choke your quarry.

For some reason that defies explanation, fishermen tend to assume that fish are stupid and will ingest anything that resembles food. This premise leads many anglers down the road to failure. Certainly there are times when a fish will eat anything including a swatch cut from the shirt on your back, but that leaves too much to chance. Those who score consistently maximize the attention they give to the bait they put on a hook. It must be the freshest available and they take great pains to preserve it in the field. They want live bait to be healthy, because a healthy bait is frisky in the water and this can make a difference.

Experienced fishermen are extremely selective when they reach in the minnow bucket, worm can, or salmon-egg jar. They'll take the time to single out a bait that looks appealing. It may be friskier than the others or the size may attract their attention, but the point to remember is that the selection is not made at random. This care in choosing a bait can pay dividends.

Using cut bait is no different. Every piece must have an appetizing look to it and be trimmed as neatly as a hedgerow on a country estate. A razor-sharp knife serves as the bait fisherman's most important ally. With it, he can trim each bait so that the edges are not ragged and the meat has an attractive appearance. It may sound like a waste of time, but it makes all the difference in the world.

HOOKING BAITS

Selecting the bait is only the first step. You must then attach it to a hook in an appetizing manner that makes it appear as realistic as possible. Where you place the hook can be critical, regardless of whether you are using live or dead bait. Even the size and style of the hook can be vital (more on that in the next section).

A live bait must be hooked so that it can swim unencumbered and so that the placement of the hook does not kill it. Minnows are among the most popular baits, but they are somewhat fragile and delicate. Even a light wire hook can damage them if you hook them through the back. That's why most

Hook size must often be matched to the bait rather than to the species you seek. By using a small hook, this herring will stay alive longer and swim without much impairment.

When a small bait is used, the hook should be of lighter wire and matched to the task.

minnows are hooked through the lips.

With shiners, bluegills, and other live baitfish including some of the salt-water varieties, you have a choice in how you hook them. If you're trolling, drifting, or if the current is strong, hooking the bait through the lips can do the job. In situations where the water is calmer or you are using a float or you simply want to live-line the fish, hook it right in front of the dorsal fin through the back. Be careful that the hook point does not sever the spine or the bait will die.

When live-lining, if you want the fish to dive deeper, put the hook behind the dorsal fin instead of in front of it. This gives the fish more freedom to move around but is a bit more difficult to control. On a few species, such as the popular pilchard found in southern waters, both the lips and the back are too soft for successful hooking, so anglers push the hook through the top of the eye sockets. The best way to keep menhaden alive when fishing for striped bass or bluefish in northern waters is to hook them through the nostrils.

Offshore anglers often troll a live baitfish such as a bonito or kawakawa for big marlin and other husky offshore predators. The standard rig is to loop some Dacron or monofilament through the tops of the eye sockets and hang the ends on a hook. The hook remains outside the fish. This very effective rig allows the bait to move freely and stay alive a long time. With bonito or any member of that family, the fish must be rigged quickly and put right back in the water. They cannot survive very long when they are handled.

Back on the fresh-water scene, a frog makes an excellent bait for bass. It can be rigged through the lips, but a better method is through the skin on one back leg. If you fish the frog on a very light line with a small hook, it will have an incredible action on the surface and should produce results.

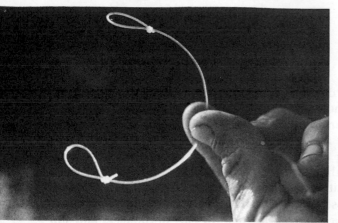

RIGGING A LIVE BAIT

Step 1. A quick way to do this begins by putting slip loops in a short piece of monofilament.

Step 2. Hang one loop over the bend of the hook and tighten.

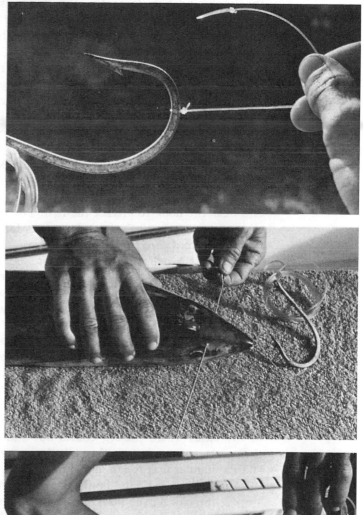

Step 3. Attach the second loop to a bait-rigging needle. When the bait is brought aboard, slide the needle in the forward part of the eye sockets and pull the loop through.

Step 4. Drop the second loop over the bend of the hook and pull tight. The live bait is rigged and ready to fish—and lethal.

Crickets and grasshoppers don't stay alive very long. The place to hook them is through the heavier thorax toward the head. Crawfish can be hooked in the tail or through the carapace or forward shell, somewhat as with a shrimp. Shrimp are among the most widely used salt-water baits and there are two basic methods for rigging them. Some anglers start the hook at the base of the tail on the inside and thread it through the body; this makes it more difficult for fish to steal the bait. The second method proves deadlier when the fish are finicky, but you can lose a lot of bait this way because it's easily pulled off the hook. Simply look for a ridge on the forward part of the head and slip the hook under it. Recently, the Padre Island Company of San Antonio, Texas, has marketed a shrimp harness that is spring-loaded and clamps over the head of the shrimp. It does not injure the bait and has excellent potential for many types of fishing.

There isn't a species of fresh-water fish, from sunfish to salmon, that won't clobber a properly presented earthworm, yet some anglers fail to hook the worm so that the most action can be achieved. If you thread an earthworm or seaworm on the hook, you destroy the enticing wiggle. You want both ends of the worm to move freely. There are a couple of minor variations in the method. The common approach is to hook the worm twice or possibly three times in the middle and let both ends dangle. Some fishermen prefer to hook the worm only once, an inch or two in from the top end. They might put two worms on the hook this way, relying on the long tail and the short protruding end near the hook to attract the fish. The important thing to remember with any worm is to keep the ends loose. As long as it will stay on the hook, you don't have to do anything more.

Crabs are a delicacy in salt water and few species of fish will turn one down. If the crab has claws, you should remove them, not only for ease in handling, but because you want the fish to take the bait without problems. Most crabs will throw their claws if you grab the pincers with a pair of pliers and squeeze.

After the crabs are declawed, slip the hook through one corner of the shell, moving the point from the bottom of the body through the top of the shell. The point of the hook should be on top of the shell; if the crab works down to the bottom, you don't want the point to hang up and you don't want it lost when a fish takes the crab.

Some crabs don't have pointed shells. In that case, insert the hook near one of the bases where the leg comes out and up through the shell. Remember that crabs swim sideways through the water and you want to rig your crab in such a manner that it can also do the same thing.

Dead bait or cut bait should be rigged with equal care. Anglers sometimes impale the bait on the hook too many times, fearing that they'll lose it or fail to hook the fish if they don't. Certain bait-stealers require more secure hooking procedures, but most fish engulf a bait quickly and effectively. They'll take the hook without any difficulty, even if it is only placed through the bait once. That, by the way, is a good way to rig a strip of bait or a piece of a fish. Some anglers will go through a second time with the hook, but that's the maximum. Hook placement should be at one end so that the strip has action in the water.

Small pieces of bait for panfish can be impaled on the hook. Dead shrimp

Crabs swim sideways. By hooking one wing of its shell, you can work the bait in a natural manner across the surface. The hook should always go from the bottom to the top of the shell. This will prevent it from snagging bottom when the crab dives for cover.

should be threaded on the hook if it is whole. Tiny grass shrimp can either be threaded or they can be hung through the carapace with three or four shrimp making up one bait.

Time takes its toll. The longer a bait happens to be in the water, the less effective it becomes. Live bait loses its strength and isn't quite as frisky as it should be. Dead bait will soften and sometimes become raggedy. Water pressure can pull a hook through the bait or cause it to lose its appeal. A hundred things can make the bait look different than it did when you first put it out. That means that you must change bait frequently. Anyone who tries to make a bait do is foolishly diminishing his chances. Fishermen often try to make a bait last for one more fish or they feel they can stick to the old bait without changing. That may work when the fish are on a feeding spree, but on those tough days, old bait will be ignored.

If you have a strike and the bait was damaged, change it. Don't try to straighten it and hope the fish will come back. Compared to the cost of fishing, bait is cheap and expendable. Buy more than you think you'll need and you won't have to worry about running out. When a bait is frayed, you can frequently repair it with a very sharp knife by trimming away the edges. No matter how you attack the problem, make certain you do something about a less-than-perfect bait. The same with live bait. If it loses stamina, change it. Put it back in the bait well, if you must, but get a new bait on the hook.

Most of the rigs for blue-water fishing are beyond the scope of this book; step-by-step instructions can be found elsewhere. There are, however, a few points to keep in mind. Neatness counts there as well as inshore. Every bait should be rigged to swim naturally or to skip with lifelike appearance. It's a proven fact that well-rigged baits catch more fish. The action in the wake of a boat will soften a bait and destroy it in time. Change these baits frequently and check to see that the new ones swim correctly.

For light-tackle fishing, a few of us feel quite strongly that the hook must be rigged outside the bait. Otherwise, there just isn't enough strength in the line or backbone in the rod to drive a hook through the bait and into the fish. Of course there are exceptions, but we're going for consistency. For short-

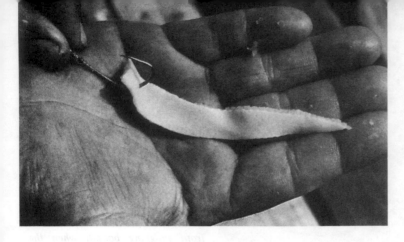

striking fish, a variation of the Ha-Ha Rig can be used with one hook in front of the bait and the other slipped along the side near the tail.

About the most effective rig for light tackle is the offshore wire rig; this is easy to make and baits can be changed in a matter of seconds. Captain Jim Paddock, a research skipper who spent years exploring remote tropical regions, came up with the method because there were times when he couldn't get baits overboard fast enough and because he didn't want to spend all his time rigging trolling baits.

UNDERSTANDING HOOKS

Hooks are tailored to penetrate the flesh of a fish and remain intact through the battle. Although the fish hook has been in existence from the earliest days of man and looks as basic a device as one can create, there are thousands and thousands of styles and sizes in use today. That alone should tell you that fishermen differ in their thinking as to what the perfect hook might be for each situation. Manufacturers report that there is little standardization among the various makers and that most styles and sizes refer to the production of a single fabricator. More important, sizes vary with style, so that you cannot name a size and have it apply universally.

Even the numbering system for hook sizes is archaic. As the number decreases toward one, the hooks increase in size. Thus, the smaller the number, the larger the hook—starting with size 32 (which is about the smallest made) and working down to number 1. Then, just the reverse is true. Hooks add an "0" after the number such as 1/0, 2/0, 3/0, and so forth. In the "0" series, the larger the number the larger the hook. A 1/0 hook is a size larger than a 1.

There are several variables in hook construction that you should know about. The weight or diameter of the wire is indicated by the letter "X" followed by either Fine or Stout. Any hook not made from standard-size wire would have this designation. A hook designated as 1X Stout would be made with the same wire used for the next larger hook and a hook numbered as 1X Fine would have the wire used in the next size smaller hook. Usually, these variations will only range through 2X and 3X, although there are special cases where a greater deviation is manufactured.

The same basic "X" system is used to define the length of the hook shank, except that the words "Long" and "Short" are substituted for "Fine" and

"Stout." A 2X Long hook would have the shank length of a hook that was two sizes larger and a 3X Short means that the shank length equals that of a hook three sizes smaller.

From a practical standpoint, many of the variations, such as type of eye, type of point, position of eye, point position, and others will resolve themselves in the final choice of a hook. Light-tackle anglers have to be concerned with penetration, holding power of a hook, and selecting a style or size that fits the bait being used. There is no universal hook, but you can certainly fish around the world with only a modest selection of styles and sizes.

As noted earlier, the breaking strength of the line you use helps to determine how heavy and how large a hook you can use. Light wire hooks penetrate far better than those made from stronger wire. The rule of thumb tells us that the lighter the line, the lighter the hook wire should be. You simply can't bury a husky hook with six-pound-test line, no matter how sharp it is. That's why light-tackle anglers often opt for small hooks, even though they are going for big fish. They know that they don't have a chance until the hook penetrates.

Everything in fishing boils down to a compromise and hook selection leads the parade. You must pick a size that is small enough to set, but large enough to hold without bending or breaking. The length of the barb is another factor. Hooks with short barbs may not hold as well, but they can be driven into a fish much more easily. Unless the whole barb is buried, the hook can come out.

Barbs also make a difference when the hook happens to be buried in a bait. The first task requires that the hook be driven through the bait and then into the fish. That's not as easy as it sounds. For that reason, whenever possible, keep the point of the hook extending ever so slightly beyond the bait.

If you run a series of experiments, you'll discover that barbless hooks offer a distinct advantage in hooking fish and they are not that simple for a fish to dislodge. You don't even need the zig-zag in the point that is typical among tiny barbless hooks. As long as you maintain pressure on the fish, the hook will hang in its mouth, barb or no barb.

In most situations, I prefer to conceal the hook in the bait as much as possible. To my thinking, it's just neater and more natural and it does make a difference on those days when fish are finicky. That helps to dictate the size hook to be used and the style. Some of the sharpshooters in the business are gravitating toward smaller hooks for much of their fishing. Surprisingly, they hook the fish better and hold well. Veterans know this, but it's tough to convince a newcomer who would much rather follow the crowd than set the pace.

Treble hooks are gaining in popularity, especially for live-bait fishing. One hook goes through the live bait and the other two stand ready to impale the first fish that comes along. Trebles are also being used in some dead-bait situations, because they leave a barb or two free of the bait. It's been the experience of many that treble hooks are much easier for a fish to dislodge during the battle, but, again, you must hook the fish first and worry about the fight later.

Light lines with small hooks and equally small pieces of bait are an advantage enjoyed by the light-tackle fisherman. The method can be deadly and it's worth remembering. When things are tough and the fish have stopped hitting, try the miniature approach and work a small bait back there. Quite often, you'll have to gamble with a very light leader, but it's fun to prove that you can get a strike and even more pleasurable when you demonstrate the skill needed to land the fish.

Short-shank tuna and albacore hooks along with the popular O'Shaughnessy pattern cover most of my assignments in salt water with the exception of some offshore work where I switch to a needle-eye hook for bait rigging and for heavy fish. Baitholder styles are good for worms and other baits. I like a sproat for plastic worms used for largemouth and smallmouth bass fishing. Smaller sproats can be used with salmon eggs if you don't want to carry a special salmon-egg hook.

As long as you have enough sizes to cover the fishing situations you will be involved in, you can usually get by with a handful of patterns. In the process, you get to know the hooks you use and develop confidence in them.

If you're going to catch fish, you must concentrate on hook penetration and that means personally sharpening every hook you tie on the line from a size 12 to a size 12/0. There are no exceptions and no excuses. It's a well-proven fact that you'll catch more fish if you work cutting edges into the point and barb of the hook. The easiest way involves a file or stone. My own preference is for a Red Devil Woodscrapers file #3915 (it used to be a #15, but they changed the numbering system).

Holding the hook with the point on top and the eye of the hook toward you, lay the file on a 45-degree angle to the point and stroke several times to create a cutting edge on that side. Then, reverse the angle of the file so it rests at a 45-degree angle on the other side and take the same number of strokes. You should have created cutting edges and sharpened the point in the process. Without the cutting edges, penetration becomes more difficult.

Hooks don't last forever and they are relatively cheap compared to other tackle items. If there is any sign of rust, throw the hook away. Should you experience difficulty in touching it up with file or stone, the hook has to be discarded. That applies to treble hooks as well as single hooks. No serious light-tackle fishermen would even think of using a hook that he had not sharpened personally.

SINKER BOUNCING

At first, everyone seemed to be catching fish. The trout stream had been stocked that morning and when the waters opened to angling late in the afternoon, it was no trick to get fish to hit any natural bait you put in the water. The torrid action didn't last long. Strikes were more difficult to come by and eventually they were the exception rather than the rule.

While most of the anglers on that stream tried in vain to reverse the trend, two fishermen at the head of one pool couldn't stop catching fish. The gentle splashing of still another trout on the surface would draw every eye in that direction like a magnet scoops up metal filings. The two were generous and good-natured, inviting a young man to fish alongside them rather than have him try to cast across their lines, but the fact remained that they took fish.

When the pressing darkness of the woods pulled the curtain down on activities, the leading angler shared a few secrets. While others were fishing four-pound-test line, he preferred two-pound test, because it performed better. More important, he noted that the typical fisherman had a brace of hefty split shots to keep his bait near the bottom in the swift stream. The successful man reported that he used much smaller split shots and more of them. His lighter line helped and he also reasoned that it gave the bait a different action. He was right.

The basic rule of bottom fishing is to use the lightest sinker you possibly can, consistent with the conditions. If it will take your bait to the bottom, that's all you need. To the uninitiated, what difference could it possibly make as long as the sinker held bottom? That's where the line separates the fishermen. Small sinkers allow the bait a more natural action and help to probe the bottom better than heavy sinkers that plummet like an anchor and hold one spot the same way.

Under the same water conditions, the lighter the line you use, the less weight you need to reach or hold bottom. The hotshot who uses ten-pound-test line while fishing summer flounder can benefit from lighter sinkers than his partner who may be relying on twenty-pound-test line.

We can all find exceptions, but the magic combination occurs when your sinker will go to the bottom and then move slowly. You want your bait to cover some territory. If the sinker doesn't allow the bait to move, impart your own action by periodically lifting the rod to pull the bait toward you and then pausing momentarily. In a fast current, make your casts upstream so that the sinker has time to reach bottom before the bait enters the productive zone. Then, use the rod tip to monitor the progress and keep the sinker and the bait bouncing downstream.

Not everyone realizes that, when they fish a current, the force of the water can lift the bait and sinker at the end of the drift. That makes it foolish to hold the rod still very long, because the bait comes off the bottom and rises somewhere into a mid-depth. In those situations, simply work it in slowly and cast again.

Even veterans can have trouble telling when a sinker reaches bottom. With the reel in freespool, the weight will plummet for the depths. Watch the line closely. You are looking for a slight amount of slack that is created the instant the sinker bounces bottom. When you see that momentary skip in the line, you're on the bottom and ready to begin fishing.

Dozens of sinker styles have been created to handle every conceivable assignment. Some are made to hang fast, while others are designed to roll around. The style you choose depends on the fishing situation. The bank sinker probably ranks as the most popular in fresh water and salt, because it sinks well and its shape allows it to be dragged over most bottoms without fouling. Dipseys also find extensive use in fresh water and for light salt-water work. Egg sinkers are favorites for fish-finder rigs.

Split shots, of course, clamp on the line and so do wraparound sinkers and rubber-core. No matter where you fish, a selection of rubber-core sinkers can come in handy. Even on the offshore grounds, they can be used under artificial squids and to separate items in a chain on the leader. Trolling sinkers are also rigged in line and at normal trolling speeds for inshore work, you can expect about six feet of depth for every four ounces you attach to the line.

The most important thing you can remember about sinkers is to choose the lightest weight you can use to reach bottom. With a little experience, you will limit yourself to a few basic sinker styles in an assortment of weights. And you'll catch fish.

SWIVELS AND TERMINAL RIGS

With the exception of a three-way swivel for certain bottom rigs, a number of light-tackle anglers tie their line directly to the leader without using swivels whenever they can. If a bait is going to spin or if you must troll it with spinning gear, you may need a small swivel. Again, size counts. Always go to the smallest swivel you can use consistent with getting the job done.

Terminal tackle should be miniaturized whenever possible. When you consider the breaking strength of light lines and match this against the breaking strength of a swivel, you don't need a heavy wire model to land fish. There's no way to escape using terminal tackle such as sinkers, hooks, swivels, and the like, but everyone can make a conscious effort to keep everything small. It just makes a more natural presentation to the fish.

Books are filled with dozens of different bottom rigs and each has its purpose. To be successful, you only need to know a few. The best all-purpose rig is what I call the Basic Bottom Rig. The sinker comes off one arm of a three-way swivel on a short length of leader and the hook is attached to the other arm via a leader. This leader varies in length, but for many situations, I like at least three feet. You can make it shorter when necessary. It's a good idea, by the way, to use lighter leader material to attach the sinker than the breaking strength of your line. That way, if the sinker hangs in the bottom, the lighter leader will break and you'll save a hook and swivel in the process.

Variations of this rig include the high-low rig in which two hooks are used, one above the other. The purpose of having one bait higher than the other is to cover two zones, especially when there is more than one species of fish. Some anglers also prefer the sliding sinker rig under the theory that a fish can pick up the bait without being alarmed by undue weight or tension on the line.

Given a single choice, I would opt for the Basic Bottom Rig. By varying the length of the leader to the sinker, you can keep the bait higher or lower in relation to the bottom. With light tackle, I also reason that one fish at a time is enough for anyone and I don't need a double-header.

Whether you buy your rigs assembled or make your own, look for those with the lightest leader material you can find. Turning to heavy leaders when they are not absolutely necessary defeats the purpose of using a light line. Most commercial rigs are made for the heavy-tackle army and some of the leaders used could pull a Jeep out of a ditch.

If you plan to fish light tackle on a steady basis, it pays to make your own leaders. Simply buy a spool or two of monofilament and you can tie up any combination you need. Remember that lighter leaders consistently catch more fish, so choose a breaking strength that will just do the job.

6

The Wide World of Artificials

The pleasures of light-tackle angling multiply when you fool a careful brown trout with a nymph that has been chewed up by a dozen other fish or you convince a deep-bellied largemouth into leaving its lair long enough to pounce on a plastic worm. Presenting an artificial and making it appear lifelike demands an extra measure of skill and concentration, but serious anglers wouldn't have it any other way. In fact, most would gladly swap you two or three fish on bait for every one they catch on flies or lures.

Mastering the use of artificials takes years of practice and a wealth of experience, but almost anyone can catch fish on these imitations if they are willing to follow a few basic guidelines. Too many fishermen ply the waters of the world with tackle boxes overfilled with lures of every description, yet they never approach the problem of catching fish with any semblance of a system.

THE CONFIDENCE GAME

No one has developed a panacea for catching fish nor has a magical lure been invented that is guaranteed to work every time. A trip to the nearest tackle shop should convince you that the marketplace has been flooded with artificials that are touted not to fail. Every lure has been tested. Every lure has probably caught fish at one time or another. No one can afford to produce a bait that doesn't work, because the costs of getting it into the hands of the consumer are prohibitive. Some, of course, work better than others.

Whether you choose to fish with a fly rod, spinning, plug, or trolling gear, every lure must be chosen with a purpose in mind. Confidence is the key to fishing with artificials and it starts at the time you plunk your money on the counter and buy the lures of your choice. You have to believe they will catch fish and that means you are anxious to give them a try. These baits should also fit into your basic approach to fishing.

If, for example, you do most of your bass fishing over deep structure, an assortment of floating plugs isn't going to do you much good. The fly fisherman who limits his selection to dry flies is missing out on several other styles that are equally effective. A good basic assortment of lures is important and it should be chosen with care to cover such variables as depth, size, color, and action.

Many dealers stock less-expensive imitations of the more popular lures as well as the originals. There are times when the bargains will work, but it makes more sense to stick with the manufacturer who developed the lure. Any bait is more than a shiny paint job. A delicate balance has usually been achieved that makes the offering perform in a specific way. Not every copy can duplicate this action and that means the price you pay can be high in more ways than one.

Confidence is equally vital on the water. Frequently, fishermen simply go through the motions of casting and retrieving without concentrating on what they are doing. A strike comes as a total surprise and they have no idea what retrieve they just used to produce the favorable results. It's far better to fish a bait for fifteen minutes and do so with enthusiasm than to flay the water mechanically. The instant you lose confidence or begin to believe that another bait might do better, it's time to change.

DEVELOPING A SYSTEM

Rick Clunn, the only person to post back-to-back wins in the prestigious Bassmasters Classic, simplified his fishing technique and began to catch more fish. Over the years, he kept careful notes on his own activities, but also recorded the results of every competitive event he could find. Studying his log books, Rick suddenly realized that regardless of where they were held, most tournaments were won by someone using a spinnerbait, crankbait, or plastic worm. Those three types of lures continuously proved superior to everything else.

Armed with that knowledge, he concentrated his efforts on learning how to fish those offerings to perfection. He ignored other types of lures and focused his attention where he knew the payoff had to be. His meteoric rise has been an inspiration to other fishermen, yet he attributes it to developing a system and sticking to it.

No matter where you fish or what species you seek, there's a system that will work for you. The common tendency is to flit from one cureall to another like a moth around a flame. When somebody catches a couple of fish on a particular lure, it can be tough to resist the temptation to start going through the tackle box. Of course, if you happen to have the lure in question, it makes sense to try it, but don't go out to buy it just because somebody caught a fish on it. That's how tackle boxes become stuffed with an assortment that defies description.

If you keep in mind that not all fish are taken on the same offering, it might give you more confidence in your own approach. Start with the most popular type of lure or one that you can work well and stick to it. It's better to fish an average lure with finesse than to be less than adequate with a good lure.

A lot can be learned from watching a good fisherman. When he ties on an artificial, he usually makes a short cast and watches the action. He wants to make certain that it performs as designed before he starts fishing with it. If it doesn't pass this test, he'll either "tune" it by adjusting some part of it or he'll tie on another one. The last thing he wants to do is waste time working something that isn't performing at maximum effectiveness.

In fishing any artificial, you must know instinctively what it can and cannot do and be able to picture the action when it is out of sight. This takes practice and few newcomers seem to be willing to invest this time. If you want to catch fish, stand at the edge of a swimming pool or find some clear, shallow water and watch what happens when you twitch the rod tip or turn the handle of the reel. Fly fishermen can also spend time studying the effect on a streamer fly or bucktail when it moves through the water. You can learn a great deal by observing. Then, when you're fishing, try to picture what you have seen.

EXPERIMENTATION

Rigid thinking has proven to be the downfall of many anglers and for good reason. Fish may be creatures of habit, but it's difficult to know what game plan they happen to be following at the moment. Those who insist on making a fish do things their way may come out second best. Eliminate any preconceived notions and take the approach of an open-minded researcher.

No one can tell you all the different ways to fish flies and lures nor would that prove very helpful, because we forget too quickly. When you ferret the techniques out for yourself, you'll be able to relate each to particular experiences and you'll start to know when and where to use each method. The important thing is to learn a general approach based on sound fundamentals. The rest comes with practice and observation.

The leading anglers in any type of fishing seem to follow the same approach. They have convinced themselves that their lures are over fish all the time and that their quarry will strike providing they find the right combination. To that end, they never stop trying and they never pause in their experiments. Concentration ranks as the most critical aspect of their work. Every instant that the lure is in the water, they know what it is doing. If a fish happens to strike, they can duplicate the retrieve or tell you the precise

Lily-pad fishing dictates a wide assortment of weedless lures.

trolling pattern and speed they were following. It isn't guesswork. They know because they remembered the data.

Pattern is the word used to describe what some fish are doing at a particular time. It applies to all species in either fresh water or salt and can be a valuable method for figuring out what lures to use and how to fish them. As you continue to cast or troll, you must try to figure out what the fish could be doing. Each time there is a strike or a follow, try to relate it to something you can recognize and repeat. You may discover that the fish are occupying a specific type of terrain or that they will only hit a lure of a certain size or that you must use a particular color. Whatever the effect, that's what you want to be able to duplicate.

Salt-water species may take up feeding positions or prowl certain areas on various phases of the tide. That's a pattern. Trout feeding on nymphs can be considered a pattern and when bass are in twelve feet of water along a sloping point, that, too, is a pattern. Northern pike may decide that the edges of weed beds make a better ambush point on a given day than the rocky shores. Fish may hit topwater baits or they could insist on lures crawled across the bottom. All of these are patterns and will help to increase your catch if you recognize them.

When you're looking for fish, the trick is to eliminate as many things as you can; that has to be done systematically. If you jump from spot to spot without reason, you may or may not find the fish. It makes more sense to fish a certain type of terrain or pattern first. Then, if it doesn't work, try something else. At least that way you are no longer fishing at random.

Some things don't make sense. Fly fishermen, for example, spend a great deal of time either choosing flies that are tied perfectly or creating their own imitations. A great deal of emphasis goes into the detail without any regard for how much a trout or salmon can see in a second or two as the offering passes the window of the fish. Everything must be perfect.

Once they begin to catch fish on a particular fly, it loses its delicate shape and balance. Eventually, the wings become chewed and it is a sorry imitation of the once-proud tie. Nevertheless, it continues to catch fish and will often outproduce a brand-new fly of the same pattern. Many aficionados refuse to admit that this happens, yet it does with regularity.

Based on these observations, one might logically question just how important tiny variations in the tie might be. The two practical factors are size and silhouette. If you can match the approximate size of the natural food and your offering has the same basic silhouette, it should catch fish. That means that if the naturals are dark, the imitation should be dark or vice versa.

Fishing the Cumilahue River in southern Chile with local expert Adrian Dufflocq, Ed Zern and I witnessed a hatch of yellowish green mayflies that none of us could identify; we learned later that Ernie Schwiebert also could not tag a name on them. That didn't stop us from catching fish. Ed and I tied on light-colored flies of about the same size and took fish up to six pounds on 4X tippets.

In fact, knowing the Latin names of insects or being able to identify hundreds of fly patterns does not insure that one will catch fish. It's far more important to be able to make a good presentation and use a pattern that represents something on which the fish is feeding.

Whenever you use artificials, there are variables. A couple stand out from all the rest in degree of importance and those are the ones on which you should concentrate. Depth leads the pack. If you insist on scratching the surface with a topwater bait while the fish are lying near the bottom, you're destined for failure. Regardless of the lure you choose, it should get down to fish-eye level. When you do fish on top, you have to select conditions when the fish will crash a bait on the surface.

The size of the offering has to rank second behind depth. Researchers have found that fish often ignore everything but a specific food to gain feeding efficiency. When you change lures, vary sizes. If there is a particular local bait that you know has become a mainstay of a fish's diet, start with that size.

Not long ago, a group of us were fishing for seatrout on the west coast of Florida. Before leaving home, I found a Mirrolure painted chartreuse on top and bottom that Harold LeMaster, one of the world's great plug fishermen and the man who created the Mirrolure, had sent me. I took this bait along more as a joke than anything else, because I was certain that none of the others would have anything like it. My plan was to convince them that they had to have a chartreuse Mirrolure to catch fish and I was more surprised than they were when it actually happened.

Lee Wulff and I were in a boat one morning and I teasingly told him that

Matching the size and silhouette of a bait can be extremely important.

he had to have a bait like mine to catch fish. Lee smiled and kept fishing. When I released the third fish, I had his attention and the next time I brought one to the boat, he gladly accepted the offer to use my rod and lure. It's hard to believe, but even though I used the same lure in a different color, I couldn't buy a fish with it. Neither could our guide who was equally mystified.

That was one of those rare days when color did make a difference. It didn't matter which one of us used the green bait, he was the person who caught the fish. Color, other than silhouette such as light or dark, usually isn't nearly as important as size. However, as you continue to change lures, you might try varying color between light and dark.

In shallow water such as the flats in south Florida and the Bahamas, the rule of thumb is that you use dark shades over light bottoms and light colors over grassier bottoms. It is true that some species prefer one family of colors over others. Tarpon fishermen often swear by orange under certain conditions. Those who fish deeper water for members of the jack family will lean toward the yellows. Offshore anglers seem to favor white or green.

FEEDING STRATEGY

Since fish are cold-blooded, their metabolisms are directly affected by water temperatures and that governs their behavior patterns. Each species has its own temperature preferences and temperature tolerances. It functions best within the preferential range and cannot survive very long beyond the tolerance limit.

From the standpoint of fishing artificials, recognizing these conditions can be important. Assuming that there is adequate cover and a sufficient supply of food, fish will seek out the most comfortable temperature. Early in the season, for example, bass will move back up into the creek coves of a lake or they'll suspend on a warm day to take advantage of the sun's rays.

Although brook trout prefer water just a little cooler than rainbows or browns (the brookie is a member of the char family), trout thrive in water from 50° to 70°. Water in the upper 50s or low 60s is optimum. During the summer when stream water warms, you'll find the fish in different lies than they maintained during other parts of the year. Look for them where the temperatures are cooler and there is plenty of oxygen.

In addition to helping you determine where fish will be, temperature plays another vital role. Artificials yield marginal results at the low end of the temperature tolerance scale. Fish are sluggish and search for food slowly. During this period, natural baits make more sense, but if you insist on artificials, they should be worked near the bottom and at very slow rates of retrieve. If you keep records, you'll discover that water temperature must rise several degrees above the minimum before fish will actively chase artificial lures. That's why it pays to carry a thermometer and to use it.

Just to stay alive, a fish has to consume at least one percent of its body weight daily in food. The process of feeding can sap a great deal of energy from a fish, forcing it to rest for a considerable period of time between feeding periods. Part of the survival plan revolves around an energy trade-off. The idea is to gain the greatest intake for the lowest expenditure of energy. Fish accomplish this in several ways.

Young fish may chase baits or lures for considerable distances, but as a fish matures and the growth rate slows, you'll discover that they are looking for the easiest meals they can find. That helps to explain why a lunker bass hesitates to chase a lure and expects its meal to venture within a foot or two of its lie.

All of us know there are times when a speedy retrieve will trigger an instant response from a predator, causing the fish to run down the escaping "prey." On the other hand, many veterans insist on using a slow retrieve for most situations so that the fish doesn't have to expend a great deal of energy. The midpoint according to some specialists is to move a lure fast enough to keep the fish from studying it, but slow enough for the quarry to catch easily.

Selective feeding, a method in which fish concentrate on one type of prey while ignoring everything else, also helps them to gain efficiency. Perhaps the most outstanding example of this occurs in the Florida Keys during late spring and early summer when the palolo worm reproduces. A spring tide late in the afternoon triggers the process and the worms break in half with the reproductive portion wiggling seaward. This section measures about two inches in length on the average.

Thousands of tarpon invade the area to feed on these tiny creatures. They instinctively know when the hatch will take place and they will forsake most other offerings while they are feeding on the worms. If you witness the event, you can't believe the constant refusals by the fish of most standard lures. Even fly fishermen cannot consistently catch these tarpon on the traditional patterns. Instead, they tie up an imitation of the worm and the results are spectacular.

It's no different with trout on a stream. They will begin to feed on a particular insect and pass up everything else. When the supply of their first choice dwindles, the fish will abruptly switch to something else. If you were to

If you choose a fly that has the same basic size and silhouette as the natural, you'll catch fish.

catch a fish and analyze the stomach contents, you would find that each species of insect rests in the stomach in distinct layers. They are rarely mixed.

This tells you that you must match size and silhouette of the food on which your quarry is feeding. Sometimes the trout will dine on a particular stage of the mayfly and ignore other stages of the same insect. If you're getting refusals, you might not have uncovered the basic food supply.

If a predator has a choice, it will select the largest prey it can handle easily. This tends to support the theory of big baits for big fish, but one must remember that if there is an abundance of a particular-sized bait, that's usually what a gamester will be feeding on.

In a series of experiments on bluefish, Dr. Bori Olla of the National Marine Fisheries Service observed his charges daily and learned a great deal about their feeding habits. As an example, he could feed them live bait of a certain size and they would eat until they became sated. Then they would ignore any other bait in the large tank. If Dr. Olla started to toss larger baitfish in the tank, the blues would begin to feed again. Apparently, food of an increased size would turn them on. It's a valuable hint to remember. If you stop catching fish on a lure of one size, switch to something larger and see what happens.

MORE ON FEEDING

Some anglers erroneously believe that gamefish feed by opening their mouths while swimming blindly through a school of bait. It doesn't work that way. Predators select and attack one specific victim at a time. They strike with a purpose and not at random. That's why the shimmering, silvery mass of a school of baitfish offers each individual member a modicum of protection. As the fish change position, it is difficult for a predator to zero in on one fish.

A friend of mine kept two bass in a fifty-five-gallon aquarium and it was always interesting to watch him feed his two pets. Usually, a hapless minnow disappeared so quickly that you would miss the whole thing if you blinked your eyes. I happened to be watching one day when my friend put about a dozen minnows in the tank. The larger bass chose a minnow and lunged for it, but the tiny baitfish dodged the attack and quickly retreated to a neutral corner. Although there were other minnows within easy striking distance, the bass stalked his original victim and suddenly tried again. He missed the second time, but continued to ignore other minnows while focusing on the one that eluded him. It took four tries before the bass nailed that food, but nothing else seemed to matter until the first victim was consumed.

Researchers tell us that a predator tries to choose prey that has become isolated, disabled, or looks different from the others. Maybe that's what happened in the example above. That's also the reason why predators will hang below and behind a school of baitfish, waiting to pick off stragglers. Knowledgeable anglers capitalize on this by allowing their lures to sink through the bait and down to the level where a predator could be lurking.

If you find a school of breaking fish on the surface, you'll discover that your lure gets clobbered about the time it comes out of the pack of baitfish and stands isolated from the rest. Veteran salt-water trollers who use umbrella-style rigs made from several tube lures use this principle to their advantage. They often resort to tubes of the same size and color with the exception of the one that trails in the center. This is purposely picked to contrast with the colors used and it usually gets most of the hits.

By schooling, predators often add to their feeding efficiency. A baitfish may be able to dodge a single attacker, but when gamefish are everywhere, it's tough for the victims to know which fish have a bead on them. In this disoriented melee, most school members are able to feed with a minimum expenditure of energy.

Such species as the pike or muskellunge in fresh water or the barracuda in the salt are built for ambush and prefer to wait for their victims to come within range. The attack comes with the suddenness of a lightning bolt and it is a straight-line affair that doesn't allow the fish to change course. If you fish for these species, you must choose lures carefully. The best ones will track in a straight line with little lateral motion. A lure that moves from side to side may zag when the fish zigs and you'll miss the strike.

Anglers who pursue pike and muskies know that once the fish chases a lure, it will often continue to expend energy in an attempt to catch it. They have learned by experience never to retrieve the bait right up to the boat and lift it from the water. Instead, they will use the rod tip and crochet a figure 8 in the water right alongside the boat. It's surprising how many strikes occur at boatside.

When a fish follows a lure and doesn't strike, you must assume that something is wrong. It could be that your quarry spotted the boat or some

Lures that are bent or twisted will not perform properly.

foreign movement above the water that scared it away. More likely, there was something about the lure or the leader or some other part of the tackle that signaled the predator that something was amiss.

Bori Olla observed the perfect example of this once when he was feeding his bluefish small striped bass. One bluefish isolated a striper and charged. The prey never moved. Sensing that something was wrong, the bluefish veered off at the very last instant and made a wide circle. Again, the blue attacked, but the bass didn't twitch a muscle or make any attempt to escape. For a second time, the bluefish broke off the charge and regrouped. This happened twice more. On the fifth try, the bass tried to dart away and the bluefish nailed it instantly. The predator expected its prey to try to escape. When that didn't happen, the blue sensed that something was wrong and wouldn't strike.

In a fishing situation, if you stop a lure dead with a fish right behind it, the fish may refuse the offering. On the other hand, you can sometimes tease a fish into striking by speeding up the retrieve when the gamester swings in behind. This can make your quarry believe its meal is escaping. Sometimes that's all it takes.

THE APPROACH

Casting accuracy contributes greatly to the success of anyone who fishes with artificials. No matter where you happen to fish, you'll find that the best fishermen have achieved a degree of finesse in their casting and can consistently put a lure right on target. If you're new to the game, take the time to practice your casting. It can be an ongoing thing in which you select imaginary targets and see how close you can come. Long casts are seldom needed, so concentrate on the shorter ones.

Once you have developed the ability to hit the target, you must spend an equal amount of time learning what targets to hit. It becomes a matter of recognizing the habitat of your quarry and then placing the lure in the most natural position in relation to that habitat. If, for example, you suspect that a bass is lying alongside a chunky log, it's foolish to drop a bait right at the edge of the log. Chances are that you'll bomb the head of the fish and spook it in the process. A better approach would be to cast beyond the log and then work the lure toward you. That way you'll cover three of the four sides in one cast: the back, side, and front of the log.

Always remember that prey do not attack predators. As we learned from Bori Olla's observation, gamefish expect their victims to move away from them or at least be unaware of the predator's presence. If a minnow charges a bass, chances are the largemouth would move out of the way until it could figure out what happened. Use that to your advantage. Try to imagine where the fish might be lying and then let fly or lure pass the spot in a natural manner.

Alerting a fish to one's presence can be a fatal mistake and probably accounts for a significant lack of success among many anglers. If you happen to fish shallow, clear water where you can observe your quarry, you can sometimes detect the effects when a fish senses something is amiss. It may not leave its lie or spook, but you can spot a degree of nervousness or you'll see the fish act a bit tense. The precise reaction is difficult to describe, but you'll recognize it when you see it.

Few of us realize that fish can spot us as easily as we can spot them. They are alert to movement and can detect a rod waving in the air or someone in a white T-shirt moving about. If you're walking along the bank, they can hear your footsteps and it makes sense to move carefully some distance back from the edge of the water. The next time you're near a lake, look for some bluegills in the shallows. When you see some, wave your arms in the air and see what happens. Then, move on until you spot some more and walk down near the water's edge. This should be enough to convince you.

If you are standing on a dock and there is a school of baitfish swimming around, wait until they are approaching you and then lift an arm over your head suddenly. The fish will instantly change direction and move away. They saw you. If baitfish can do this, so can gamefish—and lack of care could cost you a good day on the water.

Trout fishermen can explain a poor day with dozens of technical excuses, but improper wading often heads the list and it is seldom recognized. If you send ripples out as you wade, they can alert fish ahead of you. For those who insist on fishing downstream, sand, gravel, and other debris kicked up as you walk will announce your presence with the authority of a gong in an old J. Arthur Rank motion picture.

Veteran fly fishermen work upstream so that they don't telegraph their presence and so that the fish cannot see them. We all know that fish in a stream always face into the current, often selecting a lie that gives them a good window on the food passing by, yet affords them a place to stay out of the main current. As you learn to read the water, you plot a course that will put you in position to cast to the likely spots while wading those portions of the stream that customarily don't hold fish. This, of course, can vary. In some places, the fish will be along the banks and the safest route is midstream. Other waters demand a different approach and you may have to zig-zag to avoid riffles, pools, rocks, glides, and other types of habitat.

This veteran of small-stream fishing not only keeps his profile low but stays well back from the water.

FLY   FISHING

Fly fishermen often find themselves so mired in the rituals of tradition and custom that they fail to take a practical approach to their sport. Flexibility in thinking and approach can be an asset and each area should be fished in the most logical manner for that particular day.

No one knows more about the ways of a trout than George Harvey, who, for many years, taught thousands of students how to catch these wily critters at Penn State University. Watching George fish is a richly rewarding experience. He can cover a beat with the effectiveness of a vacuum cleaner. Fishing behind him is folly and if he follows you on a stream, you won't believe the number of trout you passed up.

Over the years, he has simplified his approach to the sport and much of what he does has value on any stream. His guiding principle is simply that conditions can change from minute to minute and from spot to spot. If you fish with your mind in a rut, you'll pay the price. A good angler is constantly observant and notices even the slightest change taking place.

To George, fishing with a leader tippet lighter than 6X is a mistake. He, like many of us, is convinced that fish will see the leader no matter how fine it is, but 6X is a good compromise. Usually, he'll stick to 4X or 5X, arguing that presentation is far more important.

Dry-fly fishing might be more fun than any other type, but not all anglers are successful at it. Drag destroys most efforts before they get underway. George claims that if you can float a fly over a trout for twenty-four inches drag free, you can catch the fish. This means that you must be in the proper position for the cast and you must have enough slack in line and leader to achieve the drag-free float. One way to do this is to overcast the target and let the line come up tightly against the rod. The fly will bounce back toward you and slack will be created.

To prove the importance of presentation, George stood by while three expert fly fishermen took turns working on a trout that had found a lie near a fallen tree on Pennsylvania's famed Spruce Creek. Fifteen minutes of repeated casting couldn't budge the fish. Almost all of those presentations looked perfect, but the fish didn't respond. One of the group kept asking to change fly patterns, but George insisted that we keep at it. Finally, one cast looked just a trifle better than the rest and the fish rose to ingest the fly. If football is a game of inches, fly fishing can be a game of centimeters.

Wet-fly fishermen, according to George, miss too many strikes. One reason is that they have a big belly in the fly line that creates drag. The trick is to keep the rod pointing at the line and the line fairly straight. If the rod forms more than a 90-degree angle with the line, you'll miss a lot of fish.

Lefty Kreh carefully measures the distance before dropping his fly. In limestone streams, fish can be particularly fussy; perfect presentation is the only way to fool them.

The critical time in wet-fly fishing is when the line straightens out at the end of the drift and starts to swing with the current. Trout will often strike at the moment the fly picks up speed.

The nymph has long been the favorite of most veteran anglers and for good reason. It probably accounts for more fly-caught fish than all other types combined. A weighted nymph can be deadly if you develop the touch to let it roll along the bottom and have the eye to watch the line. The slightest tick on the line can indicate a strike. For best results, a nymph should be fished on a short line and the cast should be made upstream with plenty of slack. That allows the nymph time to sink before the current washes it past the lie of the fish. The trick is to learn to work the nymph right above the stream bed where most big trout will be holding. This is done by lifting and dropping the rod tip and it takes plenty of practice before you become adept at it.

On the salmon and steelhead rivers, other techniques have gained favor. Versatility is still the key and the best fishermen are those who aren't afraid to break with tradition and who simply don't care what the next fisherman might think.

My ghillie on one trip to Iceland insisted on a number-6 Blue Charm as the only pattern that would work. To please him, I tied it on and caught a few fish, but I wasn't happy, so I started to experiment. It became obvious that other patterns worked equally well. Then, when I thought he wasn't looking, I snuck out a big saltwater streamer and started to tie it on. He turned around before I could get the fly in the water and I was immediately lectured on why that type of fly wouldn't work. Since many Icelandic salmon are caught on the common variety of earthworm, I couldn't see why a big streamer wouldn't do the job.

The fish were lying along the trailing edge of a rock formation that resembled an airplane wing and reaching them was tricky because of a high cliff at my back. After a few efforts, I managed to get the big fly in midstream and waited while it drifted toward the fish. As the line came tight and the fly started to swing, a salmon of a dozen pounds bulged the water and chased that fly right into the shallows before nailing it. After that, my friend wanted a complete set of the fly patterns I had and promised to continue with the experiments.

Direction of presentation can be important. A scant ten minutes by boat from John Garry's Bristol Bay Lodge, the Agulowak River funnels into Lake Aleknagik. Every summer, millions of two-year-old sockeye smolt pour downstream on their way to the Bering Sea. Their first major hazard comes in the form of thousands of Arctic char that take up station at the river mouth and gorge themselves on the young salmon.

Local guides usually move the boat into the river and then let it drift with the current, while the anglers cast in all directions. Our boat handler was a young lad who was trying to gain experience and he followed the basic approach. It soon became apparent to Lefty Kreh and me that the strikes didn't come as fast as they should. Fish were breaking all around the boat, yet we had to work hard for every hit and it didn't matter if we were using fly tackle or spinning gear with plugs.

We set about to solve the problem and began to monitor everything we did.

If you intend to catch large pike on a fly—like this fifteen-pounder—you should be throwing long, bulky streamers.

Two more drifts and we had the answer. If fly or lure came into the lake *with* the current, you had an instant strike. If you cast across the current, only an occasional fish would charge the offering. When the cast was made down-current, it was merely an exercise and there would be no strike. Now with thousands of char in the area, you would expect them to climb all over anything that moves. The element of competition was there and natural food was plentiful. They were in a feeding spree. Nevertheless, something was wrong when the bait didn't come from the right direction. All the sockeye followed a similar path and that's what the char expected.

Lures can be divided into several major categories and an infinite number of variations. Among these are spinners, spoons, leadheads, plugs, soft plastics, and metal jigs. In addition, several types of trolling lures are made for both fresh water and salt. Eventually, your tackle box will contain representative samples from each category, because few among us can resist the temptation of trying something new and different. There's a nagging temptation to own the latest offering to hit the marketplace and some of these innovations work very well. One question that continues to persist is what happened to last year's hot lures? Usually they are retired and something else takes their place. Over the years, however, certain standbys have endured and these are the baits all of us should focus our attention upon.

A handful of basic offerings forms the backbone of any arsenal of artificials. Those of us who travel and fish as part of our livelihood learn early in the game that there is no way any of us can tote different lures for various places in the world. Instead, we soon develop an affection for a few favorites and these tend to produce remarkably well anywhere in the world.

There are two reasons why we can catch fish on lures that may be foreign to a given area: we have confidence in their performance and have learned how to work them effectively. At times, people will tell us that a particular

By keeping the point of the hook buried in the worm, it will be weedless in the water. The worm at right is rigged incorrectly, with the hook extending through the plastic.

The spoon, available in a variety of sizes and colors, still ranks as one of the great lures.

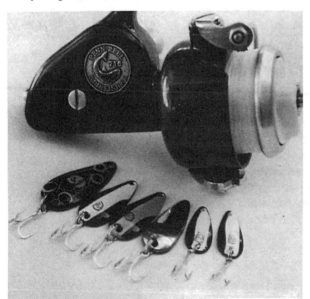

A length of surgical tubing has proven the nemesis of many barracuda. It should be fished just below the surface. When tubing gets chopped up, like this one is, fish will refuse it.

artificial will never work in the waters we are fishing or for the species we seek. More often than not, they are quickly proven wrong. It isn't a miracle and none of us are that expert in those waters, but we go with a strong hand.

In making the choice, the secret is to cover every conceivable situation with a handful of lures. You want to be able to fish every depth and you want to offer the fish a variety of actions, sizes, and shapes. You can do this with fewer than a dozen choices as long as they are available in several sizes. Of course, there might be a fresh-water and salt-water selection and sometimes we'll break it down a bit finer than that to cover trout, bass, or perhaps pike or muskies. However, many of the baits overlap.

The leadheaded bucktail certainly ranks among the most versatile lures because it can be cast, trolled, and jigged vertically. Spinnerbaits can be fished in a variety of ways for bass, covering all ranges from the surface to the bottom. A couple of topwater offerings, a darter, some medium or deep runners and you're in business.

VARIATIONS ON A THEME

A number of baits have a built-in action, making them ideally suited for the beginner and easy lures to fish for the veteran. With many, all you have to do is crank the handle on the reel and the lure will do the rest. Other offerings are more complicated to use, relying on the angler to supply the action through rod manipulations coordinated with the speed of the retrieve.

A bucktail, for example, is nothing more than a head made from lead and dressed with a tail of deer hair or some other material. By the way, as natural hairs become more expensive and difficult to obtain, more bucktail makers are switching to artificial materials such as Fishair, which sometimes looks more like natural hair than natural hair. These leadheads are often spiced up with plastic bait tails or worms and they catch fish. The problem, however, is that the angler must impart all the action or decide to retrieve it without any action.

Crankbaits with specially tuned lips cha-cha through the water with a tantalizing undulation and all you have to do is turn the handle of the reel. There are variations on the theme, however, and they are worth noting. The innovative angler is going to catch more fish. He's constantly experimenting and trying something new.

One of the most vivid examples in my memory happened on Tunica Lake in Mississippi when Bill Dance and I were fishing bass together. We were both using identical chubby crankbaits and casting in rotation. Bill couldn't stop catching bass and I couldn't start. I studied every move and tried to time my retrieve to his. To say it was frustrating is an understatement.

When I asked what he was doing, he just smiled and refused to share the secret. After several threats on his well-being from my half of the boat, he said that he would make five or six fast cranks to get the bait down to depth and then pause for a second before starting the rest of the retrieve. Armed with this knowledge, my success ratio improved dramatically both in the quantity of fish I caught and their size.

There are countless ways to work each lure and the angler who is going to come out on top will vary his retrieve and continue to vary it until he finds the formula that works for the moment. When the fish turn off, it's time to look for another way of working the lure.

Artificials have been the nemesis of many of us for years. Sometimes, they bring outstanding results and there are days when they just won't work. The challenge is always there and any fly or lure addict wouldn't have it any other way.

For deep jigging, bucktails should hang at a 45-degree angle if allowed to dangle from a loop of line. This attitude, along with its knife edges, produces an erratic action rather than a straight undulating action. It can make a difference.

The head shape and the weight help to determine the action of a lead-headed bucktail. Use the lightest weight possible for the conditions you face.

7

Working from a Boat

It's easy to fall into the trap. Today's boats bristle with so many gadgets and generate such incredible speeds that we often lose perspective. Regardless of size, fishing craft serve as transportation to and from the grounds and they provide a platform from which to fish. Electronic accoutrements coupled with maximum horsepower are nice to have, but they are support systems to be used when needed. If the focus is on pushing buttons and shoving throttles forward, the emphasis cannot be on fishing.

Whether you own your own boat, charter occasionally, or sail with a friend, establishing a routine is important. It's equally valid aboard a canoe or bass boat as it is when you set sail on a massive sportfisherman. Too many fish are missed because an angler wasn't organized and too many fish are lost because there is gear adrift in the boat that gets in the way.

Every boat has a personality of its own and you can usually recognize this before you step aboard. Skippers also vary in their approach and you can detect this by glancing around the boat. A craft that has loose equipment everywhere and no semblance of order indicates a casual attitude on the part of the owner or operator. When everything appears ship-shape, you know there's a definite pattern and you'll have to mold your own approach to the established procedure.

Tackle stowage should be the first order of business. Your gear must be readily accessible to you, yet it must be out of the way. At the same time, you'll have to share the limited space with others. Think of this when you pack for the trip and try to take the essentials, while passing up unneeded gear. Try to find out in advance how much room there will be and guide yourself accordingly.

In a small boat, you will be assigned a fishing location. On most bass boats, for example, the electric motor is in the bow and that's where the owner will be stationed. He will indicate his preferences and then it's up to you to work around his routine. Rods should be placed where you can reach them easily; if possible, tackle boxes are also kept close at hand. Some owners will place extra gear in stowage compartments, but make sure you keep out the tackle you will be using first.

Even in a small boat with bench seats, you can set up a routine. You may, for example, decide that your rods go along the port gunwale, while your partner's will remain on the starboard side. That way, there's never any confusion in trying to find another rod and reel.

As you begin to fish, concentrate on the routine you have established and follow it religiously. By doing so, you can avoid getting in each other's way. It almost becomes territorial. You take over part of the boat and the others do the same.

Unless they are back-up rods to hedge against breakage, every outfit should be rigged and ready to go. Multiple outfits provide the opportunity to have different lures at hand and they also enable you to pick up another rod if you happen to break off when the action is hot. Being forced to re-rig when fish are everywhere is not only frustrating, but it has all the earmarks of pure torture.

Casting sport in blue water frequently becomes an opportunity affair. You might start the day with standard trolling gear, but keep fly, spinning, or plug tackle at hand so that you can cast if you see a school of fish or there are fish astern when you hook up on the heavy tackle. The key is to keep the casting equipment rigged and ready. If it is buried in the cabin, you'll never get it out in time and if it is stored behind a dozen other rods, you'll lose precious seconds.

Aboard a boat with a cabin, my own preference is to stand the casting rods at the point where the superstructure meets the gunwale. Usually, each angler will be assigned one side of the boat or a specific position. With my rods on the same side and right behind me, I can get them in a hurry. Throughout the day, I repeatedly check to make certain that no one has put other rods on top of them or inadvertently tangled the various outfits.

Remember that drags should be pre-set and everything readied. Rods and reels must be out of the way, but close enough to reach with a step or two. Veteran anglers learn to build their reaction speed, so that they can grab the right tackle and get the lure in the water within seconds.

Fly fishermen have special problems that require some advanced planning and preparation. For some unknown reason, fly line will not only tangle easily but will snake its way over, under, or around any obstruction. Casting becomes an irritating chore and fish are often lost because the line cannot be cleared.

If you intend to fly fish, think about the boat ahead of time. On a windy day, loose fly line will blow around on a fiberglass deck and mat up. When you release the line on a cast, the entire coil leaps up toward the first guide and it's back to square one. By the time you untangle the mess, it may be too late for another cast.

A short Velcro strap wrapped around rigged rods in a boat will hold them in place and keep them from tangling.

There are several ways to counter this. Some anglers will carry a stripping basket with them and put the line in it. Others may use a plastic trash bucket or container lined with something that will hold the line. A roll of outdoor carpeting can work wonders if you spread it on the deck, but the disadvantage to that system is that it won't fit on every boat.

The best solution is a piece of netting weighted on the edges by rubber-core sinkers. You can throw it over the deck and over any projections that might catch a fly line. You'll find that netting over an outboard will save you the trouble of working your fly line free when it gets under the housing.

A roll of masking tape, gaffer's tape, or duct tape will also perform miracles. Use it to tape over cleats or other boat parts that look like tentacles waiting to snare a fly line. With this little bit of preparation, you can make life easier on the water.

GETTING INTO POSITION

Fishing for smallmouths with Billy Westmoreland on Tennessee's Dale Hollow Reservoir provides a premier learning experience. Not only does he know the waters as well as most of us know the layouts of our homes, but he is a master at making the perfect approach and putting the boat in the best position.

Even though the big schools of bronzebacks lie in eighteen to thirty-five feet of water during the late fall and early winter, Billy recognizes that they can be exceptionally skittish. Running his big engine full bore, he'll chop the power close to shore on the back side of a cove, making sure he spins the boat around first to knock down his own wake. Then he uses the electric motor to ease out along a sloping point that lies on the other side of the cove. When he stops and drops anchor, you are a long cast away from where he thinks the fish will be. If you happen to question his cautiousness, he'll prove he's right by showing you what occurs when you roar right up to the fish.

A stealthy approach makes sense in any waters, because fish are sensitive to sound transmitted through the hull. The scraping of a tackle box, kicking of feet, or any other scraping or thumping noises can spoil your chances. Once

It takes time and care to beat a big fish on light tackle. Gear must be chosen carefully. Note the sophisticated depth sounder for locating fish and the chum bag over the transom to hold fish near the boat.

you become aware of this, the least little noise attracts your attention like the siren and howler on an emergency vehicle.

Position can mean everything. Not only is it imperative to maneuver the boat so that the anglers can get off a cast, but the cast must be made at the precise time so that the lure tracks on the proper course through the water. As an example, it's one thing to be able to reach a log or a rock and another to place the lure so that you cover the right area on the cast. Putting a bait on the back side of where a fish might be lurking usually won't do much good.

Pike or muskie fishermen often parallel the shoreline, tossing cast after cast toward the obvious lairs. Sometimes, however, they do better if they position the boat so that their casts run alongside the weed beds or rock piles. The retrieve then brings bait or lure right along the edge rather than directly away from it. When this is done, it's often difficult for two anglers to be in prime position at the same time, but this can be worked out and there are many times when one will stand alongside the other in the bow and fish in tandem.

When you do cover a shoreline or a patch of lily pads, distance is important. If you are too close, the presence of the boat may alert the fish. On the other hand, most fish are going to be back in the cover, so you'll be working a lot of unproductive water if you hang off too far. Maximum distance also creates a problem in achieving casting accuracy. When you are closer, it's much easier to put the offering on target and that's critical.

It's also important to keep the distance relatively constant. A boat that moves in and out forces the anglers to adjust their distance constantly and they may worry more about the casting than catching fish. At the same time, you can make life easier if you follow the shoreline the right way. If one caster is right-handed and the other is left-handed, pick your direction of travel so that both are moving the rods over the water rather than the boat. That will keep the lures or baits from creating a hazard. If someone is fly fishing, station him so that the fly line is outboard of the bow or the stern. When he has to cast over the boat, there's always the chance that someone will get hooked.

In early fall, trophy brook trout start moving upstream out of Lake Mistassini in Northern Quebec. Reaching them can be a problem, since even the couple of spike camps in the area only allow anglers to cover a short stretch of water. Two of us with a pair of guides lashed a couple of canoes to the floats on a plane and landed on a lake three miles from the river. After a difficult portage, we were able to launch the canoes and had fourteen miles of the stream to cover before nightfall when the plane would return.

It became obvious that the bigger fish were at the head of a rapids or the tail of fast water. To maximize our efforts, we would shoot the rapids, fish the tail end, and then race for the next set of rapids. The key was to position the canoes so that we could fly fish and cover the best holding water. That meant moving downriver but cutting sharply to one side when an impressive spot loomed up ahead of us. With the angler in the bow and the canoe pointing downstream on the right-hand side of the river, the cast could be made comfortably and the fisherman was always in a position to strike.

Figuring out where to be is just as critical in salt water. Bottom predators love to hang around dropoffs and pelagic species will cruise the mid-depths in this region. When a fish is hooked, it will often crash dive for the bottom, trying to weave the line around an obstruction or find haven in a patch of rocks. If you're hanging atop the shallower portion, there's a good chance that the fish will cut you off as it plummets over the edge. Experienced skippers will always try to drift parallel to a ledge or reef line or they will start just before the dropoff and let the wind or tide carry them into deeper water.

In most fishing situations, the tendency is to work a bait or lure from deep water toward the shallows or from some type of cover into open water. There are times, however, when fish can be finicky about the direction from which their meal approaches. Periodically, don't hesitate to change the routine and work a lure from shallow to deep or toward an obstruction rather than away from it.

Marker buoys can be an important aid when you are trying to fish some types of underwater structure. Once you locate the target or find a school of fish, you'll probably do better if you back off and cast to the area. Keep marker buoys handy and drop them over the side the instant you find something of interest. That gives you a permanent reference point and you can then cover the area thoroughly.

ELECTRONICS

The development of the depth sounder as a sport-fishing tool has virtually revolutionized the approach to finding fish. Not too many years ago, anglers relied on trial and error coupled with a gut feeling or sixth sense to locate their quarry. Today, a properly performing depth sounder has become a necessity rather than a luxury. In fact, many boats are now equipped with two or three units.

The ultimate, at the moment, has to be a graph machine that traces the bottom contour and everything above it. Each year, improvements and innovations make these units more sophisticated and even the less expensive ones can do a reasonably good job. There are, of course, professional models that have unbelievable sensitivity. The main advantage of the recording type is the permanent record it creates. You can study the graph paper after the day is over if you want to review the places you've been.

A number of fishermen leave the graph units on while they are running and glance occasionally at the trace. That way, if they happen to pass over something interesting, they can reverse course and go back to find it.

Flasher units are still the most popular type of depth sounder primarily because they are relatively cheap. Many are exceptionally fine units and it just takes a bit longer to learn to decipher the pulses accurately. The limitation is that you must be looking at the unit to see what's happening. You could pass over a school of fish, but if you were doing something else, you wouldn't know it.

Digital readout units also make a lot of sense as a second machine aboard a boat. These simply flash the depth in numbers, which tells the angler immediately when he is over a dropoff or when the water depth is changing. Sometimes that's all you need to know.

Every fisherman should know how to read a depth sounder and operate the unit, even if he doesn't own a boat. The depth sounder provides an underwater picture and it is extremely helpful in fishing. By looking at it, you can tell when you're over a particular type of structure, what depth the fish are at, how deep the water is, and what changes are taking place.

Several companies make portable flasher units that can be carried anywhere and they are particularly valuable when you travel, rent a boat, or board one that doesn't have a machine. You don't have to own the boat to buy the unit. The transducer can be attached to the hull with a suction cup and you'll be surprised at the readings you get. Even as a guest aboard a boat, there may only be one machine and that would be mounted where your host could see it. By taking a second machine along, you can also benefit from the instant information.

Fishermen are forever overlooking water temperature as a vital factor in locating their quarry. When you troll for trout or salmon, knowing where the thermocline lies can be critical. Blue-water anglers also need to know what the water temperature is at any given spot. Bass fishermen are now learning that temperature can make a difference and they, too, measure it constantly.

The latest units mounted on boats offer digital readout of the surface temperature. Some of the other units use a needle gauge to do the same thing. They are surprisingly accurate and both types give a constant measurement. It's hard to believe that a single degree difference can mean fish or no fish.

A number of portable units can be found in major tackle shops and they are worthy of your attention. By lowering a thermister in the water, you can read the temperature quickly at any reasonable depth. With these small units, finding the thermocline is easy. That's the layer of water where, by definition, the temperature drops one-half degree for every foot of depth.

If you want to find the thermocline, move the boat into deep water and start lowering the thermometer. When the readings begin to change sharply and the water temperature drops very quickly, you've found it. Note the depth and you can then fish the areas where the thermocline meets the bottom by looking for these depths on the chart and locating them with a depth sounder.

Other gauges will measure the oxygen content of the water and also its pH or acidity. These are certainly valuable to have, but not quite as critical as a good depth sounder and a means for measuring temperature.

Along the coastlines, Loran C has replaced Loran A. The difference in letters may not mean much, but the accuracy of Loran C has amazed even the most hardened seaman. Party-boat skippers claim they can position themselves within a boat length of a spot once they have the Loran C coordinates. Those who fish wrecks, underwater humps, and other hard-to-find locations feel that Loran C is worth every penny. If you ever need help out there, you can give a totally accurate picture of your location just by reading the coordinates.

TROLLING TECHNIQUES

Practically everyone knows that the major advantage of trolling is that it makes it possible to cover the maximum amount of water in the shortest period of time. A charter skipper got my attention in a hurry recently when I heard him point out to a dockside assemblage of weekend anglers that the secret of successful trolling was to concentrate one's efforts in the areas where the fish were most likely to be. Dragging baits or lures without giving any thought to the spots being fished can be a complete waste of time. Conditions must be reviewed and analyzed on a continuing basis; the key is to make every move with a purpose.

Finding the productive ballpark can challenge the skills of even the best, but there are guidelines that can shorten the distance to the victory celebration. Lethargy has to be the number-one killer. It isn't a rare disease, but a common malady among those who pull baits behind a moving boat. The drone of the engines, creaking of the oarlocks, and the fresh air have a hypnotic effect on most anglers. They tend to sit back and relax, mesmerized by the monotony and rhythm of the scene.

If you intend to catch fish, you have to work at it. There are no shortcuts and no such thing as a relaxing day on the water. Laziness can prove expensive. When you start to think that changing a bait or checking a rod is too much trouble or not worth the effort, your production has to suffer. Anyone can learn the basic techniques, but a relatively small percentage of trollers have the drive and determination necessary to be successful.

Recognize that you must try to solve the equation with several unknowns, all of which vary from one extreme to the other. Not only do you have to find the fish, but you must then get the offerings to them in an acceptable manner.

Too many skippers simply steer a straight course at a constant speed and

Fast, maneuverable, center-console boats have opened up the offshore world to the light-tackle enthusiast. This blue marlin is about to be tagged and released after a tough battle on fifty-pound-class gear.

stream an assortment of baits and lures behind the boat. Those who quietly amass the catches that most of us envy take a much more serious approach. They know that trolling speed can be critical. Perhaps they start at the slowest speed that will work the baits or lures, but they will vary this constantly until they discover what happens to be working at the moment.

At the same time, the spread is set with great care. Experience teaches you quickly that the length astern can make a difference as well as the baits you elect to troll. These should be varied frequently and the amount of line behind the boat should also be adjusted periodically. If you have the facilities to troll at different depths, don't pass up this opportunity to experiment.

It really doesn't matter whether you troll in a river, lake, estuary, or offshore, the principles are the same. An angler who rows a short distance off a lake's shoreline might do better to zig-zag back and forth from deep to shallow and shallow to deep. Eventually, he might discover that most strikes come in a certain depth of water or only when he is heading in a particular direction. He might also find that if the water is falling fast, the fish will move off the banks, but they'll shift shoreward on a slow rise.

Even though you happen to be trolling on or near the surface, underwater depth contours can prove important. Sailfish may be over the twenty-fathom curve, while blue marlin follow the hundred-fathom mark. Gamefish may be over some type of deep structure, yet they'll hit on the surface. Almost every species of gamefish will follow some form of natural edge at one time or another. You can find these easily on a chart if you don't happen to know the water.

Speaking of edges, anytime water conditions change—such as from green to blue or from dingy to clear or there is a weedline or windrip—work back and forth across the edge looking for fish. Off the Colombian coast on the Pacific aboard Captain Jim Paddock's *Stormy*, we found a current edge where the change from green to blue was so vivid that it was startling. The current moved as a river in the sea and water from the deep was upwelling along the edge with such force that you could see it bubbling and hear it.

We did a lot of experimenting that day and found that you could barely buy a strike in the green, but the instant the baits crossed over into the blue water, it was Katie bar the door. Sailfish, striped marlin, and dolphin raced each other to the baits.

The edges of currents are usually the places to fish. Nutrients brought from the deep through upwelling cause micro-organisms to bloom when they hit the warmer surface waters. Baitfish feed on the plankton and the predators are right there at the dinner table.

Staying alert to tides, currents, or the general flow of water is important. It's worth the time to experiment going with the water, against it, or across it. That holds in both fresh and salt water, although the next example took place off the Yucatan coast between the Mexican island of Cozumel and the mainland. The Yucatan Current flows northward through the narrow twelve-mile gap and in the spring of the year the fishing can be unreal. This is truly sailfish alley, yet there are days when the fish can be very finicky.

The rule in that part of the world is that you will raise more fish working against the current than with it and it proved true. However, we discovered that we could get strikes by trolling faster than usual with the current. More experimenting taught us that when you worked the dropoff that plummeted like the rim of the Grand Canyon, you had to start crossing the current at right angles. Anything less and the success ratio suffered.

When coho fishing became popular in Lake Michigan, Captain George Seemann, one of the leading blue-water skippers, took his fifty-two-foot boat up there to check out the fishing. In a short time, his catch was as good as anyone's, primarily because he knew the secrets of trolling.

Very often, the fish were right on the bottom at a depth that equaled the position of the thermocline. Using downriggers to get the baits to fish-eye level, George worked that area. At the same time, he used other downriggers to test the intermediate depths and sometimes dragged a couple of lines on the surface.

Another skipper found that even when he backed off on the throttles, he couldn't make his boat move slow enough through the water. After considerable thought, he jury-rigged a pair of drogues or sea anchors on either side. The dragging effect slowed the actual speed of the boat, even though the engine was turning at a faster rpm.

There are times when one or two boats seem to have fish all around them and no other boat can buy a strike. That's the time to watch the successful boats very carefully and try to determine what they are doing. They may be running a range over some form of underwater structure where the fish are lying. Often, however, they are working at a different speed and you can match this from a distance by paralleling their course and setting your

When the clicker is on and a reel is in freespool, there might not be enough tension to keep the line from running out. If you loop the line around the harness lugs it will prevent this—but the line will pop free on a strike.

throttles accordingly. At the same time, vary the cockpit setup and you should eventually uncover their secret.

Someone once said that the price of a fish is eternal vigilance. Veteran trollers watch their rods and the depth sounder very carefully if the baits are not on the surface. They are looking for the telltale tick that indicates a strike. When baits are topside, all eyes should be focused on them. Not only is it important to see a strike, but you want to know when a fish invades the baits. On the offshore grounds, you can often see gamefish come into the wake, look around, and then take off. If this happens, you know that something is wrong and you'd better check the baits as well as start experimenting with the setup.

If you remember nothing more, keep in mind that trolling can be a dynamic fishing method for light-tackle sport providing you work at it constantly. Slack off or relax and you'll pay the price. Never assume that everything is all right. Check the baits and lures frequently.

SOME OFFSHORE POINTERS

With the exception of marlin, tuna, swordfish, and sharks, most deep-water denizens weigh a hundred pounds or less. There are exceptions, of course, but most fish you will catch fall into this category. That means that in most situations, you can fish with thirty-pound-class tackle comfortably and even go lighter depending on your skill and the willingness of others aboard.

For sailfish or white marlin, a twenty-pound outfit provides the perfect match. In fact, many anglers who now fish sailfish with live bait or even skipbaits prefer heavy-duty spinning tackle. Spinning wasn't designed for trolling, yet it works well when you drag a live bait very slowly. The high-speed retrieve on the reel can be an advantage. One problem is how to keep a spinning reel in free spool. The answer is to wrap a short length of bait-rigging wire or telephone wire around the forward part of the reel seat and fashion a crude finger out of the wire. The wire holds the line while you troll, but the force of a strike will pull the line free and it will pay off the fixed spool on the reel.

Veteran light-tackle anglers prefer to fish their gear as flat lines rather than

Spinning reels are now being used for trolling. When live bait is used—such as for sailfish—the problem is keeping the reel in freespool for the dropback. You can solve this by looping some soft wire around the front of the reel seat and then bending a V in the wire. The line hangs in the V and comes out when a fish strikes.

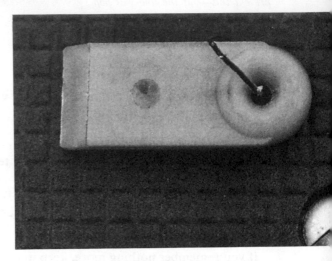

By sawing a slot in a downrigger release pin, you can insert it on the line without having to tie it into the terminal tackle. Once the line goes through the slot, it won't come out.

through an outrigger. They are concerned about the shock of a strike on the light line when it is in an outrigger pin. As a rule of thumb, twenty-pound class is marginal in an outrigger. Anything lighter than that could create a problem.

Steve Sloan, who specializes in fishing six-pound test, and his skipper, Captain Tom Furtado, developed a system using rubber bands to help absorb the shock of the strike and still keep the reel in free spool. The trick is to pick a rubber band of the proper consistency. Then, it is looped around the line and placed in an outrigger pin if it is necessary to fish from the 'rigger. Sloan prefers to use the light gear as a flat line and the rubber band is hung on the handle of the reel. On the strike, the light monofilament will cut right through the rubber band and the fish can take line in free spool.

When anglers are trying for particularly large fish on very light tackle, they try to keep the rig in the boat and raise their quarry on a teaser. When the fish comes up, the light rod, which is kept in position, is picked up and the bait is streamed back to the fish. That way, the angler can control the strike and avoid breaking the line.

Learning by his mistakes, Steve Sloan is now convinced that the use of a double line on light tackle is not really an asset, but a liability. After a lengthy

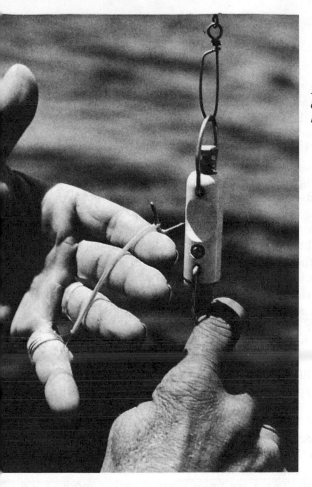

Rubber bands looped around the line and hung on an outrigger pin maintain a specific distance astern and will break at the strike. They eliminate chafing on the line.

A rubber band looped around the line and dropped over the reel handle enables an angler to keep a reel in free-spool while fishing a flat line. When the fish strikes, the rubber band breaks.

fight, most anglers lean on the fish the instant the double line is on the reel. The result is a breakoff at boatside. Without a double line, you'll be much more careful about the pressure until the leader is in hand.

Keep in mind that light line is fragile and should never be clipped in an outrigger pin or a flat line pin. If you are going to use the pins, be sure to wrap dental floss around the line or a rubber band and insert that in the pin rather than the monofilament or Dacron. It's also worth repeating that these thin lines should be checked frequently for nicks and cuts and replaced often if you're looking for big fish.

THE SURFACE INTERCEPT

Swinging the baits in front of a gamefish cruising silently on the surface without alarming and alerting it requires a cool hand on helm and throttles and the knowledge to go with it. One can't really expect a fish to hang around when it is attacked by a monstrous hulk powered by a pair of shiny buzz-saw blades. Some fish will dodge this attack on their well-being and still surface astern behind a bait, but more often, the fish will dive for the sanctuary of the depths or change course where it won't be disturbed.

Working a fish on the surface isn't really very different from other phases of the sport. The ideal is to get the bait in front of the fish without it realizing that you are in the area or anything unnatural is happening. In a perfect presentation, the fish will see the baits in front of it and not notice the boat.

Usually, a fish on top will be going with the seas. The first step is to make sure of its direction of travel and then maneuver the boat to achieve a parallel course. Using just a bit more speed than the fish so that the sudden change of engine noise doesn't alert it, inch the boat up slowly until it is past your quarry. Then, angle toward the fish's line of travel, swinging the baits in front of it. When this maneuver is done perfectly and the fish responds, you will see it suddenly become excited, light up, and move in on the free meal.

Crossing at right angles to the fish is almost as bad as running it down. In that situation, the fish sees the boat before it sees the bait and can be on the alert.

Especially when searching for billfish, this is a super situation for light tackle. You know the fish is there; you can watch its reaction; and you can keep the other baits away so that it will strike the one attached to the light outfit.

On the West Coast, fishermen sometimes prefer to cast a live bait to a surface fish rather than troll by it. In that situation, the boat must be eased up alongside the fish, but kept at a respectable distance. The cast can then be made from the bow across to the fish. There are times when it makes more sense to cast from the cockpit because of the position of the fish, but these are the exceptions. Since reasonably heavy gear is sometimes used, casting range is somewhat limited, but the technique does work.

THE RACE FOR BREAKING FISH

To an impartial observer, the race toward a school of breaking fish and the subsequent actions of the boats involved can look like a demolition derby. Everybody wants to get in on the action and, for most species, trollers compete with casters for position. Boats are usually so busy getting a competitive edge on one another and jockeying for position that they actually ignore the preferences of the fish.

Working fish on top can be an exciting experience and the dream of every light-tackle angler providing everyone cooperates and no one gets greedy. Such is rarely the case. For purposes of illustration, let's assume initially that you're the only boat in the area. It's important to realize that even though the main body of fish is cavorting topside in one area, there are plenty of other school members under the surface and on every flank.

The basic approach is to remain on the fringes of the school and make your casts toward the main body. Remember that a lure that becomes isolated stands a better chance of being hit. If you are trolling, it's easy enough to keep the boat away from the bulk of the fish and pick from the edges of the school. You can continue either of these techniques for as long as the fish are on the surface.

What invariably happens, however, is that more boats spot the activity and race for it. Some don't have enough sense to chop the throttles at a respectable distance and move in slowly. Instead, they barrel right into the middle of the fish. Trollers decide that the only way to get their lines into the carnage is to run the boat through the midst of the commotion. Casters, who until now have hung on the lip, figure that they are being aced out, so they start to close. The result is that the fish are harrassed and they crash dive.

Certain species of fish, such as tuna, can move very quickly and erratically when they are on the surface. Catching them can be a problem for slower boats. In some cases, the only solution for the caster is to run alongside the school at speed, try to hook a fish, and then stop to fight it. Another way is to anticipate where the school will be, move ahead to that location, cut the throttles and wait for the fish to come to you. Trollers also have a problem because they have to try to get in front of the fish and keep the baits there while moving at high speed.

When you're searching the waters for breaking fish, keep in mind that you won't always find wheeling and diving gulls and terns above them. The knowledgeable angler constantly watches the water for signs of splashes that give away feeding fish. Even when there are whitecaps, you can sometimes pick up the commotion, because the white water may not be moving in the same direction or with the same force as the whitecaps.

Breaking fish are also a standard occurrence in fresh water, especially in those lakes that hold large concentrations of striped bass. The same approach will work. Keep the boat away from the fish and cast into the school from the edges. Be sure to pull the power back on the big engine when you near the school. If you're alone, you can ease up quietly from a respectable distance and perhaps the fish will stay on top a lot longer than they might have.

8

Rivers, Bays, Estuaries, and Surf

Lighter lines and matching rods are becoming a way of life on the salmon and steelhead rivers across the country and in Alaska. Anglers recognize that whether they prefer artificial lures or opt for the traditional method of fishing with egg sacs, featherweight gear can make a difference. For one thing, it gives the bait or lure a much more natural action in the water; for another, it requires less weight under the same conditions to keep the offering near the bottom.

Sensitive rods and particularly those made from graphite or one of the Space Age composites have a higher modulus of elasticity and transmit the vibrations and the pickup to the angler's hands. He is better able to monitor the progress of his offering and that's the name of the game.

The rivers may be swift and the current strong, but these dedicated fishermen have learned to handle their quarry on light tackle and have fun doing it. West Coast experts such as Bill Schaadt, Dan Blanton, Bob Edgley, and Gary Loomis tackle king salmon on fly rods with light tippets or casting gear armed with equally light line. Across the continent, Bill Kozielec and other regulars in the Salmon River country delight in using ultralight spinning for steelhead, trophy brown trout, lake trout, cohos, and even chinooks. These men are skillful and agile, scrambling up and down stream to parry the surges of the fish. Bill Kozielec takes this sport so seriously that he makes his own lead strips for weight, adding or removing the three-inch lengths to match the flow of water.

In this type of fishing, feel is critical. Heavy gear robs an angler of the sensitivity he needs to get the bait in front of his quarry. Playing the fish comes later, but unless there is a strike, one doesn't have to worry about what to do next.

The area around John Garry's Bristol Bay Lodge near the Bering Sea above the Alaskan Peninsula offers some of the most fabulous freshwater potential you'll ever encounter. Rivers are choked with salmon, trout, and char and some streams flow so swiftly that one must tack a jet boat upstream or it's impossible to buck the current. Still, fly rods and spinning are a way of life. Anglers set out with lines testing between four and ten-pound test to do battle. Some go heavier for the kings, but most slug it out on lighter tackle. The primary reason, in addition to the sporting proposition, is that you get more strikes. That has to be incentive enough.

The closer an angler gets to the sea, the heavier the equipment he usually chooses. It's virtually impossible to explain why a river fisherman in fresh water will tangle with salmon on light lines, while huskier gear takes over the instant the water turns brackish or salty. In fact, the size of the quarry seldom has anything to do with it.

BASIC BOTTOM FISHING

As soon as we had loaded my gear, Bud Howard deftly maneuvered car and boat trailer through the typical airport confusion in New Orleans and headed southwest past Houma. During the fall of the year, bull redfish weighing between twenty and forty pounds prowl the passes in search of food and work the coastal shallows. Smaller reds have already filtered back into the bayous and marshes for the winter.

Bud had touted this fishing over the telephone and I was anxious to sample it for myself. It's possible to take these fish on artificials, but you stand a better chance with bait because of a red's notoriously poor eyesight. A nearby shrimper gladly gave us a bucket of net trash that included both shrimp and small fish. Once we had our bait, Bud carefully positioned the boat forward and along one side of a prominent sandbar that marked the entrance to a major pass. Because of the crescent shape of the bar, the fish had to work along the outside edge.

What made this outing a bit different was Bud's enthusiasm for fishing with light bait-casting outfits and lines that tested ten pounds. Most folks would be armed with stout sticks and corresponding reels loaded with heavy line. The beautiful part about our outfits was that we could get by with sinkers as light as one-half ounce.

There were more black drum than redfish, but both species averaged better than twenty pounds apiece and yet there was no trouble handling them from an anchored boat. The few other boats that passed us looked somewhat askance at our equipment and probably would have blamed our ignorance on the fact we were tourists except that the boat had Louisiana registration.

Russ Wilson has earned his reputation as one of New Jersey's finest salt-water anglers. He lives a couple of blocks from the water and spends as much time as possible fishing. Traditionally, marine anglers in that part of the world insist on short, stiff boat rods for bottom fishing with lines that could battle a nuclear submarine.

Fishing for fluke or summer flounder is an art that takes time to develop, because, like steelhead fishing, you have to keep the sinker on the bottom and the bait just above it. Developing that feel makes all the difference. With the standard rods, a fisherman is handicapped before he begins, but most people use them because everyone else seems to.

The secret of catching fluke lies in the tackle you use. With lines testing ten pounds and the lightest sinker possible for holding bottom, you're going to do much better. Russ prefers a medium bait-casting outfit because it is easy to handle in a small boat. He prepares his own fluke belly for bait, but instead of cutting the meaty belly section, he molds his baits out of the soft and fluttery fins. The hook is correspondingly small.

To catch fluke, the boat must drift and the trick is to keep the sinker bouncing along the bottom. That means that you must occasionally drop back a bit or take up the slack depending on the drift. If the sinker simply lies on the bottom, change to a lighter weight.

Russ Wilson catches more than his share of fluke or summer flounder. One reason is that he uses very light lines and the minimum amount of weight.

Many of the inshore bottom species are not noted for herculean fights once they are hooked. They'll struggle a bit, but can be boated without a great deal of effort on light rods and line. Some species may try to tangle you up in the bottom, but if you learn to apply pressure right away and start the fish coming up, you can usually counter that move.

Regardless of where you fish for bottom species, the most important things include featherweight gear that gives the bait a more natural appeal, fresh bait, and the lightest sinker you can use consistent with conditions. In almost every situation, if the sinker moves along the bottom, you're going to do better than if it hangs in one place.

Terminal tackle must be kept as simple as possible. Complex rigs with spreaders and other hardware don't always do the job. You'll also find that, in the case of mackerel, catching one fish at a time is adequate if you use very light gear. In fact, it's much more fun to battle a one-pound Boston on ultralight, than to take four at a time on heavy conventional gear.

CASTING AROUND

No matter where an angler chooses to fish, there are always species that can be taken on light casting tackle with either artificial lures or natural baits. The weakfish and its cousin, the spotted seatrout, are perfect examples. Redfish fit into this category and so do bluefish. Along the mangrove shorelines of Florida, you might be able to tempt a snook. In the deeper channels of the South, there are jack crevalle, mackerel, pompano, snapper, and dozens of other denizens eager to inhale an offering. All are exciting to catch, providing you tailor your tackle to the situation.

Snapper blues are a delight on two or four-pound test. Try ladyfish on six pound and use the same outfit for Spanish mackerel. If you really want to test your fish-fighting ability, tie into a jack crevalle on modest gear. The fish doesn't have to be big, but you'll know you're into a battle.

My father has been fishing light tackle for more years than I can remember and now, in his retirement, he leans on the featherweight tackle more than ever. Five days each week, he probes Biscayne Bay in search of piscatorial adventure. His basic tackle balances with four and six-pound-test line, but occasionally he "goes heavy" with eight-pound test if the situation warrants it.

The list of species he has whipped on this gear is extensive. For two consecutive years, he won the Release Trophy in the prestigious Met Tournament and then decided not to enter so that others would have a chance. Dad has been an advocate of the law of averages. He believes if he catches enough fish, a certain percentage of them will be of trophy proportions and he has proven that.

Mental attitude plays an important part when you use fly, spinning, or plug-casting tackle for tough fish. The key is to believe in what you are doing and know that you can conquer the world with the light rod. If you talk to my dad, you'll be impressed by the confidence in his gear and his ability that he constantly exudes. There's no doubt in his mind that he can whip anything that happens to swim by.

THE HIGH SURF

Ed Henckel looked out of place. Everyone around him was using the long surf rod characteristic of most coasts. The fact that he was using a one-handed bait-casting outfit with one of Pico's mullet plugs (that he manufactures) didn't seem to bother him in the least. A group of us were fishing together along Texas's Padre Island National Seashore and Ed was having more fun than any of us.

During the fall of the year, vast hordes of mullet begin to move out of the inshore waters and move south along the coast. Big channel bass, jack crevalle, mackerel, and many other species move in to attack the endless parade of bait. Like any natural barrier beach, this section of coastline has a series of bars and deeper sloughs that run like ribbons for miles and miles. The inner slough is so close to the sand that one can keep his feet dry and still cross it with a cast.

Having fished there many times before, Ed knew that he could cast a plug into the schools of bait with a one-handed rod and he was just spoiling for a battle on his choice of weapons. During the course of the days we fished that area, Ed Henckel did well with his little outfit and never felt intimidated or outclassed by angler or fish. There were a few anxious moments when the outcome was in doubt, but to Ed that was the fun of being there.

The high surf has to be considered the stronghold of heavy tackle and the last bastion of lines that resemble cables. The hardened breed of fisherman who muscles up to the cascading white water and battles the elements in a losing struggle wants plenty of power when he finally does hook a fish. Strikes can be few and far between in those waters and beaching one's quarry can become the single most important thing in the world at the moment.

Still, there are a handful of anglers like Ed Henckel who are willing to use lighter gear because of the challenge and the ultimate enjoyment they get. It's not really as risky as some would have you believe. When you think about it, lighter lines often increase the number of strikes and that can be an impressive incentive along the beachfront where fishing is tough even when it's good.

The breaking strength of the line determines the lightness of the tackle and the length of the rod has little to do with it as long as it is designed for the line that you choose. Graphite has now made it possible for rod builders to fashion longer rods that are tailored for lighter lines. One argument against lightness is the need in places to cast heavy sinkers or lures seaward for great distances. This is certainly a valid point, but one that can be countered in a couple of ways.

First, the lighter the line, the lighter the sinker you have to use in the same situation. Furthermore, if you really do have to use a larger lure, you can rig a long shock leader for casting (which many of the regulars do anyway with heavier lines). This heavier monofilament should be long enough to cover the entire length of the rod, leave enough overhang past the tip, and still put two or three turns on the reel. Once that is rigged with knots that will pass through the guides easily, you can put all the power you want into a cast and you still won't snap off the terminal tackle.

If you choose your spots correctly, you won't need the long meat sticks that are part of the scenery along the beachfront. The time to scout the surf is at dead low tide. Do it on a new or full moon when spring tides are in effect. This will show you rather vividly where the deeper holes, sloughs, and cuts lay in relation to the bars. Take the time to draw a rough map of prime areas or make notes in a log book so that you'll remember what it looks like. Some anglers make photographs and then put prints in a binder so they can refer to them frequently.

Surf fishing is usually best on incoming water, but at that time you can't always decipher the bottom contour and the best places to fish. Frequently, you can wade within casting distance of deeper cuts and you can learn to use the parallel currents and eddies to your advantage. It is here that gamefish often trap their prey and, as Ed Henckel demonstrated, you don't always have to make long casts to reach the productive zone.

Light tackle frequently must be regarded as opportunity sport. Those who fish from beach buggies often keep lighter gear rigged and ready. When the situation dictates, they can grab this tackle and capitalize on a flurry of activity.

Jetties and rock piles offer another area worthy of consideration. Neophytes usually walk to the end of the rocks and then make the longest seaward cast they can. What they fail to take into account is that bait tends to hang around the sanctuary of the rocks and that's where the predators have to venture if they want a meal. The prime spots are often right along the rocks rather than away from them.

Jetty jockeys favor shorter rods than their counterparts who use the sand as home base. The standard stick for this type of fishing may only be seven-and-one-half or eight feet long, with some anglers going shorter than that. The rods are light and they are tailored to fishing pocket water and putting a bait or lure on target. Spinning is preferred, but a few use revolving-spool reels.

Most fishermen cast away from a jetty or seaward from the beach without giving thought to where the fish might be. Veterans recognize that it's important to cover an area quickly and thoroughly, making the bait or lure pass through various areas from different directions. Direction can be important. There are currents and a normal flow of water that most baitfish will follow. If your lure traces a foreign path, it could be ignored.

When you stand in front of a slough or cut, use a series of casts to fan the immediate area. Don't be afraid to cast up and down the slough and then across it on a series of angles from right to left or left to right. When you are convinced you have fished it hard, move up or down the beach and repeat the procedure. Sometimes you can even detect a pattern in the behavior of the fish and may discover that you get more strikes when the offering comes from one direction or another.

To survive on the jetties or rock piles, you need a pair of ice creepers, golf rubbers, or something else on the soles of your boots to provide traction.

Algae clings rather tenaciously to many rocks and it can prove slipperier than a greased banana peel. It's also important to keep one eye on the tide and the condition of the sea. Each year a few unsuspecting anglers get washed off jetties and some don't survive this whiplash of the sea.

Storms have a habit of breaking up jetties and moving boulders. Often there are rocks lying on the bottom some distance off the sides or the ends of these manmade barriers. You might be able to detect their presence on a dead low spring tide, but you can also scout the territory if you have access to a boat with a depth sounder. Pick a calm day when you can maneuver easily without fear of being swamped by a wave and, if possible, work at high tide so you have plenty of clearance over the rocks.

Using the depth sounder and idling around the jetty, you can spot underwater obstructions that are probably rocks or debris that has collected. Mark the relationship of these to the jetty and try to think of where they would be if you were standing on the jetty. Take the time to make notes. Knowing what lies beneath the seas within casting range can be a valuable asset.

Along the northeast coast, the seas sweep shoreward out of the southeast, forming a calm pocket where the jetty meets the beach on the north side. Bait sometimes lies in here when the weather is gusty and gamefish move in for the feast. Before you climb out on the jetty, it's worth taking a few minutes to make some casts from the beach. Fan a series of tosses toward the jetty from the sand and cover the pockets formed on both sides. Then walk out on the jetty and begin a systematic approach.

Many experts will walk out about one-third to halfway to the end and start fishing. Casts will not only be out from the jetty, but they will thoroughly cover the region right along the rocks and parallel to the structure. Once this is completed, the angler will walk seaward about the distance of a long cast and start the fanning procedure again until the entire jetty has been fished. If you know where there are rocks beneath the sea, these zones merit a great deal of attention.

Jetty specialists like Russ Wilson feel that the initial casts can be the most important. If they have one favorite location on a jetty, they'll fish that first, taking great pains to make certain that the first few presentations are right on target.

Rocks and sand can be extremely abrasive and can destroy fishing line rather quickly. When you work this type of terrain, you must keep running your fingers over the end of the line to make sure it hasn't been scuffed or nicked. Periodically, make a cast and reel right back in, letting the entire length of line pass through your thumb and forefinger. This will tell you if the line is abraded somewhere in the middle. Should you find a weak spot, it pays to cut it out and re-rig. Nothing is more frustrating than to get a fish on and then lose it because you were too lazy to repair the tackle.

Surf fishing takes many forms and there are opportunities wherever the sea kisses the shore. In Africa, Bob Stearns and I took queenfish and other species while wading out on a point. Bob and I also fished Costa Rica together with our longtime friend, Bill Barnes, who operates the camp at Casa Mar. During the fall of the year, hordes of big snook migrate along the surf and when you find the action, it can be torrid.

The three of us had taken two aluminum boats up the coast to a small town where Bill had some business. On the way back, we passed a spot that looked good and beached the small craft. Typically, in that part of the world, even the local guides who sometimes fish commercially use bait-casting tackle for snook fishing in the surf. Favorite lures are darters, Mirrolures, and bucktails.

Luckily, we had timed our arrival right and for one solid hour the three of us caught big snook on every cast. We estimated the smallest fish at seventeen pounds and released several over thirty pounds. Then the activity stopped as quickly as it began. During the midst of the melee, I even hooked a tarpon in the surf (which is not uncommon), but broke it off as soon as it jumped so that I could get back to snook fishing.

Snook almost embarrassed me along the Caribbean coast of Colombia east of Santa Marta. A friend wanted to look at some property that his business associate owned and we stuck a couple of bait-casters in the trunk. There was an incoming tide when we arrived and, while my partner took care of business, I had a little of my own in mind.

Walking down to a large indentation in the beach, I came upon a couple of local anglers fishing for market. They had tin cans with monofilament wrapped around, a hunk of lead, and rusty hooks with pieces of cloth tied on for lures. Lying well up on the sand were a brace of snook that were better than fifteen pounds apiece.

When they saw me, both of the Colombians motioned for me to come where they were standing and fish in their spot. This was truly the type of hospitality that is lacking along most coastal sectors where it's more of an elbowing match than sport. One man caught another snook while I stood there. By winding the line back on the can, they can make that piece of cloth look like a baitfish in the water. It's something to see.

There I stood with the finest light tackle available and they were catching fish while I couldn't buy a strike. Finally, I tied on a yellow bucktail that Gordon Young of Miami had made and bounced it along the bottom. Nothing happened. By this time, I was getting desperate to produce a fish on my store-bought tackle. Remembering a trick that I had used before, I took out a pair of folding scissors I had in my pocket and cut about a half inch off the end of the bucktail. This creation had shiny Mylar strips on either side and Gordon had once told me that it sometimes works better if you just let the silver strips extend past the hair.

On the very next cast, I felt the solid strike of a snook and promptly gave the fish to my newfound friend. We only had an hour to fish, but my partner and I hooked seven fish in that time. When we left, I pulled all the monofilament off both our reels and gave it to the pair of other anglers on the beach in appreciation for their generosity in yielding their spot. Mono is hard to come by out there and they were certainly delighted to have it. As we walked off the beach, they were still winding it on tin cans.

Along Mexico's Yucatan, Lefty Kreh and I cast into the mouth of a cut that carried water from back lagoons to the sea. Rumor had it that big cubera snapper invaded this territory after the sun went down and we were going to check that out. We only had a couple of large plugs and took turns using

A small Mirrolure on a plug outfit was all it took to hook and land this thirty-pound snook in the surf.

them. Our outfits, however, were light and we had to lob the casts to handle that much weight.

The first night, Lefty had a solid strike and fought the fish with determination on a modest spinning outfit. The big snapper headed out of the cut and along the beachfront while Lefty followed. With a rod much more suited to barracuda, Lefty had his problems, but he managed to pump the fish by backing up on the sand and then reeling in the line as he ran toward the water. Eventually, he brought the fish into the shallows where he asked me to gaff it for him.

There was one small problem. The only gaff we had was a lip gaff for releasing tarpon. That cubera would lie in the wash and snap its jaws like a covey of bear traps being sprung at the same time. To make matters worse, I was barefooted and had a flashlight that was lingering on its last bit of energy. After much effort, I was able to get the gaff in the snapper's mouth and drag it up on the sand. It later weighed forty-two-and-a-half pounds.

The next evening, it was my turn and I made Lefty return the favor using the same gaff and the same flashlight. My fish was a few pounds smaller, but it gnashed its teeth just as viciously. Since we had to present big plugs, we simply worked out a system of easing them out there on the light gear. It worked; we had fun; and we caught fish that were memorable.

Lefty Kreh managed to drag this husky cubera snapper out of the Mexican surf after a long battle on ten-pound-test line. The fish covered a mile of beachfront before it was finally landed.

THE SHALLOW FLATS

The closest thing to Heaven that any of us who take our light-tackle fishing seriously will ever find on earth has to be the shallow tropical flats. There are no parallels, no analogies, no comparisons, and no training grounds in any other type of fishing. It is unique and addictive. Fresh-water anglers who have made the pilgrimage cherish the experience and long for the next time they can return.

This is a one-on-one situation. You sight your quarry first, stalk it, and then make the presentation. The margin for error doesn't exist. You have to be on target and do everything right or your offering will be ignored and rejected. Learning this form of fishing demands practice, experience, and dedication to both. It's a way of life and one must live it.

The rewards justify the challenges. Battling and beating a massive tarpon on tackle better suited to largemouth bass proves unforgettable. It's equally exhilarating to sneak up on a school of bonefish, pick one out, and make a delicate presentation that won't spook the rest of the school. Seeing the elusive permit twitter with excitement at the sight of a live crab or pounce authoritatively on a small bucktail that you happen to be bouncing along the bottom, etches memories that can never be erased. Any angler who has fished this magical type of water for the glamour species or for barracuda, sharks, jacks, redfish, snook, or mutton snapper will be back again and again.

Fish leave the sanctuary of the depths and probe the shallows for food, but every second they spend in thin water makes them more skittish and ready to abandon the idea. Sharks are right there with them, barracuda are around, birds might swoop down, and other predators are present. Sometimes they even spook themselves. If one fish panics, the entire school will flush as a unit.

If you're new to the game, the best advice that anyone can give you is to hire a competent guide, at least for the first few days. It may seem expensive, but it's cheap in the long run and you have a better chance of finding fish. Remember that you must see the fish first before you cast and that takes concentration.

Polarized sunglasses and a broad-brimmed hat are the tools of the shallow-water fisherman. The glasses should be of the wrap-around variety or have side shields to keep the sun from filtering in between the frame and your face. Unless you build a tent around your eyes, you will not have 100 percent vision. Rays of the sun reaching your eyes will make it more difficult to see. The glasses, by the way, should have a length of monofilament attached to the temple bars or some other means of keeping them on your head or around your neck if they fall. It's also a wise precaution to carry an extra pair with you at all times.

Experts often carry two or three different density polaroids, wearing darker shades on bright days and lighter ones when it's overcast. Even when it's raining, you should be wearing polarized lenses. Yellow shooting glasses (called Kalichromes) can be a valuable adjunct early in the morning and late in the day. They make things brighter and you can see waking or rolling fish at times when you might otherwise miss them.

Spotting Your Quarry

Unless you can see fish on the flats, you're going to have trouble catching them. There are tricks to spotting fish in shallow water and you should be aware of them. Assuming you're wearing polarized glasses and a broad-brimmed hat, you must then psyche yourself into total concentration. You might chat with your guide or partner, but your eyes are scanning all the time and your mind is pinpointed on every inch of real estate your eyes cover.

Flip Pallot, one of the great light-tackle anglers, with a huge permit he caught on ten-pound-test spinning gear. For catches like this one, both tackle and angler must be tuned to the task.

The important thing is to look *through* the surface of the water and directly at the bottom. Invariably, newcomers think they are doing that, but reflections of clouds and other things seem to rob them of their effectiveness. Head and eyes should be moving like a radar antenna, following a systematic search pattern that starts near the boat and covers the full area to beyond effective casting distance. The basic scan goes from beam to beam, but occasionally it's worth a look behind you. Surprisingly, fish come up on the boat from astern and it's too late when you finally see them.

Sometimes, you can concentrate on the forest and not see the trees. That's why it is important to take a long look across the water. You won't be able to see under the surface at that distance, but you can see rolling tarpon and you

Flats fishing is an opportunity game. Spinning anglers must keep the bail open, line over their finger, and be ready to cast the instant a fish is sighted.

can also spot such telltale signs as wakes running off the backs of fish, fins above the water, tailing bonefish, and what regulars describe as "nervous water," a condition caused by a school of fish that makes the water appear to ripple. During periods of marginal visibility, these are the things you look for, but they also happen on bright days and it's important to be alert to them.

Basically, barracuda will remain motionless and appear dark. Bonefish will usually be on the move and they could look dark, light, or transparent depending on the bottom and current light conditions. Schools of tarpon will be on the move, yet they can be hard to see. There are times when fish will remain motionless, lying on the bottom and you'll come right up on them before you know they are there. If you can spot them far enough away, there's time for a cast and you can catch them.

It's easier to spot movement from a boat that's staked out than one being poled across the flats. When the boat is easing along, the bottom looks as if it, too, is moving. You have to look for something moving at a different rate.

Quite frequently, something will catch your eye and you'll focus on it. Once you make the identification as non-fish or a species you don't want to catch, forget it and keep scanning. If you're in doubt and can't make up your mind on the identification, cast to it. It's better to be wrong fifty times and not miss one real opportunity than to take a chance.

Finding Fish

Before getting down to specifics, there are a few general guidelines worth remembering. Contrary to the preconceived opinions of visitors, the flats aren't overflowing with fish the year around. Much of the activity is seasonal and all of it depends to a great extent on water temperature.

The big migratory tarpon can start to show as early as January providing the water temperature on the flats is at least 75 degrees. When it drops below that, the fish move off. There are periods during the winter months when two or three warm days will pull the fish into the shallows, but the first cold front will chase them. The run continues through most of June and you can find big fish as late as July and August. At times, you'll find a few fish into the early fall. The rest of the time, catching heavyweight tarpon is a dream and not a reality.

Bonefish can tolerate water down to about 70 degrees. Local experts can find a few fish when the thermometer shows the water is down in the 60s, but that takes plenty of local knowledge. Permit also move out when the temperatures drop below about 70 degrees and the few that may stay will be very sluggish. You can find permit at any time, but the best months are early spring and again in the fall. During May, June, and into July many of them move over the wrecks in deep water to spawn.

As long as the temperature is comfortable for them, you'll find bonefish. Peak periods are spring and fall, with the fall of the year being a bit better. During the summer months, very warm temperatures may keep the fish off the flats during the heat of the day and most fishing takes place in early morning or late afternoon. Since visibility is limited during those hours, you either have to spot waking fish or work shallow enough water where the fish will tail.

Tides make everything happen on the flats. Some areas are only good on incoming water and others come to life when the tide is falling. Many spots produce under both sets of conditions if you know where to look and others harbor fish during a brief tidal stage. To complicate matters, there are places that are super when there are spring tides with higher highs and lower lows. Some spots just don't produce when there are spring tides. It takes time, local knowledge, and a lot of experimenting to find the best places.

Then there are the habits of the fish. Tarpon, for example, will move through deeper water with the tide or they'll angle across it. One of their favorite habits is to let the tide push them up against the edge of a bank or flat, so that they can follow the contour downtide looking for food. If you know where this happens, you can stake out and wait for the fish to come by. On other flats, you have to stalk the fish as they glide across in search of a meal.

The bait or lure must land in front of and beyond the fish, so that the retrieve will bring it into view. You must note the direction in which the fish is travelng and how fast.

Bonefish and redfish usually move onto a flat from the downtide side, attracted by the scent of food. They tend to feed into the tide where they can put their sense of smell to maximum use. On some flats, the fish move right up with the incoming tide as high as they can and then trade back and forth waiting for the water. When they get up as high as they want to go, they'll turn and work back into the tide.

You may want to follow the downtide edge on some flats or work up as far as you can and then scout the area ahead of you and to the sides. Depth is critical. If you don't know the right depth from experience, it pays to zig-zag in and out until you start seeing fish.

There's no substitute for a silent approach. The main motor should be turned off a respectable distance from the area you want to fish and the approach made via pushpole. The poles are fiberglass and range in length from fourteen to twenty feet with a sixteen-footer or an eighteen-footer among the more popular. Actually, the length of the pole depends on the depth of the water and whether or not there is an elevated poling platform on the boat. In deeper water, some anglers use electric motors to follow the fish, but there's no substitute for a good man on the pushpole.

The direction in which you pole can make all the difference. You want to follow the contour of the right depth or at least run an intercept. The stage of the tide should help to determine where on the flat you will be. As the tide becomes higher, you move up more, but as it starts to fall, you drop back with it. In some places, it's a good idea to work parallel to the edge of a channel from which water is rising to flood the flat. The fish will come over the edge and you'll be there for the intercept.

Wind and sun also are important considerations. If possible, try to get both of them at your back. Otherwise, you have to make a choice: whichever one is more of a handicap should be at your back.

Keep in mind that fish are bolder and more aggressive on a flood tide than they are when the water is ebbing. They'll linger and look much more when the water is rising and they probably won't appear to be in a hurry. You can follow them effectively and often get a shot after a long stalk.

On falling water, it's a different story. The fish become much more skittish and are concerned about being left high and dry. You'll notice that they move a bit more quickly and don't linger. It's also worth noting that in some places your boat can get stranded if you're not careful. The tide drops quickly and you have to get off the flat or out near the edges even though plenty of fish may still be above you.

Stalking fish on the shallow flats is a challenging experience. Captain Dale Perez silently poles a client in search of sharks. The angler must be ready to cast as soon as the fish is sighted.

The Presentation

Any fishermen who ventures across the flats with only one species in mind is missing out on a lot of fun. Part of the pleasure comes from the variety of fish you can catch and the different types of tackle you can use. It is not uncommon for two anglers in a small boat to carry sixteen to twenty rods between them. Each person will have an assortment of fly, spinning, and plug gear if he is competent with all three types.

If your main target happens to be bonefish, you should certainly have a rod rigged for sharks or maybe two rods ready for them: one for heavyweights and a lighter one for the smaller sharks. Another outfit should have a tube lure on it for barracuda. Then there are the bonefish rods and you could very well have another for permit or tarpon.

Each rod must be rigged and ready to go, stored out of the way, yet placed where you can reach it quickly. When things happen on a flat, there usually isn't much time or advanced warning.

You have the choice of natural or artificial bait. Shrimp is the basic offering for bonefish and it should be impaled on the hook working from the tail toward the middle. The tail is usually broken off to make it less wind resistant and to enable it to move backward in the water if you lift the rod. As you stand scanning the water, the bail on the spinning rod should be open, your finger on the line, and the right amount past the tip top for a cast. You must keep the shrimp in the water alongside the boat or it will die.

With a shrimp, you can cast closer to a fish than with an artificial. Still, it should be about three feet ahead of the fish and about four feet beyond. The instant the shrimp splats on the surface, lift your rod tip so that the shrimp will skitter a foot or two across the surface and then sink. The bonefish should smell it out and pick it up.

Flats expert Flip Pallot goes a step further. He wants his offering to land uptide of the fish whether it is natural bait or an artificial, because that's the direction from which it expects its food to come. He'll even pause momentarily until the fish heads in that direction before he casts. With a tailing fish, of course, you can drop the bait a mite closer, depending on the circumstances.

When there is more than one fish present, you must be exceptionally careful to place the bait or lure where it won't spook another member of the school. In some waters, that's not easy because you think you see all the fish, but you don't. If the bait lands too close to a fish or the line crosses one, it's adios. That's why it often makes sense to pause an extra instant if there is time and try to identify every fish in the school.

One of the most difficult casts occurs when a school of fish is moving directly toward the boat. There's a tendency to overcast the fish and not allow enough time for the bait or lure to sink into position. It's often better to cast short and wait for the fish to come to the bait. When they are just about there, they should get the smell of the shrimp and pounce on it. You can sometimes help matters by lifting the rod tip so that the shrimp jumps off the bottom; then let it settle. That should do it.

Once you spot the fish, you should never take your eyes off them. Surprisingly, you might not pick them up again very quickly and that could cost you the cast. Beginners have a great deal of trouble at times trying to monitor both fish and lure. You should be able to watch both at the same time and know the relationship and relative position of one to the other.

Leadheaded jigs are the prime artificial for bonefish. You can also use a small plastic worm tail or grub rigged with a slip sinker. Follow the same approach you would with live bait including the presentation from uptide if possible. Most of the uninitiated want to hop the lure along the bottom at a reasonably fast speed. There are times this will work, but a much better approach is to hop it in place once or twice and let the fish pounce on it and ferret it out.

As a basic rule, use the lightest weight bucktail you can under the circumstances. For tailing fish, you don't want to go over a quarter ounce and you'll rarely need heavier for cruising fish. In very shallow water and on a grassy bottom, a flat jig and one that resembles a clenched fist are among the best.

Since you're fishing by sight, you can monitor everything taking place. If you have cast too far beyond the fish or ahead of it, take whatever action is necessary to get the jig in position. If you miss altogether, crank in as fast as you possibly can and get ready for a second cast. There's no time to waste. You can also see the reaction of the fish. If it's eager, you only have to show it the jig and it will grab it. If the fish hesitates, you might use other methods such as speeding up the retrieve. There isn't much time to accomplish the whole operation, so it's worth the risk to gain a commitment.

Permit are fished very much as for bonefish, only a live crab to them looks like a sundae with a cherry on top. These are fished best with spinning gear. The technique isn't very complicated. When the fish is within range, cast the crab in front and beyond it. Remember that permit are almost always on the move and sometimes change course quickly. As the crab hits the water, keep the rod tip high and start to reel slowly. You want to swim the crab across the surface until the permit sees it. When it does, it should charge. The instant you see the fish move toward the crab or you see a swirl where the fish was a second ago, drop the rod tip and open the bail. The crab will dive for the bottom and the permit will engulf it. Wait until the fish moves off about ten feet, close the bail, wait for the line to come tight, and set the hook. You've just set the stage for the thrill of a lifetime.

Permit will also hit bucktails. A sand color or light brown is touted among the best shades by the experts. Many are taken on bonefish jigs because they happen to be on the line and there's no time to grab another rod. They'll sometimes strike a plug and I've had them chase tube lures moved at flank speed for barracuda. Catching permit on a fly is one of the supreme light-tackle triumphs—and quite rare.

For most light-tackle aficionados, tarpon are the premier fish of the flats. It's amazing how a hundred-pound fish can glide through the water undetected, but it happens. If you can get a shrimp or a crab in front of them, they should take it, but most anglers use artificial lures. There are several on the market, but most amount to some type of weighted head and a tail. In past years, sliders with weighted cork and hackle were the favorite offering because you could make them hang at mid-depth. Tarpon are often on the deeper flats in three to eight feet of water and it's important to get the lure down to eyeball level or just above the fish. More tarpon are missed because the lure doesn't get down than for most other reasons. You'll soon discover that they are moving much faster than they appear to be, yet the strike usually is slow and it doesn't even look as if they changed their swimming speed.

The trick is to ease the lure along in front of them and keep it moving. Newcomers are sometimes so shocked to see a big fish follow their offering that they freeze and the tarpon loses interest. Silver kings will hit a variety of artificials ranging from bucktails to sliders to plastic worms to plastic squids.

At times, a fish will peel off from the school and follow the lure, failing to take it. When this happens, try speeding it up for a short burst and see if this makes a difference. Sometimes, the fact that its meal is escaping will motivate the fish into action.

There are exceptions to all the rules, but no one can be prepared for every eventuality without putting in time on the water. The nemesis of many visiting anglers lies in casting. They are used to tossing lures at random and have no experience in throwing to a moving target. The best advice is to practice at home and then practice some more. Set up targets and work until you can hit them without thinking. Don't worry about long casts. Most of the action takes place within seventy-five feet of the boat and even closer. When visibility is limited, some of the casts are within twenty or thirty feet. That means that in addition to accuracy, one must develop a speedy delivery. It's a matter of practice.

Redfish, snook, and trout are also found on some flats along with other species. You already know how to cast to a specific fish and work the bait or lure by it in the most natural manner. On shallower flats, where redfish have their backs out of the water, the choice of lures is important. You'll need something that will float and not hang up in the grass. In fact, the choice of lures is usually dictated by the type of flat and the depth of water in addition to the species.

Barracuda and Sharks

Flats fishermen have a tendency to become so enamoured with tarpon, bonefish, and permit, that they overlook some of the fastest and most impressive action in the shallows. Both the barracuda and shark have been underrated and maligned for years, yet they are great gamefish and certainly worthy of your attention. I wouldn't dream of fishing the flats without having a couple of outfits rigged for these two toothy denizens.

Some of the largest barracuda move into the flats during the winter months when there are cold snaps. That's the same type of weather that forces bonefish into deeper water and the tarpon are long since gone. You can, however, find the cuda at any time of year in varying sizes.

They are a particularly curious fish and exceptionally wary. Once they see you or the boat, they can be difficult to fool in spite of their formidable dentures. The trick in catching them usually hinges on making long casts with a lure fashioned out of surgical tubing and then moving the offering as fast as you can. This brings out the killer instinct in the fish and strikes can be spectacular.

Sharks are an extremely fragile part of the sea's ecological balance. Researchers are now asking that unneeded sharks be released unharmed.

No one knows more about making tube lures or tube-lure fishing than Captain John Eckard of Key West, Florida. I have seen John tease cuda into striking that the rest of us had long given up on as uncatchable.

Tubes are an illusion. They look like a creature undulating through the water, but they are actually spinning. At the same time, however, they do create sound and that's important. Most anglers work a tube lure by making a long cast well past the fish and then cranking as fast as possible with the rod tip held high to keep the lure on the surface. It's surprising how far a barracuda will come to catch that lure.

This primary technique works a good part of the time, but John Eckard has a better way. He believes that if you can keep the tube just under the surface without breaking the skin of the water, you'll get more strikes and fewer follows. To accomplish this, he slows the retrieve slightly and he weights his tube lures more. Instead of using a quarter-ounce slip or egg sinker in front of a tube, John will go to a half ounce.

The average tube lure for barracuda is about ten to twelve inches long, but John finds he has better success with tubes that are fifteen to eighteen inches long. Chartreuse is the number-one color, followed by fluorescent red. Tubing should always be kept coiled so that it retains some natural bends. When you rig it, use number 6, 7, or 8 stainless steel wire. You have the option of single hooks or trebles. One thing I learned from John is that the middle hook should be slightly forward of the center of the tubing. Said another way, if you are using sixteen inches of tubing, the center hook should be slightly less than eight inches from the head. Otherwise, you'll miss a greater percentage of fish.

Frequently, it becomes a race when you fish a tube. The fish is in hot pursuit and it becomes a question of whether it will grab the lure or see the boat and turn off. Some anglers slow the retrieve before they get too close to the boat and try to tease the fish. Whatever you do, keep the rod to the side so that if the fish hits and jumps simultaneously, it won't come right at you.

Some of the sharks you'll see on the flats will make you shudder. Their dorsals will knife through the water like a sail and their tails will beat back and forth like windshield wipers on a stormy night. It's surprising how high on a flat a shark will venture, constantly looking for an easy meal. Unlike their brethren in deeper water, these shallow-water marauders will put up a spectacular fight, making long runs that burn line off the reel.

There are also plenty of smaller sharks on the flats and they are a great deal of fun on light and ultralight gear. You can be ready for both sizes and you may find that they save the day when fishing is slow. Basically, sharks like warm water and you'll see larger ones during the summer months, but when bonefish and tarpon are on the flats, the sharks can be formidable.

Although we picture them as wanton killers, most sharks have poor eyesight and must rely on their sense of smell and their ability to home-in on distress vibrations to find their prey. That's why you will see one suddenly appear as you're fighting another fish.

Natural bait invariably proves much more effective than artificials because they can find it with their sense of smell. For smaller sharks, a live shrimp or even a dead one is perfect. Simply hook it on a light rod rigged with a wire leader and cast it in front of the cruising shark. You'll see the fish circle and it should find the shrimp easily. If it doesn't, reel in and cast again.

Balao makes the ideal offering for larger sharks. Hook it right through both jaws and the head, breaking off the beak. The balao gives you plenty of weight for long casts and it has a couple of irresistible advantages. By keeping the rod tip high, you can work it across the surface in front of the shark like an artificial. Then, when the shark sees it, simply stop reeling, drop the rod tip, and let the shark pick it up. When you set the hook, hold on!

The real fun of shark fishing is to get a big critter to strike an artificial. They'll hit almost anything if they can see it and are in the mood. However, they pass up artificials with frustrating frequency and getting one to strike isn't always a breeze. You can try several fish and then one will just clobber the lure.

Darters and chuggers worked on the surface are good because the shark can home-in on the noise. It's important, however, not to make too much commotion or you'll scare them. The cast should be made at right angles to the eye and alongside it if possible. Remember that sharks don't see well and have trouble finding the lure. At times, they'll get behind a plug and just nose it, making you think they'll strike.

Plastic squids such as those used for offshore trolling and teasers make an excellent lure. Fluorescent red is a prime color. The squid should be weighted with a light sinker so it gets down quickly. The tentacles flutter as it drops and this is effective.

After a while, you may become addicted to catching Nature's greatest predator.

9

Special
Offshore Techniques

A prophet named Mohammed once reasoned that if the mountain wouldn't come to him, he would go to the mountain. Light-tackle anglers, however, have struggled for years with techniques tailored to bring their quarry within range in what might be termed a semi-controlled situation. By setting the stage carefully, they try to get the fish to come to them so that they can either cast or drop a bait back.

Learning the principles is important, because they can always be modified and applied to a variety of circumstances in both fresh water and salt. Once you know the basics and let your mind wander, it's amazing how quickly you can get a start on trying to solve a problem of luring a particular species within range of your offering.

CHUMMING

Few species can resist the *hors d'oeuvres* that signal a free lunch. By putting natural food in the water, you can not only attract fish but stimulate their desire to feed. Because of the competition in a chum slick, fish are also more aggressive and will sometimes race each other to the nearest tidbits.

Areas where fish are concentrated provide the best places to chum. Among the more obvious are reefs, wrecks, structures such as towers or oil rigs, groupings of coral heads, humps, and any other bottom configuration that can be considered a fish haven. In addition, chumming can be quite successful in diverting passing fish or holding a school near the boat.

In Bermuda, for example, the summer months offer superb chumming

154

opportunities for yellowfin tuna, blackfin tuna, amberjack, bonito, rainbow runners, and many others. West Coast anglers use live anchovies to hold schools of albacore. Shark chumming is a way of life and a long slick will pull these predators in to investigate the source, which happens to be the transom of your boat.

Unless you have a tide or current to carry the chum and its scent, the results can be disappointing. That's why this technique works best when there is a flow of water. The boat, of course, must be positioned carefully so that the flow will carry the chum back toward the target zone. If you intend to fish a structure, you must anchor on the uptide or upcurrent side. When you are fishing the edge of a bank such as they do in Bermuda, the chum must move

Chumming is the perfect way to lure big fish within range of featherweight gear. This yellowfin tuna picked up a bait drifted back by Bermuda's Pete Perinchief. Captain David DeSilva holds the gaff.

from the shallower regions off the edge into the deep. Cruising gamefish will pick up the morsels or the scent and start tracing it to its source.

The chum you select depends on the area you fish and the species you seek. In most situations, the primary chum is an oily fish such as menhaden, mackerel, herring, or others that will cause a long slick to form well behind the boat. In other places, small baitfish make up the basic attractor and, although they are usually dead, they could be alive as in the case of anchovies for albacore or yellowtail.

Veteran chummers like to keep other goodies on hand to sweeten a slick, particularly when they start to attract fish. When bluefishing in the Northeast, they'll toss in killifish or sand eels. Tuna fishermen may have a variety of offerings ready and start using large chunks or whole fish when the big bluefins suddenly appear. Pilchards are used down south and so are the gleanings from the net trash generated by shrimp boats.

Along parts of the coastline, the basic chum is either ground-up fresh or frozen blocks that are placed in net bags and hung from the transom so that the washing effect of the water spreads it. If you use ground fish that is fresh, you simply mix sea water with it and then ladle it over the side.

The secret of chumming is the creation of a continuous slick that moves off at an even rate with no break in it. When a mesh bag is hung over the side, the water takes care of this, although some anglers will occasionally shake the bag to release an extra amount of chum. If you have to ladle chum overboard or toss in whole fish or chunks, the procedure is a bit different.

The rule of thumb among chummers is that as one batch of bait begins to disappear from sight, it's time to put the next in the water. Even if all hands on board are busy fighting fish, you must maintain the chum slick. There are no excuses and no exceptions. If you don't keep that slick going, you can lose the fish out there in a matter of moments.

Theories vary on how much chum to put out at one time. Some oldtimers feel you merely want to whet the appetite of your quarry, while others like to chum rather heavily and keep the action at full tilt. If you concentrate on what you are doing, you can usually sense what's taking place. On difficult days, you might chum heavier and when you have the fish coming, ease off just a bit. Aboard many boats, anglers rotate in handling the chumming chores, so that there is always one person who is not fishing and can keep the slick going.

Fishing a Chum Slick

How you fish a slick depends on where you happen to be and the species you are trying to catch. In the more common situation, one baits up with either the same thing used as chum or a slick sweetener and drifts it back. The exception is when live bait is used as chum such as you would do for albacore on the West Coast. The trick there is to cast the live bait as far away from the boat as possible. It will then try to swim for the safety of the hull and a predator should nail it on the way.

Nothing is more important when fishing a dead bait in a slick than to keep it swimming constantly. There will be times when you can hold a bait in one

Frozen blocks of chum are available in most tackle shops. Slip the block into a mesh bag and hang it over the side; water action will keep the slick going.

This handful of anchovies and hog-mouthed fry will lure fish right behind the boat.

place and get strikes, but you'll do a lot better if you let the bait drift with the natural flow of the current.

As chum is ladled over the side, it starts to float away and sink at the same time. It's really following an inclined plane toward the bottom and the slope of that plane is governed by the force of the current. In a fast current, it will take longer for the chum to reach the bottom. By drifting the bait, it follows the line of the chum and is more likely to be found by fish in the slick.

Free-floating a bait is easy if you become a line watcher. Start by stripping off three or four rod lengths of line and keep an eye on the line as it starts to straighten. Just before it comes tight, strip more line on the surface of the water. With a little practice, you'll develop the timing. You don't want the line to come tight for an instant. If it does, the bait will begin to rise and you'll be above the plane of the chum.

By watching the line, you can also tell when you have a pickup. The line will begin to move off much faster than the tide is carrying it and that's your clue. Engage the reel, wait for the line to come totally tight so that you can feel the pull of the fish, and then set the hook.

If you do enough chumming, you'll encounter days when it's tough to pick fish. Perhaps it's because you haven't brought much into the slick, but it also may be due to the fact that you're using too large a bait. Try small hooks, lighter lines than usual, and a very small piece of bait. Speaking of bait, always use fresh offerings and change bait if it has been mashed by a fish or if the water has softened it.

Another trick worth remembering is one that is used by Boyd Gibbons of the "Coral Sea" in Bermuda. He has a small chum pot with a sinker on a short line. When the fish are down deep or when he first starts chumming, Boyd will fill the pot and lower it down as deep as possible before tripping it. The next load will be a little higher and the third pot full will be still higher. This method helps to bring the fish up quickly.

To bring fish up from the depths, you can use a small chum pot lowered with a sinker. A second line is used to trip the pot when it reaches the desired depth. Each drop is shallower than the one before, bringing the fish to the surface.

Dick Kondak used an innovative idea when he was desperate off the Hump near Islamorada. Blackfin tuna were the target and there was one boat on the scene that had chum and was bailing fish. Being a sportsman, Dick didn't want to invade their slick nor did he want to disturb their fishing, but he recognized there were plenty of fish in the area. Moving a respectable distance away, he cut up baitfish and inserted small egg sinkers in each piece. That gave him enough weight to throw the bait a considerable distance from his boat. By shortening each throw, he was able to lure a couple of fish near the live baits he was drifting and managed to get his fares some blackfin. The other boat remained in the thick of the action and everybody was happy.

In some situations, the fish are close enough to the boat so that you can almost pick the one you want and drift a bait back to it. If you're fishing for species that don't show, such as bluefish in the Northeast, keep drifting the bait until you cover a significant distance. Then reel in and do it again. You might even have one member of your party try a small sinker ahead of the chum when you are probing the slick to find fish.

The other method of fishing a slick works well in tropical waters when the chum attracts multitudes of small fish and you are looking for the huskier denizens. Usually, the underwater sounds of small fish feeding will be a rallying cry for the heavyweights. Since the water is exceptionally clear, you merely have to watch the activity in the water carefully. When bigger fish pass through the slick you'll see them. In fact, you should notice that the smaller creatures move out of the way and let the others have the chum.

You then have the option of either using bait or artificial lures. With bait, simply drift it back to the fish you want or cast it out and let it sink in the vicinity of your target. Since you can eyeball everything taking place, you can almost steer your bait to the fish you want or at least keep it away from a smaller critter.

If you decide on artificials, you can cast them toward the big fish and monitor the response. Often topwater chuggers will grab the attention of husky predators because they know they are in a feeding situation. Bucktails also work and can be effective because you can vary their depth quickly.

Artificials can certainly be fished in a slick where you can't see your quarry. It's usually better to catch a fish or two on bait so that you know they are in the slick before switching to lures. Then make long casts down the slick and retrieve the offering toward you.

Chum can be used to hold fish, such as dolphin when you find a school, in open water. Most offshore trollers don't carry chum, but they have plenty of balao or other trolling baits. Just cut them up into little chunks and toss them over the side. The dolphin will start feeding on them and stay around. You can then use bait or cast artificials.

As aggressive as dolphin can be, they sometimes become particularly finicky when you are trying to hold the school. Assuming you are using artificials, switch to another color or a different lure if you get refusals on two or three successive casts. Another trick is to cast well past the fish and then retrieve much faster than you ordinarily would. This can turn the dolphin on and you'll pick up a few more. Keeping one hooked fish in the water all the time also helps to hold the others.

Chumming is as valid on the inshore grounds as it is in deeper water. Striped bass are chummed with everything from clams to grass shrimp and other species can also be brought to boatside via that method.

Captain Bill Curtis, one of the world's leading bonefish guides, uses a chumming technique that was originally developed by Captain J. T. Harrod. Bill picks a sandy bottom where he knows bonefish will cross during a particular stage of the tide. He'll stake the boat out a comfortable cast from this spot with the sun at his back. When the angler is ready and has baited up or tied on his favorite artificial, Bill will cut up several shrimp and toss them out on the flat. Bonefish have a particularly acute sense of smell and the scent of the fresh shrimp will lure them into the area. More important, they'll mill around looking for more tidbits. Bill then points the fish out to his customers and tells them to cast. In an average year, he'll guide almost three hundred days in all kinds of weather and there won't be a half dozen when he fails to produce a bonefish for his customers.

TEASING FISH

Light-tackle enthusiasts who insist on probing blue water for outsized challenges master the art of teasing fish early in the game. It's somewhat akin to being a quarterback and dropping into the pocket to throw a pass while the other team is blitzing. There doesn't seem to be much time to make the play, yet there is enough if you're able to stand there and concentrate on your job while ignoring the charge. With practice, you'll be able to function effectively, but you'll never hold down the excitement of the scene.

Teasing takes several forms. On the offshore trolling circuit, it can be used to raise billfish or other denizens and then cast to them with fly, plug, or spin. Another application in the same waters is to get a big fish in position where you can drop a bait back on relatively light gear.

Captain Rick DeFeo, one of the best light-tackle guides on the seas today, has honed the technique to perfection and one marvels at how he can remain so matter-of-fact while playing tug-of-war with a sailfish or marlin. Rick will rig daisy chains of plastic squids plus some other hookless offerings and drag them behind the boat. Nearby, he has a couple of teasing outfits armed with natural baits that have been carefully sewn to a swivel. The stitching job is extensive so that the fish cannot pull the bait off easily.

When a sailfish, for example, comes up on a daisy chain of squids, Rick will drop a natural teaser back and switch the fish from the artificial to the real thing. At the same time, all the other outfits are taken out of the water quickly and then the original daisy chain is pulled when the fish becomes interested in the natural. It then becomes a process of letting the sailfish mouth the bait, then pulling it away. Each time the sail comes back more aggressively, its body a vivid neon color. When Rick feels the fish is ready, the boat is slipped out of gear and the cast is made.

A good cast will be slightly behind the eye of the fish, but alongside. As the artificial comes into view, the sail should turn off and try to grab it, venting its

Teasing fish is an offshore trick that produces exciting results. Veterans actually pick the fish they want, get it excited, and then substitute an artificial for the live bait. This blue runner was just yanked away from a barracuda as an amberjack approached.

frustrations on the new offering. If that doesn't happen, Rick will yank the natural teaser out of the water and the fish will start looking for a meal that was right there an instant ago. The next thing it sees is your lure. To do this, the teasing rods are usually longer than a standard outfit, which makes it easier to jerk a bait out of the water.

Ideally, the fish will turn on the new artificial and take it going away or at least in a crossing situation, which results in a better chance to hookup. If the angler misses, the natural goes back in the water and the boat is put back in gear until the fish is worked up again. It takes cool courage, but it's exhilarating to watch and to be part of the activity.

The same basic procedure can be used with other species. Not everyone will switch a fish from an artificial teaser to a natural one, but Rick believes that he can prepare a fish much better if it gets the taste, smell, and feel of something good to eat.

Instead of casting artificials, you could slip a natural bait back in the wake and get a hookup on very light line. This is the basic procedure for those who fish six-pound class or even lighter lines. Mike Levitt took a record sailfish on four-pound test using a similar hooking technique.

Nothing excites Steve Sloan more than the challenge of trying for very big fish on very light lines. He has set a number of records over the years on six-pound test and has also boated an 862-pound black marlin for a world record on thirty-pound class. It only took him thirty-seven minutes to land that fish.

Through constant experimentation, Steve has developed a teasing system that works for him, especially when it takes a big bait to raise the fish, but you have to use a smaller offering on the light rod. The procedure starts by trolling a pair of big baits on two eighty-pound outfits plus the usual teasers. These baits are rigged hookless. When a billfish comes up, the teasers are pulled out of the way. At the same time, Steve tells the captain to put the boat in neutral. The boat still has forward motion, but a slick glide is created for at least forty to fifty feet astern.

In the slick water, the fish can see the new bait coming back to it and the strike is spectacular. Seldom will a marlin or sailfish turn away from the offering being free-spooled. When he's using line up to twenty-pound test, Steve prefers to rig the bait so that the hook is on the outside. This improves the hooking rate, because he doesn't have to pull the hook through the bait, which can be tough to do on light line.

Over reefs and wrecks, there's another type of teasing that proves particularly effective. It involves the use of live bait, though dead bait can also be used. Usually, the first step is to chum big fish up near the surface. Then, a live blue runner or some other live fish is used to tease the fish. It works wonders on species like amberjack, cobia, and other denizens of the reefs.

You have to be quick to keep the bait away from the predator. By dangling it in the water and pulling it out, you can get a fish so worked up that it loses all natural caution. When that happens, just lift the teaser out of the water and slap something else down there and the fish is all over it instantly.

The same thing is possible with dead bait, but you have to lob it out and swish it back and forth across the surface, making a commotion in the process. One day out in the Gulf of Mexico off Key West, Bob Stearns and I had amberjack and cobia all over the surface. I was trying to tease some fish for Bob when an amberjack of about sixty pounds wrapped its lips around the goodie. There was no hook in the teaser and I struggled to pull it free. The huge jack wouldn't let go and I had the fish half way out of the water trying to wrestle the bait away from it. Bob was busy trying to get a cast off and a half dozen cameras sat idle in the boat during the whole episode. What a picture it would have made.

It's always been my contention that roosterfish could be teased into taking a fly using a similar technique. After discussing this with Bill Barnes, he tried it on the Pacific side of Costa Rica with a modicum of success. It does work and I believe it can be refined into a technique that will become commonplace in the near future.

Roosterfish can be very stubborn when it comes to hitting artificials, sometimes following the lure for an extended period of time. Anyone who has cast for these great gamefish knows that you get a lot more follows than strikes. You can catch them on light casting tackle if you troll the lures and one method that worked well for me involved a topwater chugger. Again, the scene of this action was in Costa Rica.

We were working from small skiffs and roosters were abundant in one large bay. Instead of using the spoons and other lures that are preferred for this

Artificial baits will raise sailfish, but they should be teased on a carefully sewn natural strip bait. Bonito belly makes one of the best teasers; it can be folded over, Panama style, or two bellies can be sewn together.

fish, I decided to experiment with a big chugger that made a lot of surface commotion. Keeping it back in the wake, I had the guide run the outboard at a reasonable speed and waited. It wasn't long before the first fish appeared behind the sputtering chugger and followed it. Nothing would happen once the fish got behind the lure. That's when I decided to appeal to its instinct to keep a meal from escaping. By dancing the rod tip sideways, I would chug the lure at a faster speed. The fish would quicken its swim rate to maintain the distance. As it did that, I dropped the rod tip and let the plug drift back suddenly. Invariably, the roosterfish would grab it as it started to fall back. It produced fish time after time.

KITE FISHING

If someone tells you to go fly a kite, it may be sound advice. The fishing kite can be an effective light-tackle tool for presenting a live bait or for trolling a dead one. In fact, there's no better way to interest a gamefish in a live offering, because the line and the leader are kept out of the water and the only thing seen is a bait in a distress situation. Because the baitfish is in trouble, it gives off low-frequency vibrations that will bring predators in a hurry.

Although the kite has been used as a fishing tool in parts of the world for a long time, its use among offshore sport-fishermen can be traced to the early efforts of the late Captain Tommy Gifford and then to Captain Bob Lewis of Miami. Right after World War II, Tommy started using the kite and the results were so fantastic that Bob Lewis knew he had to try one. Gifford gave Lewis his first kite and Bob soon mastered the technique.

While Bob Lewis was experimenting, he figured out that a single kite of a given density could not be used in all wind conditions. Eventually, he determined that one had to have three different models to fly in light, medium, and heavy breezes. Most of the fishing kites in use today were either made by Bob Lewis or are manufactured to his specifications. All are the same size, but the cloth density changes in each model.

Kites are handled from a short rod with a large, drum-type reel and are always fished downwind. You can use monofilament to fly the kite, but multifilament lines are better because they don't have the stretch. Anglers have the option of fishing one or two lines from each kite and they are simple to use. Two clothespins or light outrigger clips such as those made by Captain Al Black of Marathon, Florida, are hung from the kite line. A pair of swivels spaced about forty feet apart hold the pins or clips in position.

To keep the bait right on the surface or let it drop below, you have to be able to adjust the length of the line. This is done by inserting the line through a small plastic ring and putting the ring in the pin. A paper clip works equally well. If you are using a clip like the one that Al Black makes, the line can be fed through without anything on it.

The first clip is about fifty or sixty feet from the kite, but it could be as much as a hundred feet from the end. Flying the kite is easy. The breeze will just lift it and you can always use the boat to help if you're having trouble. As the pin comes off the spool, attach the fishing line to it and let both the kite line and fishing line out together.

Good, frisky, live bait is important. In Florida, blue runners or goggle-eyes are favorites for sailfish, but live balao, pilchards, or mullet will also work. If you fish other waters, simply pick popular baits and use them.

A kite allows you to fish your baits out of the wake and away from the boat. Some skippers prefer to troll slowly, but others like to drift if conditions will permit, because they feel that gamefish can hear the distress signals better if the engines are turned off and things are quiet.

You can, of course, keep the kite out there and do other types of fishing at the same time. If you wanted to deep jig, that could be done off the upwind side of the boat while the kite was flying on the other side. Keep in mind that a live bait can be relatively small and still raise big fish. That's why the kite is such an effective light-tackle method of getting fish. It is used throughout south Florida and carried elsewhere by well-traveled skippers, but it still hasn't achieved the popularity it should.

There's no reason why it couldn't be used when fishing for striped bass to carry a bait over areas that you can't reach with a boat. Certainly those anglers fishing the offshore canyons around the coastline can do well with a kite and live bait. The strikes can be spectacular and you will often see a predator streak across the surface directly toward the hapless baitfish. Again, where and when you use it is a matter of imagination and how innovative you want to be.

Captain David DeSilva, one of Bermuda's premier light tackle skippers, uses his kite in a number of ways. He may be up on the bank and discover that the current is wrong and he can't get the chum slick to flow over the edge. When that happens, he flies a kite over deep water and hangs a live bait out there. It works.

Not long ago, I was fishing with David way up on the bank where we had chummed up a wide variety of fish. Pretty soon, some rather husky barracuda started to appear and they would hang well back in the slick, making occasional forays through the schools of baitfish we had attracted. It was something to see a cuda chase down its prey. No matter what we threw at them, however, they refused.

One member of our party had never caught barracuda and was anxious to tangle with some of the heavyweights that we could see. David solved that problem in a hurry by rigging his kite. All he had to do was move a live bait about seventy-five feet astern and a barracuda had it faster than you could read this sentence. Kites are worthwhile having on board and, if you take your light-tackle fishing seriously, you may want to carry your own.

DEEP JIGGING

There's no middle ground. You either like deep jigging and become addicted to it as part of the light-tackle scene or you do everything in your power to avoid it. The variety of fish you can hook using this technique will amaze you, but it's grunt and groan work to pry some of those critters out of the depths. Deep jiggers have strong arms and backs, because that's the nature of the game.

If you think of this method as *vertical* jigging rather than deep jigging, the concept will become more apparent. It can be done in thirty feet of water or one-hundred-eighty feet of water and the procedure is the same. You can figure that two-hundred feet is the outside limit, although there are some hard-core addicts who will probe deeper than that.

Standard tackle would include twelve-pound or fifteen-pound-test line. Some beginners will insist on twenty-pound test, but the lures don't work as well as line test increases. Gordon Young, a Miamian who not only makes the finest jigs available, but practices the sport himself, now prefers to deep jig with six-pound test. That, of course, is an extreme and not meant for everybody (including me).

The rod you select should be on the stiff side and boast plenty of lifting power. If the tip collapses, you cannot fight a fish and you'll find that the jig doesn't have the proper action. Most anglers either use spinning reels or plug reels such as the Ambassadeur 6500 or the Daiwa Millionaire 6H or the Shakespeare President series. A few will go to larger reels, but they really aren't always necessary and they take some of the challenge away.

The leadhead itself is the heart of the system. Design is important and so is the weight. Remember that you want to use the lightest weight you can under the conditions. Under typical circumstances, you can get down to two-hundred feet with a two-and-one-quarter-ounce bucktail on fifteen-pound-test line. If there is a strong current, you may have to go to four ounces. With twenty-pound line, four ounces could be the standard instead of two-and-one-quarter.

Opinions differ on the perfect shape, but the better ones have a knife edge on at least the bottom side. Arrowheads, spear shapes, and a tapered wedge shape are among the best. These will fall faster and they will produce an erratic upward action when jigged. In fact, you should perform a simple test on a leadhead before you decide to use it. Loop some line through the hook eye and let the lure hang freely. It should be facing upward at a 45 degree angle. Any jig that hangs horizontally and parallel to the deck just won't have as much action.

The heart of the system lies in a truly vertical retrieve. Those who try it for the first time, find it difficult to resist the temptation to make long casts away from the boat. If you don't work the lure vertically, however, you won't do as well.

The lure should be freespooled and allowed to drop without any drag, directly to the bottom. This is usually done on the upwind side, but if there is a strong wind or current, a short cast downwind will help. When the lure reaches the bottom, the boat will have drifted down on it and you'll be vertical.

Under some conditions, it's tough to tell when you're on the bottom. If you're having a problem, watch the line. When the lure hits, it will go slack for an instant. Jigging is done by pumping the rod and reeling up the slack as the lure falls back. You can work it all the way to the surface using this method and cover every level of water.

Experts use just a bit of finesse. If they are interested in bottom species, they may bounce it on or near the bottom several times, letting out additional line before bringing it up. When they get into mid-depth, they sometimes change the rate or type of retrieve to make it more erratic for some of the pelagic species. This will come with experience. Once you reach the surface, simply repeat the whole procedure.

It's equally important to monitor the progress as the lure falls. Sometimes a fish will grab it on the way down and you may feel a bump or notice that the line has picked up speed. If that occurs, engage the reel, wait for the line to come tight, and set the hook. If you don't feel a fish, continue the drop.

A plain bucktail or leadhead will work under some conditions, but those of us who deep jig a great deal will hang a plastic worm or some other dressing on the hook. It may or may not make a difference, but you'd have trouble convincing us of that fact. You can also use bait on a jig and that will definitely improve its performance. It becomes a matter of preference whether or not you want to fish strictly artificial. A balao, small baitfish, or even a strip will work well.

Most fish will take the leadhead as it drops, but you won't feel the strike until the next lift. Even though the fish appears to be hooked, set the hook again anyway. Fish can hold a lure in their mouth and then let it go, so it's worth the effort to bury the barb. Jig hooks are relatively large and have heavy wire. In order to set them with a light line, you should file or hone cutting edges on every hook.

Another trick that some of us use is to put eyes on leadheads using a felt-tip marker. All you have to do is take a black marker and make a dot on either side of the head. Does it make a difference? It's hard to say, but it can't hurt. Some of the best jigs have Mylar outside of the bucktail, nylon, or Fishair; this also helps. Everyone has their own color preferences, but white is by far the most popular in deep water and white with green is also an excellent combination.

DOWNRIGGERS

Long before any of us knew what a downrigger was, a group of dedicated light-tackle fishermen in the Northeast used to probe the depths with a makeshift arrangement that centered around a chicken-leg drail. If the term confuses you, a chicken-leg drail is about two to three pounds of lead shaped somewhat like a chicken leg and thigh would look on your dinner plate. There were metal rings on either end of the lead and we simply attached a length of heavy parachute cord or some other line to it. Using heavy wire, we then secured an outrigger clothespin to the other end of the drail. This device allowed us to fish deep yet avoid the miseries of wire lines or heavy weights that made it impossible to fish with light gear.

By running a swivel on the line and putting one end in the clothespin, we could adjust the length while it was underwater. Light trolling sinkers also helped to keep the bait or lure deep, but the drail took the line down. All you had to do was lower it over the side and then tie the heavy line off on a stern cleat.

The downrigger developed as a tool of the salmon fisherman and skyrocketed into popularity when coho and king salmon were planted in the Great Lakes. Every boat had to have at least a pair of these gadgets and some craft bristled with as many as a half dozen or more. They took different shapes and had varying degrees of sophistication. Some were fully automated and ran electrically. Others had a drum and a crank.

The shape of the lead weight also varied, with the cannonball configuration about the most popular. A few were molded in the shape of a torpedo and there is the odd one that resembles a space vehicle. Experts argue that the shape does make a difference in performance and in raising fish. However, the cannonball is still the most popular—perhaps because West Coast salmon fishermen employ breakaway sinkers in the cannonball shape.

Salt-water anglers have greeted the downrigger with mixed emotions. Those who have tried the units usually swear by them as an effective tool, but it's hard to get the traditionalists to look at something new and different. Along the Northeast coast, they work wonders on bluefish and striped bass, enabling fishermen to reach the proper depth with light line and not be bothered with the problems associated with wire line.

Downriggers are as important offshore as they are along the coastal waters: they can put a bait or lure at any depth you desire. The common tendency is only to think of the downrigger as a vehicle for dragging bottom or reaching the depths.

Veteran Florida guide Arlin Leiby has been using downriggers on a daily basis for almost five years and talks of them in glowing terms. He agrees that people ignore them where fish are easy to catch by other methods, but insists that once an angler uses them, he wouldn't be without them. Arlin's main business is guiding light-tackle anglers and the downriggers allow his customers to fish twelve to twenty-pound test with ease on big fish and get the bait to fish-eye level.

If he's trolling offshore, Arlin will fish the downrigger lines about the length of a standard flat line. He has come to believe that the sound of the weight and the wire moving through the water attracts fish and that the next thing they see is a bait coming by. Much of his fishing is with live bait and he often trolls two downrigger outfits from four to eight feet below the surface depending upon sea conditions. In gusty weather, he'll lean toward eight feet and go shallower when it's calmer. Those outfits produce plenty of sailfish as well as other species.

Arlin likes to fish the downriggers in conjunction with his depth sounder. If he is over a reef or wreck, he might lower a unit to a hundred feet or more; he can adjust the depth to match the concentrations of fish he reads on the machine.

Farther up the coast, Captain Hugo Uhland has been doing a considerable amount of work with downriggers in salt water and he, too, insists that every boat should be equipped with them. The feeling among downrigger specialists is that most fish feed below the surface of the water and even if you are trolling skipbaits, dragging one or two offerings on downriggers can make a difference.

Right now, a handful of experts have been experimenting with the use of Cyalume lightsticks manufactured by American Cyanamid in conjunction with downriggers. The theory is that the light will help to attract fish to the downrigger and then the bait will become visible once the fish is in the area. In the years to come, you will probably witness an increased use of downriggers in salt water.

HIGH-SPEED TROLLING

Although high-speed trolling was not developed specifically as a light-tackle technique, it does have ample application. By definition, high-speed trolling is anything faster than the normal speed at which the bait would be swimming, but in practice, it can range from 7 to a maximum of 20 knots.

Because of the speed, there is no dropback necessary and a fish will either hook itself or you'll miss it. The fast pace not only allows anglers to cover the maximum amount of water, but they can often troll while moving from one spot to another.

From a light-tackle standpoint, the strike creates tremendous strain on the line and the drag has to be set precisely. However, it's a method that will cause huge marlin to crash a small bait and that puts the game in the light-tackle ballpark. It's marginal with twenty-pound tackle, but you can get hookups on thirty-pound and fifty-pound line without having to troll the typically large marlin bait.

Hawaiians have been using trolling lures at high speed for a long time but only recently has the technique gained acceptance in other parts of the coastline. One reason that it has taken hold centers on the fishing efforts now being expended in the far offshore canyons. Not only can boats troll these lures going out and coming back from the fishing area, but they can scout the territory in a hurry once they are there. It's a long run, so time on the grounds is at a premium.

Lures have to be designed for particular speed ranges. There was a time when the world thought that a cup-nosed model was better than anything else, but this attitude has been changing. Islanders place great emphasis on the design of the head, using inner-tube material and vinyl seat covers for the skirt. Others, however, use varied approaches. Jet lures with holes for water to pass through have become favorites on some coasts and the shapes of lures now run the gamut from rocket-tapered straight runners to blunt-nosed scooters and darters.

Experts disagree on whether a lure works better when it digs and dives, working the interface of the water, or when it runs a foot or two under. The weight of the lure coupled with the length of line behind the boat and the boat's speed determine where in the water it will be. Some of the newer soft plastic lures such as those made by Mold Craft of Fort Lauderdale seem particularly light, yet they have excellent swimming qualities and produce fish. Design can often be more important than weight. A true ballistic shape, for example, seems to ride best.

When you do find a lure that works, mortgage your home, finance your car, but don't sell it or give it away. No one knows why, but even among lures that look identical, one will work better than the others. That's the trolling bait you want to keep.

Popular theory has it that you need a big lure if you intend to catch blue marlin and other huskies of the seas. Not so, say those who have done their homework. The eight to twelve-inch range is by far the more productive and they will produce smaller as well as bigger fish. A great deal seems to hinge on the shape and the commotion or lack of it made in the water. Straight runners aren't spectacular, but they catch fish.

The flatter the face of the lure or the more scoop it has, the slower you have to troll it. Straight tracking lures are the truly high-speed jobs. At certain speeds, it's possible to combine both types and, if you do, fish the erratic runners from the outriggers and the straight trackers on the flat lines.

There are a couple of other things worth remembering. Because of the drag in the water, you need a stouter rod to handle a trolling lure at high speed and still have enough reserve power to weather a strike. Outriggers on smaller boats that are not supported with spreaders and stays may need some beefing up. One way is to run a line from the rigger to the bow. Also, since the boat is going in one direction and the fish in another, you need reels with extra line capacity. A blue marlin could easily strip a small reel before you ever stopped the boat and got it turned around.

In spite of the tendency to use heavier tackle with high-speed trolling lures, look at it as an opportunity to hook fish on thirty-pound or fifty-pound line. If you pick up tuna, sails, white marlin, wahoo, dolphin, and other species, the tackle is better suited to the chore. When the big blue marlin strikes, you're in for some light-tackle fun.

NIGHT SWORDFISHING

When Jerry Webb of Pflueger Marine Taxidermy landed a 348-pound broadbill swordfish and his cousin, Jesse Webb, boated a 368-pounder on July 5, 1976, off Miami, angling history was made. Until then, swordfish were caught during daylight hours by first spotting them on the surface and then trying to bait them. The Webbs performed their act at night and brought the swordfish, once the province of only the very wealthy, within the grasp of the average angler.

Longliners baited swordfish for years at night off the Florida coast, but no one paid attention to the fishery. Once Jerry and Jesse proved it could be done, others followed right behind them and the sport mushroomed overnight. The fish range in size from as small as fifteen or twenty pounds to several hundred pounds and there's no way to tell the size of the one about to strike. For that reason, it is customary to rely on heavy gear; eighty-pound line is about the average. However, as an angler catches a few fish, he begins to think in terms of the challenge that lighter tackle brings and, in the months and years to come, I believe you will see more and more people fishing swordfish with very light tackle trying to set new records. That's why the procedure is included here.

Although most of the fishing is done during the spring, summer, and fall, the limiting factor seems to be weather conditions. Boats must drift at night and that's somewhat uncomfortable unless the seas are relatively calm. On the east coast of Florida, most of the swordfishing is done in the Gulf Stream where there is at least 1,000 feet of water. Swordfishing has also been successful off California, canyons off the East and Gulf coasts, and at such places around the world where these fish are seen during daylight hours.

Research shows that the broadbill comes toward the surface during the night hours, but returns to the depths at the first sign of dawn. That's why the night action is so much better.

Doug Smith, a young Fort Lauderdale angler, caught his first swordfish right after the Webbs and has shared his knowledge with a number of others. The approach he uses is typical and will give you an idea of what to expect. Although the longliners use a variety of baits successfully, sport fishermen opt for large squid that are about eighteen inches long and weigh about a pound. They are rigged on heavy monofilament, under the theory that if a shark eats the bait, it will bite through the mono and you won't have to battle it very long. Cuban night sharks are a nuisance on the Florida grounds.

Hooks are 12/0 or 14/0 with a ring eye instead of a needle eye to accommodate the monofilament. Specialists feel the larger hooks are neces-

The development of night-fishing techniques for swordfish has enabled countless anglers to catch this great gamefish.

sary to avoid pullouts. Swordfish have particularly soft mouths and a smaller hook will work loose more easily. The hooks are carefully sewn in the squid so that they will not come out and to keep the bait from being jerked free when a swordfish plays with it.

Depth is one of the major variables in swordfishing and the trick is to fish three or four rods with each set up differently. The first bait is kept within fifty feet of the surface. To do this, a light sinker of about two ounces is hung from the swivel. Egg sinkers are the preferred type and they are looped on with eight-pound-test monofilament, which will break off once a fish is hooked. About fifty or sixty feet above the swivel, a balloon is tied on the line to act as a float. It, too, will break on a hookup.

The second outfit is rigged to fish at about one-hundred-fifty to two-hundred feet. Everything is the same, except the balloon is omitted and as much as a pound of lead is hung from the swivel. Three hundred feet deep is the range for the third bait and this is accomplished by hanging even more weight on the swivel. Up to two pounds may be necessary, depending on the breaking strength of the line and the water conditions. In a strong current, you'll need more weight, but it takes less weight to get lighter lines down under the same circumstances. Downriggers are a little-known but effective way to maintain baits at a specific level.

Cyalume lightsticks have become an essential part of the rig. These produce light through a chemical process and repeated tests by both longliners and sport fishermen show that they account for increased catches. At first, the Cyalume lightstick was inserted inside the squid. Some anglers even break the sticks and let the liquid impregnate the squid. However, most anglers prefer to hang the Cyalume from the swivel. It seems to work well there and offers another advantage. When you are fighting the fish, the Cyalume serves as a marker to show where your line is in the water and to give you an idea of how far away the fish happens to be.

The Cyalume can help indicate the depth at which you are fishing if the water is clear. In the Gulf Stream, you can see it down to about two-hundred feet. That means that the lightstick on the high rig should be plainly visible, the one on the middle one barely visible, and you won't be able to see the Cyalume underwater on the rig beyond two-hundred feet.

Another way of telling depth is by the angle of the line. Your shallow line should be at about a 30-degree angle; the middle line at 45 degrees; and the deep one as nearly vertical as possible.

Most swordfish strikes are spectacularly disappointing. Although some fish will crash a bait and move off swiftly, the majority swat it with the bill, mash it, toy with it, and drive you crazy. It might be nothing more than a few notches on the click mechanism on your reel, but that could be a strike. Patience is a virtue. It may be a full two or three minutes, or even longer, before the fish comes back. You have nothing to do but wait and think about the emptiness that suddenly has conquered your stomach.

The fish may come back several times or move off and stop before moving off again. What you are waiting for is the fish to start moving at an increasing rate of speed. When that happens, lock the reel in gear, wait for the line to come tight, and set the hook. Even then, the broadbill might turn and ease toward the boat without putting up much of a fight. You'll see the Cyalume come closer and closer. Then, when it's about fifty feet away, the fish will realize it's in trouble and that's the moment you'll know you are tied to a swordfish.

Light-tackle anglers will lose their share of big swordfish, but you can almost bet that some of the new records will be set using this method. It's much easier than trying to get a fish on the surface during the daytime. For the daytime enthusiasts, if they can average one fish in a season, they've had a good year. The percentages are much greater at night.

10

Salt-Water Fly Fishing

The flat-bottomed garveys of Barnegat Bay were a way of life back in the 1940s and their shallow draft enabled them to negotiate the treacherous bars and shoals that punctuated the estuaries of southern New Jersey. At least once a week, my dad and his cronies fished from one with such legendary skippers as Captain Holmes Russell and Captain Owen Ridgeway.

These were men who were born to the sea, carrying with them a family tradition that went back to the earliest settlers of our shores. They were fishermen and good ones. When I pestered my father enough or could live through a week without getting into trouble, I was allowed to accompany him. During the summers and into the fall, the standard technique was to anchor off one of the jetties in the inlet and chum with grass shrimp on the outgoing tide for the striped bass and big weakfish that were plentiful in those days.

For some reason, my father always insisted on light tackle. He may not have known all the sophisticated reasons for its use, but he did realize that he caught more fish with it and that the gear enabled him to develop a delicate feel when working the chum slick. Spinning hadn't become a fact of life yet and it was virtually unknown in America. Revolving-spool reels were the standard fare and I can remember using the knuckle-busting bait-casting mills and small bay reels of that era. Learning how to drift a bait without drag was a frustrating experience, but one well worth mastering.

Periodically, Dad would take a fly rod with him. He had always fished for trout and even cast a fly for largemouth bass when he didn't use a conventional outfit. It occurred to my father that he could have fun catching striped bass and weakfish on the same tackle he used in fresh water. After all, the fish

172

were in the chum slick behind the boat feeding on live grass shrimp and a small fly probably looked like the real thing to the fish.

I can remember vividly that the Mickey Finn was one of his favorite patterns and wondered how a yellow and red streamer with a little tinsel could ever represent a shrimp. Dad had been teaching me to use the fly rod in fresh water and, after considerable urging—the type that is characteristic of determined young boys—he let me try the fly rod in salt water. It wasn't easy, but by casting and then letting the fly drift back, I was able to catch a few striped bass and weakfish.

In those days, anyone seen using a fly rod in salt water would be accused of combat fatigue or ready for the funny farm. Twenty years later, the angling world still wasn't ready to accept the light wand, although a handful of stalwarts carried the banner on boats and beachfront. Today, marine angling with a fly rod is not only recognized but a growing legion of fishermen are trying it because the fun can be spectacular.

Fly fishing must be looked upon as an opportunity sport. There are some who insist on using that type of tackle in situations that border on the impossible, but it just doesn't make sense. You'll find that the best fly fishermen in the world have put the technique in its proper perspective and know when and when not to use the tackle.

That doesn't mean that they aren't out there trying to develop new techniques and improving on existing ones. It does indicate, however, that they choose the time and the place and the conditions with care. Whether you are new to the game or have been at it for a while, it makes sense to find the fish with other types of tackle and then switch to fly when conditions warrant. Some types of fishing, such as tarpon on the flats, lend themselves particularly well to fly-rod sport, providing the wind is semi-cooperative and visibility is good.

Chances to fish a fly rod exist everywhere and run the gamut from Boston mackerel to sailfish and marlin. One cannot assume that just because a person has caught a large fish on a fly—such as a sail or a hundred-pound tarpon—that he oozes experience. You have to pay your dues along the way and fish for a variety of species both large and small. Each demands a specialized approach and each brings its own rewards.

A CLOSER LOOK AT TACKLE

Marine fly fishing has become much more sophisticated today than it was a decade or two ago. Back then, many experts insisted that they only needed a single fly rod for any assignment and they were probably right. First, there weren't that many tackle options open to the pioneer in the way of rods, reels, or lines. Second, the number of species considered fly-rod targets was extremely limited and those of us who loved the sport were busy trying to figure out new ways to catch fish. Progress takes time, at least until a certain stage of development is reached.

Today, an angler has more tackle choices in salt water than he does for lake or stream fishing. Not only can he use many of the fresh-water designs, but he has a vast array of gear tailored specifically for his use.

Instead of thinking in terms of a rod, focus on the line first, since it is the weight of the line that carries the fly to the target. If you're going to use small flies, it doesn't take a very heavy line to do the job, but the bulkier and more wind-resistant an offering becomes, the heavier the line you must have to do the same job.

Keep in mind that wind plays a part and there are few days on the marine scene when there isn't a breeze. Just try to pick up a fly rod and the zephyrs will develop out of nowhere. In a breeze, you need a heavier outfit to do the same work.

If you insist on challenging the heavyweights of the sea or flats, you're going to need a fish-fighting tool and that's much more important than castability. You can, however, get both features in the same rod if you choose carefully.

Advertising claims can be misleading. Regardless of whether a rod is made from cane, fiberglass, graphite, or a new composite, the ultimate test is its fishability. If it doesn't cast well or fails to produce the needed reserve power to beat a big fish, you've wasted your money. In fly fishing, the rod is critical. This is not the place to cut corners. Buy the best one you can afford, but remember that price is not necessarily an indication of quality and performance. Try before you buy.

We talked earlier about choosing a rod, but the key points are worth reviewing. If you plan to fight husky fish with it, the rod should be able to lift at least five pounds of dead weight off the floor with six inches of line extending past the tip. If it can't, look for something else. For casting, a rod should boast good recovery from vibrations and have maximum dampening ability. Every time the tip moves up and down or from side to side, it puts shock waves in the line and that makes it more difficult to cast. You want a rod that will help you to throw tight loops and, when you find one, buy it.

Unless you're going to use very light leader tippets, a rod for fighting a fish should never be more than nine or nine-and-a-half feet. Longer rods are available in graphite and composites, but these are more for specialized casting situations and won't generate the power to fight big fish. If you do want to use light tippets, you must stick to a rod for lighter lines or a longer and softer one.

In the heavier rods, you should have an extension butt. Salmon fishermen in the early days insisted on a six-inch extension, but this is totally impractical in salt water. A butt that extends two inches behind the reel seat is all you need and it should be permanently attached.

There is no such thing as a single rod for all purposes and, unless you limit your fly fishing to one or two species in a particular situation, you'll probably need at least two rods to cover the waterfront. Eventually, you'll have more. As a general rule, a rod capable of handling a 10-weight line works well for most smaller species and will be a basic, all-purpose tool. Many anglers choose a rod for 9-weight and one for 12-weight or 13-weight lines as the two that they buy first. The heavier rod will handle bulky flies and it becomes the

Salt-water fly fishermen often prepackage leaders in plastic bags. The numbers indicate the breaking strength of the tippet and shock tippet: 15/88 means fifteen-pound tippet with an eighty-eight-pound-test shock.

fish-fighting tool. The lighter one is ideal for smaller fish and can also be used when you want to fish with six-pound-test tippets.

When you choose a reel, you must consider how serious you are about fly fishing and whether you plan to tangle with big fish on a regular basis. There's no question that reels like Bob McChristian's Seamaster are superb and a dream to own, but you don't have to spend the money for typically small fish or an occasional big one. The main points to consider are line capacity and a drag that will work smoothly. For average fish, drag isn't nearly as important as long as you have enough line. Two hundred yards of Dacron backing plus a fly line makes an adequate combination though you may want more if you're going to take on anything that swims.

The modern fly fisherman has learned that several different types of lines for each rod increase his effectiveness and put more species within range of his fly. That's a significant departure from the days when a floating line was all one seemed to need. Whether you use a full fly line or a shooting taper with running line, it should be weight forward. The exception is lead core, which is only made in level lengths.

When very long casts are needed or you want the line to sink rapidly and deep, shooting tapers are the answer. A full length fly line is easier to handle when casting and it is certainly the first choice of anyone who fishes the shallow flats. In flats fishing, you often have to pick up quickly and cast again. This is not possible with a shooting head, because you have to strip in the running line first.

Wherever you fish, don't overlook the potential of the super high-density fly lines or heavy lead core. Gaining maximum depth is only one advantage. If there is a strong current flowing, they will get a fly down quickly before the line bellies and straightens. Some anglers even use them for sailfish on the surface, because the super-fast sinker or lead core will put the fly a couple of feet down in a second or two and timing is important. The important part is that you can control depth with them if they are used properly.

Most salt-water fly-rodders use a butt section of leader with a loop in the end. The tippet and shock tippet are looped to this so that they interlock.

Dan Blanton holds up a brace of San Francisco striped bass. Shooting tapers are his favorites; they enabled him to make the long casts needed to cover a lot of water and take these fine fish.

Any streamer fly can be made into a popper instantly by slipping a cork on the leader and sliding it over the eye of the hook.

FLY PATTERNS

Compared to fresh-water patterns, salt-water flies are far more basic in their appearance and tend to suggest rather than imitate a tasty morsel. There are exceptions, of course, when tiers try to duplicate a natural food, but it doesn't happen often and one can question how effective it really is.

A number of factors are important in choosing flies and you should be aware of them. Size coupled with silhouette ranks first on the list and its significance cannot be overemphasized. Two factors play a role. If there is a supply of natural bait in the area of a given size, your fly should try to duplicate this. That doesn't mean the fish won't hit a larger fly, but if they are specializing on a particular size, that's the place to begin. The second thing to remember is that certain species show a preference for flies of a particular size most of the time. Let's look at some examples.

You can fit a ripe canteloupe melon into the mouth of a hundred-pound tarpon, yet it will eagerly eat a fly that is four inches long. There are places where tarpon fishermen may resort to six-inch or seven-inch flies, but this is the exception. Smaller tarpon also prefer smaller flies. Bonefish cannot inhale a very big fish because of the size and shape of their mouth. If you're trying to tease a sailfish with a strip bait that is ten or eleven inches long, you can't expect the fish to pass it up in favor of a five-inch fly.

Fly choices should be made after you have studied the situation. Don't be fooled by the fact that "everybody" seems to be using a certain size or pattern. At times, it makes sense, but you'll find plenty of occasions when your own instincts may prove better.

In making a basic selection, choose patterns of various sizes or have several sizes of the same pattern. Vary the colors between light and dark with a few bright ones thrown in and don't forget black, which can be deadly. Mylar added to the flies gives them "flash" in the water; this can be important. If you tie your own creations, add the Mylar to most streamers. You can always cut it off later if you don't want it.

When salt-water fly fishing took hold on the West Coast, many of the first anglers had only a scanty knowledge of what flies to use, so they developed their own. Dan Blanton, a talented fly fisherman, came up with his Whistler series, while Ed Givens, another serious angler, developed the Givens Barred-N-Black. These were bulky flies, presenting a wide silhouette in the water. They work particularly well at night and in places where the water is murky and visibility limited. Some of us believe that because they are bulky, they create more low-frequency sound when they push through the water and the fish can use their lateral line to locate the target. They also do a job in clear water.

Harry Kime is one of the early pioneers on the West Coast and in Mexico's Baja; his accomplishments and innovations are legendary. Harry ties almost all his flies in white and then uses felt-tip markers to change the colors or create whatever pattern he wants. One of his favorites is a psychedelic display of pastels tailored to match the same erratic pattern on the teasers that he uses.

Fishermen often overlook the sink rate of a fly. If you're fishing redfish on the very shallow grass flats, you want an offering that is bushy and Palmer-tied so that it won't sink deep and hang in the grass. If bonefish or tarpon happen to be your game, you must get the fly down to their level in a hurry. Not only does the amount and texture of the tying material affect this, but the hook size can also make a difference. The bigger and heavier the hook, the faster it will sink.

While we're on the subject of hooks, it's worth reviewing some of the aspects of penetration. Regardless of the size of the fly, you're going to have extreme difficulty trying to set a hook larger than 5/0 or 6/0. Veterans like to use smaller hooks and some even try to find hooks with lighter wire for easier penetration.

You may get some ideas of your own based on the practice employed by the handful of anglers who are among the best at catching bonefish. Writers have said for years that the average bonefish fly is tied on a 1/0 hook and, if you consider what everyone who fishes for bonefish uses, they're probably right. The leading experts, however, tie bonefish patterns on size 6 hooks and many of the largest of the species landed on fly were caught on hooks that small. The reason for the smaller hook is that it allows a much more delicate presentation and you can place the fly closer to the fish, increasing the chances that it will be seen. Bonefish flies are either tied on keel hooks that ride with the point up or they are tied in reverse on a standard hook so that the point will ride up.

Many of today's flies are tied with a rather sleek appearance to make it easier to cast them through the air. If you have to cast to a specific fish and fight a wind in the process, you want an offering that can cut through the air rather than one resembling a shaving brush.

PRESENTING THE FLY

Things are different in salt water than they are in fresh. A trout, bass, or pike will maintain its lie and you have plenty of time to study the situation

John Emery is about to remove the fly from a redfish he hooked in extremely shallow water. The rod and reel are about the same size one might choose for trout. In very shallow water, the fly must be dressed fully so that it will sink very slowly.

and even change fly patterns. Creatures of the sea are usually on the move, making speed and accuracy the prerequisites of good casting. That in itself is enough to throw the convert. He is also bothered by the fact that he has to use a longer and heavier rod armed with a big fly and a shock leader that can hamper casting. Add to that the need to make some long casts and the mountain facing the beginner seems impossible to climb.

It's pretty well accepted that a lot of salt-water fish are caught within a relatively short distance of the boat and there are times when very short casts are necessary. Don't let that lull you into believing that you don't have to develop into a long caster. If you can only throw sixty feet of fly line, you're operating under a serious handicap. Perhaps you never had to use more than thirty-five feet for trout, but this is a different ballgame. An angler who can reach an *honest* ninety feet under reasonable conditions, can cast sixty feet without a great deal of effort. If, however, sixty feet happens to be your maximum, a fifty-foot cast can be straining things.

When you're blind casting, long presentations enable you to cover the maximum amount of water in a minimum amount of time. You'll also encounter many situations where an eighty-foot cast spells the difference between fish and no fish. It takes practice and technique to cast properly. The purpose of this book is not to teach the actual casting, but to let you know what you should be able to do.

The key to blind casting centers on one's ability to make a reasonably long cast with a minimum of false casts. Fresh-water anglers develop the damaging habit of false casting forever, and some keep the fly in the air more than in the water. In salt-water work, you want to be able to pick up about thirty-five feet of line and shoot line on a total cast of seventy to eighty feet. There are no false casts; it's merely a pickup and a shoot. To achieve this, you must be able to double haul, which is a technique of tugging on the line just before the backcast and forward cast are made to increase line speed.

Coupled with the ability to double haul is the skill of throwing tight line loops. A narrow loop will cut through the air easier and you'll get longer and more accurate presentations. When you master those skills, you can blind cast all day with little effort. You'll pick the line off the water, shoot some line on the backcast, and make the cast. More important, the fly is fishing most of the time and it isn't in the air.

Spot casting proves the nemesis of even some of the top-rated tournament casters, because it is something they haven't taken the time to practice. Remember that you must develop speed of presentation as well as accuracy. The fly must land in the right place and you don't have much time to get it there because the target is moving.

Lefty Kreh is by far the best fly-casting instructor in the world today, at least from a fishing standpoint. He insists repeatedly that if you can't get the

The secret of fly fishing on the flats is the ability to hold the fly in hand until the fish is spotted. Most fly casters have never practiced the technique of presenting the offering quickly and accurately from this type of starting position.

Speed and accuracy are the secrets to good presentation on the shallow flats. The bait or lure must be placed in front of the fish and allowed to sink to the depth at which the fish is swimming.

fly to the fish within six seconds, you will probably be too late. Unless you practice the method, you'll never do it.

When you fish the flats or for billfish on the offshore grounds, the fly is held in one hand and the rod in the other. About fifteen or twenty feet of fly line hangs past the tip top of the rod and the rest of the line is coiled at your feet. That's the way you stand for however long it takes until you spot the fish you want to catch. Rolling your wrist, you make a high forward cast, releasing the fly from your other hand as the line tugs it free. Double hauling, you shoot more line on the backcast, and then make the presentation to the target. Notice that repeated false casts have been eliminated. With that technique on a typical day, you should be able to reach at least sixty feet and possibly more. For longer casts, you might require one additional false cast to build up line speed. With that extra cast, however, you should be able to throw a whole fly line.

That's the way the game is played and if you intend to have a chance at most of the fish you see, you have to be able to handle the tackle with that type of skill. There will be times when you merely have to get the fly twenty feet from the boat or forty feet, but you have to be ready to cover the waterfront.

If you're a right-handed caster and standing in the bow of a skiff facing forward, you can probably cast directly ahead to anywhere off the port beam or from nine o'clock to twelve o'clock. What happens if a fish shows off to your right? Most casters must shift their feet and change position before they can begin to cast. That runs the risk of making noise that will be transmitted through the hull and there is always the danger that you will step on the fly line in the excitement and blow the whole thing. If you practice it, you can learn to release the line on your backcast and make the cast from port to starboard. If you develop more skill, you can learn to turn your hand in the air and push a forward cast to the right without changing position.

It is not my intention to make this whole thing sound complicated and frighten prospective salt-water fly-rodders away. Quite the contrary. My goal is to help you find the enjoyment in fly fishing that I have had over the years and shortcut many of the frustrations that I had to endure.

Remember that you can expect plenty of wind on the water. At times, it will seem impossible to buck; this may well be the case. However, you can also develop the skills to make the wind work for you or at least minimize its negative effects.

When you are trying to achieve maximum distance with a shooting taper, the water haul can make life easier. The first step is to false cast so that you have the correct amount of running line past the tip top for the start of the cast. With a shooting head, there is a point at which the head feels and performs right and you must find this. Once you know where it is, you can reach that approximate position of overhang quickly. The water haul is nothing more than making a weak forward cast and allowing the shooting head to fall on the surface of the water. Even if it is a lead-core line or fast-sinking, the water haul will work.

The instant the line lands on the water and before it has had a chance to sink, make the regular backcast. Then, make the full cast. What has happened is that the surface tension of the water tends to hold the line and this extra force loads the rod to the maximum. It's like pulling a bow all the way back before releasing the arrow. When that loaded rod comes forward, it really catapults the line. Water hauling is easy if you are willing to spend a little time practicing it.

If you are a right-handed caster, you will double haul with your left hand just before you make the forward cast and the line will shoot off the deck and through the guides. Instead of dropping your left hand, hold it open and allow the line to shoot across it. This gives you constant control. Should the cast be too long and you see that you will overshoot the target, simply clamp the line with your fingers and the fly will drop. Equally important, if a fish should strike the instant the fly drops on the water, the line is under control and you can set the hook.

As the fly lands, transfer the line from your left hand (just the opposite if you cast left-handed) under the first or second finger of your rod hand. This finger holds the line loosely against the cork, providing continued control.

The strip method of retrieve provides an effective system for recovering the fly and you can make the offering do almost anything. Using the rod to impart action is a frequent and terrible mistake, because you are seldom in a position to strike the fish or make another cast. Start the retrieve by putting the butt of the rod at your belt buckle with the tip pointing directly at the fly and stopping just above the surface of the water. The rod remains in this position throughout the retrieve. Everything else is done with your left hand (right hand for left-handed casters).

Action is imparted to the fly by tugging the fly line. To do this, reach behind the rod hand and grasp the line. Everything depends on how you pull the line. A short, sharp tug will cause the fly to dart forward a short distance. If the pull is long and steady, the fly will swim that far. The frequency of the pulls determines how fast the fly will move. It's surprising what you can do using this method.

When a fly fisherman hooks a big fish he must clear loose line from the deck at once. To do this, make a "guide" with your thumb and first finger and let the line feed through it.

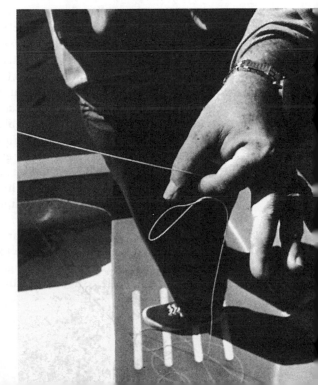

Since the rod is always pointing at the fly and the tip is low to the water, you are always ready to set the hook or to make another cast. When it's time to recast, simply make the pickup, shoot line on the backcast, and go to the target. If a fish strikes, you're ready to lift the rod tip to set the hook.

When you are spot casting to fish you can see, it may become necessary to recast in a hurry. You could be off the mark or the fish might have changed course about the time you released the line or they may not have seen the fly. There's very little time to get the fly in front of them and if you worry about stripping all the line in before you cast again, you'll waste precious seconds.

The preferred technique is to reach as far forward as you can with the rod, keep the line tight, and pick up the entire length. It may sound impossible to do, but there are anglers who can snatch a sixty to seventy-foot length off the surface in one motion and lay it right back down in front of the fish. Remember that once you make the pickup, you go right back to the target.

FISHING THE FLATS

The greatest advantage of fishing the flats is the ability to see the response of your quarry. Too many of us assume that the fish didn't know what it was doing when it turned away from our offering, but that's a pitfall to be avoided. When you get a refusal, it's for a reason and you had better search for the answer.

Fishing for tarpon near Key West one day, Bob Stearns and I watched several schools of big fish flush from our presentation. We were using the standard-size tarpon streamer that usually proves successful for us. It didn't make sense until we began to analyze the situation. This was the first day the fish had shown after being chased into deep water by a cold front and they were exceptionally nervous in the shallow water. I suggested to Bob that we try a much smaller fly pattern than usual and he agreed. We couldn't stop hooking fish on flies that were smaller and darker in color. The next day, things returned to normal and we went back to the standard patterns.

Though fly lines come in a variety of colors, they seldom make a difference except to the angler. There are times, however, when fly-line color can spell victory or defeat. Jack Kertz and I were fishing tarpon together in another spot. When it was my turn to cast, the fish would explode before the fly ever reached them. He had no trouble catching fish. Although I hated to admit that the problem was the brighter line I was using, I decided to test the theory. Jack lent me his outfit and I made a cast to the next group of fish. Bingo! I then asked Jack to cast with my rod and the fish flushed. There was no question that Jack's dull fly-line finish made a difference. Since those early days, a few of us talked the fly-line makers into dying some of the tarpon lines gray.

Trying to determine how far ahead of a fish to make a cast can be a problem. What you really have to consider is the sink rate of the fly and the speed at which the fish is moving. Both can be deceptive. Big fish appear to be gliding slowly, but they are really moving faster than you think. It's better to

Learning to spot a bonefish underwater takes practice. Polarized sun glasses are a great help.

cast too far ahead and wait for the fish to reach the fly than to be too close. Flats veterans often use an intermediate or Fisherman's fly line that will sink very slowly. This helps the fly to get down and it keeps the line under the grass that sometimes drifts on the surface.

Sharks can fool you. The dorsal fin rides clear of the water and you use that fin as the guide for making the cast. The problem is that the head is a few feet forward of that dorsal. As a general rule, on a fair-sized shark add at least three feet to the lead you would normally use and you should be right on the money.

Tailing bonefish are fun to work and can prove to be a challenge to your casting skill. You want them to be able to see the fly, so you must get it close to them. However, if you get too close, the whole school explodes and disappears. Use a small fly such as one tied on a number 6 or number 4 hook and try to time your cast. The ideal is to drop the fly uptide and relatively close to the fish. To do this, wait until it tails and has its head down. You can get the fly closer at this moment, but if the fish comes up before the fly lands, you could be in trouble.

You learned earlier that sharks have poor vision and that taking them on fly can be a tough assignment for the fly-rodder. Surprisingly, a dozen sharks in a row may ignore a fly before one pounces on it. The cast must place the fly right alongside the eye of the fish. At the same time, you merely want to give the fly movement and keep it in the area. The retrieve should be painstakingly slow. Mylar should be added to the fly and, if you tie your own, put a bright collar on it such as orange, red, or fluorescent green. This patch of color at the head may not mean much to the shark, but it will enable *you* to see the fly and that's vital. When you can keep your eye on both fly and fish, you can work it more effectively.

When a school of fish is swimming right toward the boat, there isn't much you can do. Once they get too close, they'll see you and flush. The correct procedure, however, is to freeze and remain perfectly motionless. Don't even twitch your nose. Sometimes the fish will swim right on by or at least they won't panic. Once they clear on the other side, you can flip a fly out and frequently get a take.

Speaking of schools, one of the problems in casting to tarpon or bonefish is that you can't always see or identify all the fish. If the fly line passes over the back of a fish or the fly lands too close, you'll have to look for another school. When you can identify most or all of the fish, try to pick one on the fringes on your side and don't try to get one on the far corner. The toughest shot is when the fish are going away from you. You have little choice but to make a desperation effort. However, if one or two fish are not packed in tightly, try for them. Make the cast to the side of the outboard fish and hope that they'll see it and turn.

During periods of low light and even in the middle of the day, schools of fish give away their position by creating a V-wake or a condition known as nervous water. Many cast to the point of the V as the van of the school. Actually, the lead fish are well ahead of the wake and if you don't cast considerably in front of that area, you're going to spook the fish.

OFFSHORE FISHING

The late Joe Brooks had actually talked me into it. He convinced me that catching a yellowfin tuna on fly in Bermuda waters was the next thing on the angling agenda and arranged with Pete Perinchief for me to go down and give it a try. Although Pete and the late Louis Mowbry, head of Bermuda's Aquarium, were friends, they were completely skeptical as were Boyd and Teddy Gibbons who ran the Coral Sea.

It wasn't until the next to last day that we finally had yellowfins in our slick, but Pete insisted that all of us use regulation tackle first before fooling with a fly rod. After battling one of those brutes on twenty-pound tackle, I wasn't that sure about what Joe had told me. Finally, the chance came and I made a cast among the hog-mouthed fry that Boyd Gibbons had just tossed on the water. The tuna were picking up the bait, but they ignored the retrieved fly. My choice was a polar bear pattern named the Blockbuster that I helped to develop along with my close friend and expert fly tyer, Bub Church.

The second cast fared equally poorly and, when the third was ignored, my mind was searching for a solution. "Throw another handful of chum," I instructed Boyd and, as he did, I put the fly right in the middle of it. Instead of retrieving, however, I stripped some slack line into the water and let the fly float completely dead with the chum. The Mylar and polar bear offering looked exactly like a hog-mouthed fry. The tuna moved in swiftly, picking up the tidbits. Suddenly, I watched my fly disappear in the maw of a yellowfin and the battle was on.

No one believed it would last long and they teased about cutting the line now or just popping the leader. After twenty minutes, however, they began to

Pete Perinchief removes the fly from an almaco jack. The fish picked up the offering in a chum slick as it was drifting with the natural bait.

suspect that we might accomplish our mission. When the battle ended, a fifty-three-pound six-ounce fish lay on the deck, establishing a world record at the time and proving that tuna could be taken in a chum slick. Jim Lopez has since surpassed that catch with a number of exceptional ones and others have hooked and caught tuna that way. In fact, a year ago, I had a seventy-pounder up to the boat and lost it at the last moment when the leader frayed.

The point of all this is that a fly fished dead in a chum slick can be a potent weapon. Since that day in Bermuda, I have tried the technique for many species around the world and recommend it to you. If you have dolphin alongside the boat and are keeping them there with tidbits of cut bait, you

There are no small tuna. Some are only bigger than others. Fly fishing for these great gladiators provides one of the ultimate thrills in angling.

may find that they won't hit the fly when you retrieve it. Switch over and let the fly drift dead. The main requirement is that the fly not even shudder or twitch. If it floats free, the fish will pick it up.

Norman Duncan developed a similar method for taking big barracuda when they strike a fish about to be landed. You can't fool those wily devils by retrieving a fly, but if you toss a big white streamer alongside a piece of the fish that was hit and let it float away, the cuda probably will come back and eat it. If there is any movement to the fly, forget it.

Anybody who has the chance wants to catch a sailfish on fly and some skippers have the procedure down to a routine where even a beginner can score. It was a lot different when the late Dr. Webster Robinson set angling history on January 18, 1962, aboard the *Caiman* off Panama with Captain Louis Schmidt. Using a hookless bait, the skipper teased up a sailfish and Web hooked it on fly. It sounds easy, but it took a lot of calculating on Web Robinson's part to figure out the whole technique.

I spoke to Web at length about it and he gave me my first sailfish fly shortly after that. From what he told me, I credit him with not only developing the technique of teasing billfish, but formulating the whole teasing concept for fly fishing. Everything else is an offshoot.

Theories go back and forth. For a while, most of us who tried for sailfish used sliders or poppers. Then it seemed to make sense to use a large streamer fly that could be worked under the surface. One reason was that it was easier for the sailfish to take the bait below the waterline than on top. Now, though, I again believe that a popper may be the way to go because it helps to attract the fish's attention in a hurry.

It can be tough to get the fish to lose interest in a foot-long hunk of bait and settle for a fly. In fact, tandem flies are now being used that are longer and bulkier for just that reason. But the sound of the popper on the surface gets

Teasing a sailfish to the fly requires teamwork between boat crew and angler. The fish must be excited with a natural or artificial bait before the fly is cast. Here the angler stands ready while the captain and mate work together to bring the sail within range.

attention in a hurry and, when the fish turns, you can pull the teaser away.

The ideal cast is alongside the eye of the sailfish, but slightly behind it so that the fish turns away to strike. It's important to keep the fly line on your side of the teasing line. If you cross, you'll tangle and have problems. Perhaps the most critical part is to get the fish teased up and excited. If you make the presentation too early, the fish might lose interest. Veterans try to do this by letting the fish eat a natural bait without hooks and then pulling it free.

Catching a wahoo on fly is a magnificent accomplishment and something that had been done only a couple of times and at random until Stu Apte and Bob Griffin came up with the technique in Panama at Bob's Club Pacifico. During the rainy season, great concentrations of wahoo move in, but you just can't go around tossing a fly at random. Unlike the sailfish, it's tough to tease a wahoo and hold it in the wake while you make a presentation.

Stu and Bob found that if they trolled a conventional rig, they had a chance. Here's how it worked. When a wahoo crashed the regular trolled bait and was hooked, the skipper would stop the boat immediately. Stu then cast blindly back in the glide path of the boat using a lead-core line so that the fly would sink a bit. He then retrieved rapidly. Sometimes, other wahoo would be with the first and they were looking for a meal. The fly was visible in the slick water and the technique proved effective.

There are many tricks that can be used on the offshore waters and you'll begin to learn and remember them as you gain experience. Lefty Kreh came up with a way to get a cast into a school of moving fish in a hurry. Assuming the boat had no super structure or at least one that could be negotiated, he would place a right-handed caster on the starboard side of the boat. The rod would be pointed directly astern and the fly line streamed far enough back to allow for a comfortable cast. As the boat came up on the school, it would be thrown in neutral and all the fly fisherman had to do was bring his arm forward using a double haul. The backcast was already in the water and tension had loaded the rod fully. He had a perfect cast and an exceptionally quick presentation.

With cobia or amberjack over a wreck, there's another thing you can do. You already know about using a live bait as a teaser, but you can also use a hookless chugger-type plug. One person makes a long cast with the chugger and starts the retrieve. When the lure is within casting range, the angler drops the fly right behind it and matches the rate of retrieve. When a fish comes up, it sees the fly and you're in business.

Going back to the live-bait approach for a moment, the thing to use in that case is a huge popper with a face about the size of a silver dollar. The man on the teasing rod holds the bait over the side and gets the fish near the boat. Each time the husky critter lunges for the live bait, it is jerked out of the water and then put right back in. You have to be quick or the fish will grab it before you can get it away. Finally, when fly-rodder and teaser are coordinated, the caster yells "now" and the bait is removed. In its place, a large popper hits the water.

The trick is to have simply the leader extending past the tip top of the rod. You slap the popper on the surface and swing the rod to make it gurgle. Then, pick it up and repeat the procedure or shift the rod tip and work the popper

A variety of different density lines now make it possible for fly-rodders to dredge the bottom; this fisherman was there, as this flounder proves.

back and forth. The fish should charge and engulf the whole thing.

Another teasing method involves the fishing kite described in the last chapter. Instead of rigging the live bait in an outrigger clip where it can come out, you set the clip so it won't open. The fish can now be raised or lowered by reeling on the conventional outfit or putting the reel in free spool. You can then tease a fish and toss a fly. The live bait becomes airborne and the fly lands on the surface.

Wherever you fish a fly rod, you can find ways to make life easier or your techniques more effective. Many of the methods described here can be adapted to other situations or modified to work for you. Equally important, try to do some of your own innovating. Not only is it fun, but the world of fly fishing is always eager to have something new to use. Fly fishing in salt water is one of the light-tackle angler's greatest challenges; and it still needs pioneers.

Dolphin are relatively easy to hook on the fly. Note that the angler is using his fingers to increase drag pressure.

11

Hooking, Fighting, and Landing Fish

The true excitement of light-tackle angling focuses on the challenge that comes from battling a fish on gear tailored to the task. In many situations, the fish is so hopelessly outclassed by the equipment that one need not do more than yank the creature from the water or wrestle it aboard a boat.

When the tackle is matched to the species you seek and the conditions under which you must fish, you have a chance to demonstrate skill and finesse. In many instances, the fish has every advantage and the only way one can win is by working the tackle to the maximum without exceeding the upper limits.

Through the years, dedicated anglers became experts at fighting fish successfully on light tackle. In the process, they developed techniques that make it easier for all of us and they are worth investigating. The one thing you'll notice is that these specialists are extremely fussy about their gear and how it is rigged. They concentrate on the most minute details and try to stack the deck in their favor by stringing a lot of minor points together. Any of them will tell you that fish are landed the night before. What they mean is that they take the time to put every item in top working order and then combine that with thoughtful hook-setting and fish-fighting methods.

THE HOOK

You can't fight a fish until you hook it. Too many fish are missed because the angler doesn't consider a number of factors before he ties the hook on the

193

line. One can offer dozens of excuses on a missed strike, but lack of a little planning was probably the chief cause.

Hook manufacturers stock thousands of styles and sizes. It's an expensive policy for them, but they know that the right hook makes all the difference. Certain styles perform better on specific assignments and your first task is to match the hook to the situation. Experience will help a great deal, but, in the beginning, educated tackle dealers or other anglers can help.

Special hooks are made for the plastic-worm fisherman, designed to hold the artificial in place while the point is buried inside to keep it weedless. Steelheaders and trout fishermen who use salmon eggs will find several styles of small hooks to accommodate the bait. There are baitholder models for other forms of natural baits and pike fishermen even have the option of using a wide-gap hook that works well on that species.

Because of their deeper penetrating shape, siwash hooks are used for salmon in salt water and are also finding advocates among trolling-lure users. Small tuna and albacore hooks are in many marine tackle boxes and the O'Shaughnessy has been a popular pattern for years. Other styles are standards for big-game fishing and there are light wire hooks for flounder and smaller denizens. The point to remember is that the style of the hook can make a difference and should be tailored to the species you seek.

Size also plays a key role. If you are using four-pound-test line, there's no way you're going to drive a 1/0 heavy wire hook into a bony mouth with any consistency. You may get lucky now and then, but you'll miss a lot of fish in the process. Some of us are coming to believe that fish often set the hook themselves via jaw pressure, but it's still easier to get a hook in a fish when the wire is lighter and the size is appropriate.

On the other hand, you have to consider the strength of those jaws and sometimes reach a compromise. If a fish can spread a hook, then you have to pick a middle ground that gives some hook-setting properties as well as hook strength. A number of veterans argue that it is far more important to get a fish hooked and worry later about the hook holding.

Once you have selected the proper hook, the next task is to sharpen it. The fact that you just pulled it out of a brand new box does not eliminate the need for further sharpening. This rule has no exception. If you intend to hook fish, you file or hone the hook or hooks you are going to use. The leading light-tackle anglers in the world today sharpen every hook.

You must accomplish two things when you hone a hook. The first is to create a point that will hang on the flesh in a fish's mouth the instant it touches. Unless the point hangs, there is no way for the hook to dig in. Second, a hook must have cutting edges to facilitate penetration. These cutting edges actually slice through and help to bury the barb.

Some fishermen take the time to triangulate a hook, which means that they flatten the bottom or outside of the point and then put cutting edges from the point to the barb. This takes time. The resultant hook looks like an old triangular bayonet with cutting edges on all three corners. My own preference remains with the single cutting edge and two flat sides with a semi-round bottom. It's quicker to do and the hook penetrates just as well.

If you have to fish in heavy cover, replace the treble hooks with weedless ones—but be careful not to upset the lure's balance.

The procedure was outlined earlier but is worth repeating. Hold the hook with the point on top and facing away from you. Lay the hone or file on a 45-degree angle to the hook and make a few passes. Then, shift the sharpening tool to the same angle on the other side so that the finished strokes will create a sharp edge on top of the hook point. Some fishermen do this on the inside along the barb. Either method works. It's pretty much the same as full triangulation, only you don't flatten the bottom. If you want to test the point for sharpness, run it across your fingernail. When it hangs, it's sharp enough.

My own favorite sharpening tool and one that I have used for years is the Red Devil Woodscraper's #15 file. The only problem with it is that it can rust if you don't take care of it. I keep mine sprayed liberally with a demoisturizer and that seems to work well.

When fishing for certain species that boast particularly hard or bony mouths, you might want to work on the barb as well. If a hook style has a particularly long or flared barb, it makes sense to use a file on it and take it down to the minimum size consistent with good holding power. The barb hinders penetration. Sometimes, only the point hangs in the flesh and the fish is subsequently lost because the hook didn't get in far enough to reach the bend.

Bill Barnes and I were trying to photograph tarpon jumps one day and neither of us wanted to fight a fish to the boat. We figured that if we mashed the barbs on the hooks, the silver king would make a few spectacular jumps, throw the plug, and we could look for the next fish. It didn't work that way. Instead, we discovered that our percentage of hookups increased and we couldn't get rid of the fish. With a sharp point and without a barb, the hook would bury to the bend the instant we came back on the rod. A fully barbed hook made it necessary to use repeated thrusts to drive it home and we weren't always successful.

It's virtually impossible to convince the average angler of this, but *you don't lose many fish on barbless hooks*. And you hook a lot more fish *without* a barb. Tom Mann, a bass-fishing champion and lure manufacturer, tried it after I mentioned our experiences with tarpon and he reported similar results. According to Tom, it really made a difference in the number of hookups. If you still have doubts, pick one of those golden days when the fish are plentiful and you've caught enough to satisfy your appetite. Then give the barbless-hook theory a try.

The position of the hook in the bait can improve your hooking average. Too many anglers bury the hook in a hunk of meat or hide the point in a plastic worm. The problem becomes one of driving the hook through the bait before you even have a chance of getting it in the fish and that's tough to do on light lines and correspondingly soft rods.

If you're an offshore trolling enthusiast, there are several ways to rig baits with the hooks on the outside. Bass fishermen might bury the hook in a plastic worm to make it weedless, but there's a way to do this that can help. When you insert the hook, push it all the way through the worm and then back it up so that the point rests inside the worm. What you have done is put a channel in the soft plastic that will make it easier for the hook to travel.

With cut bait, don't make the mistake of pushing a hook through the soft flesh and letting the point remain buried behind the tough outer skin and scales. The point has to be able to come out if you intend to hook a fish. It's a matter of common sense. Put the hook in position so that it can spring out and do some damage. On a skirted lure, if the plastic or rubber covers the point of the hook, you'll miss every fish that strikes. Finally, if you hang up in the rocks or on a tree or anything else, check the point of the hook and touch it up with a file.

Fly-rodders who use popping bugs for bass or in salt water sometimes run into a problem that slips by unnoticed. On some offerings, the shank of the hook is too short or it isn't placed far enough back. The bend and point of the hook ride under the body of the lure and there isn't enough of a gap to hook a fish. Check this on the lures you use.

Topwater chuggers that have a wide mouth and taper back to the tail can create another problem. The tail hook should be large enough to extend wider than the front of the lure. Otherwise, a fish could hit the head and slide right over the plug without ever getting hooked. On some lures, I even turn the back treble hook so that a single barb extends over the top of the lure's back. My thinking is that a fish will get hooked if it comes over the top. All you have to do is tighten the screw-eye a half turn.

HOW TO STRIKE A FISH

Largemouth bass fishermen insist that the only way to set a hook in their quarry is to snap their arms upward and literally try to turn the boat over. This method was originally meant for plastic-worm fishing, but it now seems

By turning the points of weed-guards downward, you can prevent painful injury to your hand when handling a fish; and the lure won't spook a fish that misses and gets its nose jabbed with a sharp piece of metal.

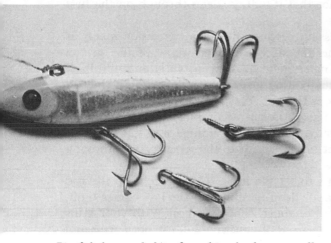

Big fish have a habit of crushing hooks on small plugs. If you carry a supply of replacement hooks, you can restore the lure in minutes.

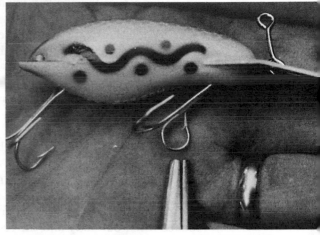

By bending the front hook inward on the forward set of trebles, you can make a diving plug somewhat more weedless.

to apply universally in bass-fishing circles. At first glance, it seems to work, but it also has limitations. For one thing, if an angler is sitting down, he doesn't get much leverage in raising his arms, because he's eliminating the use of the rest of his body. If you watch some of the leading pros on the tournament trail, they do a lot more standing than they used to and primarily for this reason.

How you set the hook depends on many factors. You must consider the bait you are using. If the hook is buried inside, such as it is in a plastic worm, it takes plenty of force to move the hook through the worm before you can even begin to drive it home. The breaking strength of the line must be considered, because that dictates the limitations on the force you can use. The farther a fish is from the rod, the more difficult it is to set because of the stretch in the line. Many of the leading monofilaments have as much as 30 percent stretch and when you pull back on the rod, you aren't doing much to the hook end. If a fish has a soft mouth, you must, of necessity, be delicate in striking. If you are trying to plant the hook in a tough-mouthed denizen, it takes extra power to do the job. All of this and more must be part of your response when a fish takes bait or lure.

If you put a scale at the end where the fish would be and then lift the rod above your head and beyond a 90-degree angle, the readings will surprise you. It may feel good to your hands and arms, but there is very little pressure down at the other end where it counts.

Can you drive a nail better with one long swing of a hammer or several shorter ones? Those of us who challenge some of the husky denizens of the sea and estuaries opt for the latter and prefer to use a series of short, sharp strokes rather than a single long one. Our reasoning is that we can drive the barb in by stages rather than take a chance that it will go clean through on the first pull.

To maximize your effectiveness in setting the hook, as much slack as possible must be taken out of the line. If you can get some of the stretch eliminated, so much the better. Anglers tend to react instantly and pull back on the rod when a fish strikes. Usually, that just does enough to alert the fish that something is wrong and it drops the bait. For positive hooking, you want a tight line between you and the fish. You can accomplish this in two ways depending on the species and the situation. Either you must wait until the fish moves off and the line comes tight or you can help the situation by cranking on the reel handle until the line is tight.

Almost everyone lifts their arms to set the hook. If you do, keep the rod directly in front of you, reel down; or drop the tip until the line comes tight, and then pull upward with a series of short, sharp strokes. With your arms locked into your body and the rod in front of you, you will use both arms and back to set.

In many situations, striking sideways with the rod low and parallel to the water makes a lot more sense. The ability of your body to rotate adds a great deal more power to the strokes and it's a more forceful set. At the same time, because the rod is parallel to the water, the strike has a different effect on bait or lure.

When you raise the rod, you pull an offering toward the surface. If it's already on top, the tendency is to yank it clear of the water. Assuming the fish misses the bait the first time around, there might not be a second chance because the fish may not find the bait. With a side strike, if you don't hook up, the bait remains in the vicinity of the fish, giving you another opportunity for a second hit.

Fly fishermen have a number of hook-setting methods that apply to their type of fishing. With fragile leader tippets, for example, and fine wire hooks, you can bury the barb by using the slip strike. Instead of holding the fly line as you raise the line, which is the typical striking method, just snap the rod upward. When you do, a certain amount of line will feed through the guides, but there will be enough resistance on the fly line to set the hook. This combination helps to prevent the leader from breaking.

In a lake or when you're fishing well below the surface, you can set a hook with a fly rod simply by tugging on the fly line. Since the rod isn't raised, the fly remains in the same relative position just in case you miss the fish. Sometimes, while a fly is being retrieved, a fish will come up and inhale it. The whole scene is so close to you that there is no room to raise the rod to set the hook. When that happens, all you have to do is make a roll cast and the hook will be set. If you analyze the roll cast, the line actually comes toward you before it goes out and has the same effect as if you were to tug on the line.

The next one is hard to believe unless you've tried it. Nymph fishermen have to set the hook in a hurry. By the time they lift the rod, it can be too late. One very worthwhile method is to snap the rod *down* toward the water when you sense a pickup. If you were to watch what happens in slow motion, you would discover that the rod tip really goes *up* before it goes down and it is this upward motion that buries the barb.

Salt-water fly-rodders have other problems. Some fish are soft-mouthed and one need only lift the rod to set the hook. Not so with tarpon, sailfish, or other concrete-jawed monsters. When you're dealing with those critters, you've got to generate all the power and force you can. The method used to get this full force is simply to double haul when you want to set the hook. You pull the rod with one hand and, at the same time, haul on the line with the other. Remember that you are going to set several times.

WHEN TO SET THE HOOK

Knowing how to set the hook is only half the battle; when to set it can be equally important. A pike or muskie fisherman realizes that his quarry usually grabs its prey in the middle and moves off with it before turning it around to swallow the bait head first. If you're using live bait for these huge fish, you're going to miss a lot of takes if you decide to set the hook right away. You just have to wait it out until the fish has ingested its prey and starts to move off again.

Plastic-worm fishermen differ in their theories on when to set. Most believe that when they feel the pickup, the bass has swallowed the worm and any delay in striking could cost them a fish. A minority still feels it's better to let the bass ease off and then set. You can make up your own mind, but try both ways before you do.

With natural baits, timing can be everything; there's no way to cover all bets. It becomes a matter of trial and error. If you start to miss fish, wait a bit longer or strike slightly faster than you have until you develop the timing *for that day*. It can vary. You'll find situations when you'll hook fish if you strike quickly. Come back tomorrow and you discover you have to hesitate.

When a fish takes a bait, it must first expel the water that came in with it and then try to swallow the bait. The same thing happens with artificials unless the fish detects something is wrong. Then it can eject that bait *fast*.

If you're nymph fishing with a fly rod, you have to be about as quick as a mongoose trying to grab a cobra. The fish can pick up and reject the nymph before you can react. Usually, the only signal you get is a slight twitch of the tip of the line and you almost have to watch for that rather than feel it.

In most other situations, with the exception of a few species that are notorious bait stealers, you have more time to set than you think and sometimes it pays to delay. A bonefish, for example, will pick up a leadheaded jig and throw it back on its crushers because it's used to feeding on crustacea. You can actually wait until the fish moves off with your artificial.

I ran a series of experiments one time at Lake Verret, Louisiana, where we were using plastic, weedless frogs in some heavily covered surface water. There were plenty of bass eager to explode all over the lure, so it was perfect for a study. It had occurred to me that I was missing a lot of bass when I tried to set the hook the instant the fish exploded over the lure. Taking the opposite tack, I decided not to strike the fish and let them grab the plastic frog. The results were amazingly superior. The real answer lay somewhere in between and I found that if I paused before setting, I did much better.

When you can see a fish take your bait or lure, you certainly have the advantage in timing the hook-setting operation providing you can resist the impulse to set immediately. Tarpon fishermen on the shallow flats try to wait until the fish turns away with their offering in its mouth before they try to set. In fact, experts often tailor the strike to the type of take. If a fish is moving from right to left or left to right, they'll sweep the rod low to the water in the direction *opposite* that in which the fish is traveling. If, however, the tarpon is coming right at them, they force themselves to wait until the fish has turned away and then set.

Fishing plugs in slightly deeper water, Bob Stearns prefers to let a tarpon almost pull the rod out of his hand before he strikes. The method works well because the fish has taken all the stretch out of the line.

In using natural baits, the size of the offering affects the timing. If the fish can swallow it easily and rapidly, you set much sooner. If the bait looks big for the fish, you'd better allow plenty of time.

Offshore fishermen have their own set of rules, especially for billfish. The standard procedure involves a dropback in which the bait is freespooled to the fish. How far you let the fish run off with the bait is a matter of speculation; there's no stock answer. You learn to judge each situation individually, but there are some guidelines. With sailfish, for example, veteran skippers feel that they want to keep the fish within the spread of baits and they'll use a short dropback. Some even prefer simply to drop the rod tip and pull the bait back toward the boat, repeating the procedure until the fish gets excited and crashes it. Still others favor the long dropback, giving the fish plenty of time to take the bait and swallow it. This is another situation you'll have to play by eye.

Captain David Rose, who used to fish the Panama coast for black marlin, taught me a boat-handling trick that you should know about. When a marlin hit a bait, most skippers would keep trolling during the entire dropback. Then they would speed up the engines to help the angler strike the fish. The only problem with that standard procedure was that the fish was two-hundred yards behind the boat or even more and the hook-setting effectiveness was minimized. David had a different technique. The instant the fish hit the bait, he stopped the engines. Then, as it took line on the dropback, he would ease

Striking a fish with the rod low and parallel to the water often makes sense. This keeps the bait in front of the fish—in case you don't hook up, the hook is pulled forward instead of up.

the boat into reverse and start backing down on the fish. The trick was not to gain line, but merely to keep the fish from taking more line during the time it was swallowing the bait. When it came time to strike the fish, the big black marlin would be close to the boat and you could set the hook with power. It really worked.

Running the gamut from lifting a fly rod when a trout gulps a dry fly to dropping back on a big billfish or waiting for a swordfish to move off at an increasing rate of speed demonstrates the variations in hook-setting techniques. The point to remember is that nothing remains static. You have to vary your approach just as you would in working a lure. If you're missing fish, something is wrong and you should set out to remedy the situation.

THE BATTLE RAGES

Almost all fishing reels—with the exception of some very light fly reels and a few older bait-casting mills—boast a drag mechanism designed to allow line to slip at a predetermined pressure. Setting the drag correctly can be critical. The time to do it is before you start to fish.

There are general guidelines worth remembering. The lighter the breaking strength of the line, for example, the lower drag setting on the reel. When we talk of these adjustments, it is usually in terms of percentages of unknotted line strength. That means that if you were using ten-pound test line and the drag was set at 15 percent of the breaking strength, you would have 1.5 pounds of drag on a straight pull. The percentage is important, because it enables us to make comparisons and to do the actual setting regardless of the breaking strength.

Remember, also, that drag is measured on a straight pull with the rod tip pointing directly at the scale. In other words, the basic measurement eliminates any additional friction caused by the rod or the rod guides. When someone talks about percentages of drag, it's important to make sure he is referring to this straight pull off the reel. If you measure the drag through the rod, there are too many variations, because rods differ in degree of stiffness and in the amount of drag they create.

The key to light-tackle fishing is the ability to depend on the delicate addition of drag with your hands and to set the mechanical drag on the reel to a workable minimum. Drag is a cumulative measurement involving many factors. If you have a spring scale and a friend willing to help, you can run your own tests and discover quite a bit about what's happening when you fight a fish. Suppose you were using ten-pound-test line and had the drag set at 15 percent. As you started to move the rod vertically from the horizontal measuring position, you would discover that the needle on the scale would continue to pull downward. The amount of drag is increasing and you did nothing more than lift the rod to the fighting position.

At the same time, it's critical to recognize that the minimum amount of drag occurs when you point the tip of the rod directly at the fish. The old adage about keeping your tip up could, in some instances, be the worst advice anyone can give you.

Drag increases as the amount of line in the water increases. As the diameter of line on the spool drops, the drag grows proportionately. That's why you want to start with a full spool of line on the reel.

With a fly reel, you can put your fingers on the line or against the flange and instantly increase the drag. Put your thumb on a baitcasting reel or cup the spool of a spinning mill and you've done the same thing. You also have the option of using your rod hand to force the line against the foregrip on the rod or hold it between your fingers. All of these methods increase the drag, but the beautiful part is that you can release the drag and go right back to the basic setting simply by removing your hand or fingers. That can be done instantly and there's nothing to bind or catch. As a word of caution, never put your hands on the line when a fish is running at burst speed. The line could cut deeply into your flesh. The time to apply hand pressure is when the fish has stopped running or it is moving off at manageable speed. And substituting a thumb or finger for mechanical drag could lead to serious burns or bruises.

In almost every situation, the best advice anyone can give you is to set the drag before you start and then leave it at that setting. Make further adjustments with your hands and fingers. Newcomers are forever trying to change the drag setting and invariably they succeed in breaking the fish off. Once the drag adjustment knob or the starwheel has been set, leave it there.

The latest offshore reels use a drag lever to increase or decrease the amount

A finger on the spool enables you to apply drag pressure. Some reels, like this one, also have a flange on the spool for applying drag.

Thumb pressure on the spool and against the line will increase the drag on a bait-casting reel. You can remove the pressure instantly by moving your thumb.

Fingers cupped under the spool of a spinning reel are the proper way to increase the amount of drag.

of drag and they also have a pre-set knob that allows you to set the lever within a predetermined range. This must be done before you start fishing or you'll be in trouble. Although most anglers do use hand pressure on fish, veteran light-tackle enthusiasts Dick and Kay Mulholland take a different approach. Their game is monstrous blue-water fish on light gear and they are masters at it. Using one's hands can be impractical with thirty-pound tackle or even fifty-pound gear when you're battling half a ton of marlin. Dick and Kay feel that they have developed the skill to use the single drag lever for all adjustments. It is their belief that once you learn how to use this, you know exactly how much drag you are applying at any moment. This, of course, is only possible with the drag lever offshore reels.

As a general rule, light casting tackle should be set at 15 percent of the unknotted line strength, providing there is ample open water to play a fish. That's more than enough to set the hook and that's about all you need. There are exceptions. If you're trying to snake a fish out from under a dock or you're afraid your quarry is going to bury its nose under a log, then you have to increase the amount of drag. Under those circumstances, 25 percent or even 33 percent will do the job. You can add more pressure with your fingers.

A large number of bass fishermen crank the starwheel down on their bait-casting reels and try to bully a fish away from cover. This might work on the smaller bass, but they occasionally run into a trophy fish and pop the line or pull the hook. It's better to learn how to use hand pressure and work a give-and-take arrangement with the rod.

Even if you have to lock down on a reel with your hand, you can dip and extend the rod and then try to pull the fish back toward you, weathering each surge by yielding just a little bit. It's difficult to accept this method unless you've seen it work. A skilled angler can keep a fish out of its hole even though there might only be three feet between the fish and its goal. You drop the rod at the surge but pull back almost instantly with a smooth pull. This can be done with a fly rod to keep a salmon from reaching fast water and it can be done with spinning, bait-casting, or other tackle.

One of the most important lessons to learn is that the rod is not a boom and the reel is not a winch. They are tools and must be used correctly. Most anglers have been taught that the whip of a rod tires the fish. I've never been certain that is true and feel that you beat a fish either by convincing it to give up (which can be done, particularly with a big fish) or by forcing it to battle so hard that it uses up its oxygen.

It's unfortunate that many fishermen merely maintain a tight line and feel they are pressuring a fish. So often, you can observe a fish just dogging it in a current or parallel to a boat and the angler holds on. Nothing is really happening, yet the person with the rod feels he is doing everything possible.

A fish should always be battled to the maximum ability of tackle and angler. If you can land a fish too quickly to satisfy your needs, then switch to lighter tackle. Merely holding the rod until the fish dies of old age or gives up from boredom deprives you of learning the fish-fighting skills that are very much a part of light-tackle sport.

You're like a boxer when you fight a fish, taking line when you can and giving when you must. Nevertheless, you keep wading in trying to get the fish closer and closer. If you pause or if you are forced to rest, the fish will regain its strength faster than you can. Remember that the longer the fish is in the water, the greater the chance that you will lose it.

Invariably, when we hook a fish that we know is big, we baby it. We get cautious and try not to make a mistake; but in doing so, we increase the time and reduce the pressure. The longer a fish is in the water, the greater the chance for angler error or tackle failure. That spells disaster. Any time someone begins a fish story and announces how long he battled the fish, you can assume that he lost it. When you hook the big one, you're in a barroom brawl and you'd better be in there slugging. It's been said that if you aren't more tired than your quarry, you weren't fighting to your maximum capabilities.

THE SLUGFEST

Once you set the hook, you can assume that the fish is going to run. Feeling the steel in its jaw is a new experience and one that demands an instant response. How far the fish runs depends greatly on the species, its size, and where you happen to be fishing. A critter hooked on the shallow flats may streak a couple of hundred yards for the safety of deeper water. A bass four feet from a log may only want to travel that far.

Your response is dictated by the habitat. If you're in open water, there's nothing you can do but let the fish run. If you try to snub it short, you'll pop it off; so let it go. If you have to keep the fish from reaching the log or any other obstruction, that's different; we already discussed dropping and raising the rod.

Whenever you fight a fish, it should be in front of you and you should be facing it. Keep the rod in front of you, also, so that there is room to maneuver if you must. The instant the fish stops, you must start to apply pressure and continue doing so throughout the battle. Your mind must be on what you are doing and you cannot lose your concentration. This is not the time to share jokes with your buddies nor is it the time to pause for a soft drink or sandwich.

Your first task is to regain line and you do that by pumping the fish. Pumping is nothing more than using the rod as a lever. You lift upward, dragging the fish toward you, and then crank in the controlled slack as you drop the rod tip. This procedure is repeated continuously for as long as the fish comes your way. When it makes another run, you let it go until it stops and then start pumping again.

The type of pump depends on what the fish is doing. If it is deep, you should lift slowly and steadily, trying to raise it. If the fish is on the surface and you get it coming toward you, the pumps should be short and fast. You'll find that you can sometimes regain line faster with short pumps than trying to go the maximum distance. In fact, don't be afraid to start with the rod tip right at the water and lift from there.

When you hook a fish on the shallow flats, it will run instinctively for deeper water, dragging a couple of hundred yards of line. The trick is to hold the rod as high over your head as possible, to keep the line out of the water. This reduces drag and prevents the line from nicking or chafing on underwater obstructions.

Nearly everybody pumps by moving the rod vertically. That's the only choice you have when a fish is deep and the water is even deeper. However, for a fish on the surface or in a shallow lake or stream, you may discover that side pressure is more effective. The rod is kept low to the water and parallel to it. The idea is to make the fish tack from one side to the other, much as a sailboat would sail into the wind. Remember Sosin's Law, which says, "Where the head of the fish goes, the tail is sure to follow." The idea is to move the head of the fish and keep moving it.

If you let a fish dog it in the current or just hang out there, you stand a good chance of losing it. You have to make the fish use its strength and, especially with light tackle, swim your way. You can do this with side pressure. With the rod on one side, keep working the fish. Then, switch the rod 180 degrees to the other side and force the fish to turn and swim in that direction. Each time the fish turns, you are shortening the distance. It's amazing how this works, particularly when you are trying to fight a strong current as well as the fish.

In each battle, there are a number of test points and you must recognize these and meet them. The fish starts to surge away from you, yet it isn't quite as strong a surge as others have been. You decide to test your quarry and you increase the drag slightly with your hand on the reel and, at the same time, start to drop the rod tip. There's an instant of indecision. If the fish increases its power, drop the rod tip and let it go. However, quite frequently, you can prevent the run from happening and get the fish coming your way again. These points can be critical with a big fish.

The main thing in fighting a fish is developing a feel for your tackle and the amount of pressure it can withstand. Your knots must be 100 percent of the unknotted line strength so that you know how much pressure you can apply. If you have no idea at what pressure the knots will break, you must baby the fish and that can be costly.

Rods are often an excellent indicator of the amount of pressure you are applying. They are, of course, a shock absorber and should always boast a certain amount of reserve power to prevent them from "bottoming out." There will be a few times during the battle when you may have to put everything the rod has into moving the fish, but this usually comes in the later stages. When your quarry is active, keep adjusting the angle of the rod so that you have some reserve left. Remember, also, that when the rod is pointed directly at the fish, you have the minimum amount of drag. A few anglers insist on fighting their fish directly off the reel, but this taxes the reel and eliminates the role of the rod. Those who persist in this method have never battled a truly out-sized fish.

SPECIAL SITUATIONS

Quickness, alertness, and the ability to apply continuous pressure are the major ingredients in fighting a fish. There's little margin for error with light lines and that's what makes the game so much fun. It's a one-on-one test and only you can win or lose.

More fish are lost at or near the boat than at any other time. If you learn to anticipate, you can prevent this from happening a good part of the time. There are two types of errors: either the fish surges suddenly and breaks the line or the fish gets under the boat and cuts you off. All of us know that a fish is going to make a sudden surge or last bid for freedom the instant it sees a net, gaff, the boat, or you standing there in waders. All you have to do is anticipate it and be ready.

When a fish surges, it shocks the line. The ability of the line to absorb this sudden spurt of energy depends on its length and there certainly isn't very much when the fish is right in front of you. The line can't handle it so it breaks. You already know the surge is coming and you also know that the least amount of drag occurs when you point the rod tip directly at the fish. Anticipate. When the fish makes that lunge, drop the rod tip and point it right at your quarry. Don't fall into the trap and try to stop the fish. That breaks the line. As soon as the fish moves off, you can come back up to the fighting position and try to stop it delicately. Remember that it takes more pressure to *start* a drag turning (called inertial drag) than to keep it turning.

Fish also have a habit of diving under boats instead of surging away, and you must be ready for this as well. If a fish goes under the boat, put the rod tip in the water as far as you can reach and try to get the line under any obstructions on the hull or the engine so that you and the fish are on the same side once again. You have to be quick. If you hesitate, the fish can cut you off or come up on the other side and fray the line. Aboard a big boat, make sure you are always on the same side as the fish. Don't stand on one side of the cockpit with the fish off in the other direction.

The procedure for handling jumping fish is similar to that used for fish surging near the boat. When a gamester is in the water, it maintains a neutral buoyancy and weighs only a fraction of its actual weight. Once that fish is airborne, not only do you have the full weight, but you have the problem of mass or weight multiplied by velocity and that comes out trouble in any language. At the same time, if a jumping fish lands on a tight leader, it can sever it instantly. If the same fish lands on a loose leader, the damage may not be serious. Finally, if there's no pressure on the line, the fly, lure, or bait stays in the vicinity of the mouth and there's a chance to rehook the fish. If you think that's a dream, talk to some of the tarpon guides.

No matter how far away a fish happens to be, when it leaps clear of the water or its head starts to come out, drop the rod tip and push the rod as far as you can in the direction of the fish. It's the same type of lunge a swordsman would make and it's called bowing to the fish. What this does is throw controlled slack toward the fish and relieve the strain on the line. The leader goes slack and the weight and force of the fish is negated. Just as soon as your quarry drops back into the water, regain the fighting position and continue the battle. Stay ready, however, for other jumps that might come. This, by the way, is just as important with trout on gossamer threads as it is with tarpon, sailfish, and other spectacular jumpers.

Stream fishermen and surf fishermen make a similar mistake in fighting

When a fish jumps or surges away from the boat, drop the rod tip and push the rod directly at the fish. This reduces the drag and helps to counter the sudden increase of pressure on your tackle.

fish. They often remain rigidly implanted in one spot and refuse to move. When they lose a fish, they often wonder why. If a fish is moving along the beachfront, stay right with it and hustle along the suds so that the fish is always in front of you. The line should never be at an angle with the breakers or the sand.

Recognizing trouble before it develops can save a fish. In a fast-moving stream, a big trout or salmon will usually move with the current and, before you know it, you're here and your fish is down there. Knowledgeable anglers always have a mental picture of the terrain and can react without thinking because they know what has to be done. There's no way to get a fish back to you if the current is strong, so you have to work your way down to the fish.

Anticipation can save a big fish. The moment you hook up, get downstream of your quarry and continue to maintain that relative position. It's much easier to handle a fish if you are abeam of it or below it. Once the fish gets downstream from you, you're in trouble and the additional force of the water can put critical strain on light lines or leader tippets.

Typical of that situation was a river in Greenland where the fish were in fast water and then the river smoothed out for a short distance before turning and tumbling down a chute. If you didn't get the fish before the turn, it was all over. We had to start running as soon as we hooked a fish. If we were fast enough, we reached the dogleg before the big Arctic char and could lead it into calmer waters. If we hesitated, it was all over.

Speaking of streams, rivers, tidal currents, and other types of moving water,

You can generate plenty of power with a light fly rod if you stay abeam of the fish and drag it across the current. Note that the line is passing through the author's fingers so that he can control the amount of drag.

the real trick is to stay parallel to the fish and drag it across the current. If you insist on trying to force the fish upstream, you could lose it.

When you fish the tropical flats, you face another set of conditions. The bonefish or tarpon is going to make a run for deep water. You can bet that whatever direction the fish takes, there's a dropoff somewhere in front of it. Seldom will a hooked fish run into more shallow water. Flats have vegetation that includes sea fans, grasses, and often a hard, coral bottom. If the line rubs against anything, you can start retying the knots, so you have to hold the rod as high over your head as possible. This keeps much of the line out of the water to minimize line drag and it also helps to eliminate the chance of the line brushing against an obstruction.

Grouper and other bottom dwellers will make a beeline for a grotto, rock pile, or wreck the instant they are hooked. If they reach it, you're in trouble. Stopping them is another problem. Sometimes the fish will merely put its nose against some rocks and hold there. With the stretch in the line, you cannot generate enough power to move the fish and so it is a stalemate that usually results in the line fraying or you simply breaking the fish off.

Veterans employ a trick that you might want to file away for future use. They will slack off on the line and wait for a reasonable period of time exerting no pressure on the fish. Then, when they are ready, they take up the slack slowly until the line is almost tight. At that point, they start pumping and reeling as hard and as fast as they can. It's a desperation method, but it does work sometimes. If the fish thought it was free, it might venture out of the hole and the idea is to start it coming your way before it can get back there.

Fly fishermen have a couple of unique problems based on their method of fishing and the fact that they are probably using a single-action fly reel. Unless you must keep a fish from finding sanctuary or an escape route that's only a few feet away, a husky critter should be played directly from the fly reel. The strip method doesn't work because if the fish were to make a long run, the line might tangle and break the fish off. The only time you might have to clamp the fly line is where you have to stop a fish right away or lose it.

When a fish is first hooked on fly, it might not make a long run. If it doesn't, reel in the slack line that resulted from the retrieve and get the fish "on the reel." When your quarry does take off, your immediate concern must be the loose fly line either at your feet in the boat or floating downstream. Focus your eyes on that fly line and forget the fish. Take the thumb and first finger of your line hand and make a loop around the line, using this as an additional guide. Until the fish is "on the reel," make sure the line will flow smoothly to the stripping guide on the rod.

USING A BOAT

Although some anglers prefer to do battle from a dead boat, your fishing machine can be your greatest asset in fighting a fish. In fresh water, you may use a boat when a bass crochets your line back in the lily pads or a steelhead takes off downstream in a mighty West Coast river. The boat, however, really comes into play in salt water where fish make exceptionally long runs and some of those brutes will clean the clock if you don't get after them.

The closer a fish is to the boat, the more pressure you can exert on it. When a gamester makes a long run, there's little you can do at that extreme range other than try to work it back toward you. If you're successful, that's fine, but if that fish makes a second long run, you're in trouble. Skilled light-tackle troops take off after a fish in a hurry. If they are on the flats, they will either pole or motor after the critter and on the offshore grounds, they either back down or run forward and achieve an intercept.

If you happen to be trolling and a fish strikes, there may not be much time to swing around and start after the fish before the reel is stripped. With a fast-running fish, it usually makes sense to run bow forward, but take a course to one side of the fish so that the line isn't cut off by the boat running over it.

Skiffs and center-consoles have to run forward because of the problem of

Side pressure often makes more sense in fighting a fish than simply pulling back on the rod.

water coming over the transom or flooding out the outboards. When you do run toward a fish, remember to keep the fish off to one side. Most folks run right behind their quarry and the line streams out of the mouth and right over the fish's back where the leader could be cut or frayed. If you run alongside the fish, the leader not only comes out of the side of the mouth but the angler can exert side pressure to drag the fish toward the boat rather than trying to pull the fish back. A fish's head turns from side to side, but it doesn't go up and down.

The final stages from a boat are critical. That's when a fish will find a comfortable pattern and ease back and forth, maintaining a steady distance. If that happens, you have to keep trying to drag the fish toward you. Hanging on merely increases the risk of losing the fish.

In deep water, some species may sound. When a fish goes to soundings and you're topside with light tackle, it's a dangerous game. You have to get the fish to the surface and, if your adversary is big enough, it has to come up itself. When a big fish dies down there, you don't have a chance to drag it up on light line.

The usual procedure is to get over the top of the fish and use vertical pumping to try to force it up. Sometimes, it's a give-and-take battle with you gaining by the inch and the fish taking all the line you recovered and then some by the yard. If the fish sulks, you have to stay in there and keep trying to lift it.

There are a couple of tricks that work with billfish and they might help with other species if you are desperate. The first is to ease off on the pressure and move the boat away until the angle between you and the fish is from 30 to 45 degrees. Then, tighten the line and try to pump the fish. If this change of angle doesn't get the fish started, slack off again and slide the boat around 180 degrees. Take up the line slowly until it is tight and then strike the fish hard, trying to pump and pull. There are days when this tactic will bring the fish right back up to the surface. Whatever you do, keep trying. The longer the fish is down there, the less your chance of victory.

If you ever get in a situation where you can't follow the fish or you're on shore and your quarry is smoking line off the reel, the only choice you have is to back off on the drag. The common practice is to tighten the drag to stop

Fish almost always explode near the boat, especially when the angler puts maximum pressure on his quarry. Remain alert! Be prepared to counter any moves the fish might make.

the fish, but this leads to instant disaster because the amount of drag increases as spool diameter decreases. All you can do is keep loosening the drag. Some anglers try a do-or-die trick of taking all the drag off. They are hoping the fish will think it has won its freedom and stop moving away. Then, they try to put the pressure on and get the fish coming their way.

When you are pumping a fish up from the depths, there might be resistance levels. Once you get it past one of these zones, it will come easily until the next one. Keep that in mind and be ready to act. When a fish comes up a little more on each pump, don't stop and don't hesitate. Maintain the steady pumping rhythm and keep working the fish.

THE FINAL MOMENTS

Long before you are ready to land your quarry, you should have reached a decision on whether or not you intend to keep the fish. If the fish will be turned free, you want to minimize the amount of time it is being fought. The trout purist who plays a fish until it is totally exhausted and then plans to release it is making the trout's survival questionable. Lactic acid builds up in a fish as a by-product of muscle exertion. If the build-up isn't too great, the body can dissipate it through basic processes. An excessive amount, however, can cause the fish to die later even though it swam away. Even after a long fight I want to chance releasing a fish anyway, because I know if it goes into the creel or fish box, it definitely will not survive.

When you do want to release a fish, get it to the boat or to your side as quickly as possible and then turn it loose with a minimum of handling. With the trout, for example, a pair of hemostats can work wonders. Simply clamp them on the fly and shake. The fly will come out and the fish will swim away.

A bass can be immobilized by pushing one's thumb in its lower jaw or letting the belly of the bass rest in the palm of your hand. Take the hook out as carefully as possible and release the fish.

If a fish is hooked deep, the best procedure is to cut the leader as close to the mouth as possible and turn the fish loose without pulling on the hook. Gills are also sensitive areas and the last thing you want to do is get your hands or fingers in them. The same goes for eyes. Northern pike fishermen have a habit of grabbing the fish by the eye sockets, but it makes more sense to hold the fish across the head.

Release can be equally damaging to a fish when you squeeze its internal organs. A better method is to use a rag or glove to get a steady grip on the fish rather than hand pressure.

In a stream, you may want to slide the fish up on a bar or sandy spot. This must be done carefully; every attempt should be made to keep the fish from flopping in the shallows. Remember the word "slide," because that's what you're trying to do. To be successful at it, you have to get the fish on its side or at least reasonably tired. Reel down as close to the fish as you can so that you have control. Then, with one steady motion, start it toward the spot you picked and keep the fish moving at a fairly good pace. If you are successful,

A strong fish must be eased out of the main current and into calmer waters.

you can slide it right up. If the fish surges away, give it line and try again. Whenever possible, use the current to help you. It's easier to control a fish across the current or against a gentle flow than it is when the fish is being swept downstream.

Surf fishermen encounter problems similar to the stream angler who wants to get a fish on a gravel bar. The problem in the surf comes from the waves. As each one recedes, there can be a powerful undertow or back pull. If you try to drag the fish against this flow, you can break it off. Timing is the key. Ease off when the flow of water is back to sea and then try to surfboard the fish toward you on the next wave. You'll go back and forth a few times, but it can be done. When you get the fish coming, it's much easier to run up on the sand than to try to reel. Just hold the rod parallel to the water and run right up the sand, letting the wave carry the fish. When that wave recedes, the fish will be high and dry and you can get to it before the next wave comes.

Netting a fish is easy if you remember that the creature cannot swim backward, at least not with any degree of efficiency. That means that you always net head first and that the last thing you want to do is try to scoop the fish with the net. Simply place the net in the water at approximately a 45-

Whenever you have the option, a net is a better choice than a gaff.

degree angle with the surface and have the angler swim the fish right into the net. Once the fish enters the net, scoop it up and into the boat.

More people get into trouble by trying to come up behind the fish with the net and scoop it out tail first. The fish keeps swimming out of the net and this comedy of errors continues until the fish is inadvertently knocked off the hook.

Speaking of nets, you should use one rather than try to lift a fish over the side. Too many fish are lost when fishermen think they are going to lift it out of the water and into the boat. Another important point is that when you have a choice between netting and gaffing, use the net. It's much easier and you stand a better chance of landing your quarry.

Gaffing is a bit more difficult. The first step is to triangulate the point of the gaff or at least file some cutting edges on it. The principle is no different from that for fish hooks. You need quick penetration and cutting edges help.

If you intend to release the fish, a lip gaff is in order. It may take a little longer to get it in place, but when you slip a gaff into a fish's mouth and through the lower lip, the fish is unhurt. If it's a husky critter, you may have to hold the point of the gaff against the gunwale until you can release the fish.

Wrapping a line coming from the gaff around your wrist can be a dangerous practice. If a big fish breaks loose or you can't control it, there's no way that you can get that line off your wrist and you could be in serious trouble. There are also cases on record where somebody did that with a medium-sized fish and when the shark came and grabbed that catch at boatside, it looked as if it might take the gaff man as well.

With a larger gaff, you should bury the point swiftly, accurately, and without missing. Gaffers can create problems if they insist on slashing wildly at the fish rather than using a standard approach. The basic method is to put the gaff in the water, have the angler swim the fish over it, and then lift sharply. No two people gaff a fish alike, at least not among experts. Each has his preferences and some are worth noting.

When you do hit a fish with a gaff, it must be a positive movement. If a big fish is involved, gaffers try to strike with all the force they can and throw the fish off balance or even turn it over. Some will reach across the back and others come up from the belly. Either way works if you've had some practice and are confident.

Captain Boyd Gibbons of Bermuda is a master at gaffing and he told me he tries to do two things. First, he moves the gaff in from behind the fish so that the fish doesn't get a good look at it and so that it is behind, not in front of, the leader. Second, he waits until the fish is facing away from the boat before he strikes. That way, if he misses, the fish will bolt into open water and not dive under the hull.

Sharks can be tricky when you gaff them. Many species have the habit of spinning around and they can twist a gaff handle right out of your hands. There are gaffs made for sharks with sleeves that allow the gaff to turn while you maintain your grip. Another item that is available for sharks is a gun that fires a 12-gauge shotgun shell on impact and another item that injects CO_2.

One of the easiest ways to release a fish—and it is a legal method in most tournaments—is simply to touch the leader. As soon as the leader is in hand, it can be yanked and, if it is monofilament, will probably break near the hook. Otherwise, simply reach down with a knife and cut the mono or use pliers on wire leader.

Sailfish and some of the smaller marlin are often billed. A deckhand wearing gloves reaches down and grabs the bill of the fish and holds it. This can be tricky if you've never done it before and it is certainly not the recommended procedure for beginners. If you do bill a fish, you always take a hand position that will push the bill away from you if the fish should surge forward. The wrong way is to put both hands together and pull the fish toward you. Your hands have to be placed so that the bill cannot reach you.

Researchers have come to rely on the efforts of sport fishermen in tagging certain species of fish. These tags, when recovered, aid in helping the scientists to compute migratory patterns and growth rates. Most of the work

Getting a release gaff into the mouth of a tarpon isn't always the simplest task. This one had other ideas. It exploded at boatside.

By placing a small release gaff in the lower jaw of a fish, you can hold it alongside the boat while removing the hook. This tarpon will be pinned against the gunwale, the hook extracted, and then it will be turned loose.

Although he is pressuring this small tarpon toward the gaff, Chico Fernandez is alert and ready to drop the rod tip if the fish should surge away. More fish are lost at this stage of the battle than at any other time.

carried out by the National Marine Fisheries Service involves billfish, tuna, and amberjack. The American Littoral Society (Highlands, New Jersey 07732) has had its own tagging program for many years. They record data on all species of fish and will be happy to send you information if you are interested in participating.

On big fish, the tags are placed in the shoulder near the dorsal fin. A tagging stick is used in conjunction with a dart-type tag. At the time the tag is implanted, a card must be filled out noting all of the catch data.

Scientists tell us that fish sometimes survive when anglers are certain they were dead. There are a number of cases on record of fish that simply sank out of sight bleeding heavily. They may have been considered dead by all hands on board, but the tag was later recovered, proving the fish lived.

In releasing a fish, it's important to get the fish in the best possible condition before turning it loose. The principle applies for panfish as well as marlin. Rather than let a fish sink to the bottom and lie there, you can give it

Unneeded fish should always be released. Satisfaction should come from inward confirmation of skill and not from throwing a stringer of fish on the dock.

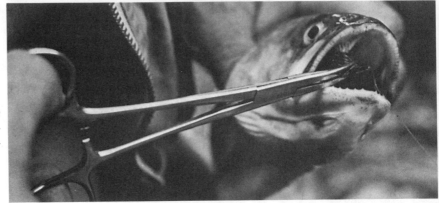

Surgical forceps, needle drivers, or similar instruments are perfect for removing hooks.

artificial respiration and help it to regain its regular breathing. In some instances, a fish is disoriented and need only be placed upright before it scoots away. With most fish, however, it is necessary to hold them gently and move them back and forth in the water. This forces water through their gills and helps them to glean oxygen. Usually they are suffering from an oxygen deficiency and will respond to the new flow of water.

Keep moving the fish back and forth until it swims out of your hand. You can either hold the fish gently by its mid section or grip it near the tail. With some fish, you have to work for a few minutes before you see results, but it's worth the effort.

What do you do if the fish is too big and heavy to work back and forth through the water? You would probably be aboard a boat, so hold the fish along the side of the boat and kick the engines ahead slowly. The forward motion of the boat will do the job. This works well with billfish.

If you happen to haul a fish out of the depths, its air bladder expands and you can't get it back down. There are a couple of ways to remedy the situation. One scientist who worked on lake trout told me that he used to take a needle and puncture the air bladder. It would deflate and the fish could get back down. He said that the wound healed quickly. Another method we used in salt water was to throw the fish into the water nose first. If we could get it down just a little bit, that sometimes helped.

There's one other idea that I have saved for the end of this chapter, because it applies more to those who seek truly large fish on light gear. When you deal with a big fish, there is often a moment or two when the fish seems confused or disoriented. It could come within the first few moments of the fight and it could come at any point down the line.

A number of veteran anglers feel that you must be alert to this when it does happen. You should try to land the fish at that time even though it might be far from ready. Most of us will watch that moment pass, reasoning that it won't be long before the fish is ready, but we might be wrong. If you're aboard a boat, you can often get down on the fish quickly and finish the battle right there.

Ted Naftzger has caught more swordfish than anyone and he has taken every one of his fish on the surface during the daytime. He's one of the top light-tackle anglers and an extremely factual and knowledgeable man. Ted tells the tale of a world-record swordfish he once had that jumped and was bleeding profusely. The fish lingered on the surface and seemed to be in its death throes, while Ted and his crew watched excitedly. They made no move toward the fish.

As Ted put it, that fish must have pulled out a styptic pencil, because it got stronger and stronger as the hours passed and finally earned its freedom.

Light-tackle sport is opportunity fishing. It demands quick reactions and an even faster response from those who intend to master it.

Wiring a billfish can be tricky. One must be prepared for anything. This black marlin went airborne the instant the leader was grabbed.

12

The Flow of the Water

If you've come this far, you are well aware that light-tackle fishing has many facets and there are many challenges at every level of skill and dedication. The beautiful part is that each angler has the opportunity to follow his own guiding star and pursue those areas that are most meaningful to him. Once one shrugs off the rigors of peer pressure, he can recognize that this is a one-on-one scene with only an individual and a fish in the arena.

Some phases, of course, require team play, but it still comes down to the solitary angler. Light tackle can quickly become a way of life and, if you are to be successful at it, it must become a way of thinking.

The methods and techniques that have been outlined are only a beginning and there will be new ones coming all the time. Because light-tackle aficionados share their findings, all of us can benefit and improve our own skills.

We have a great deal to which we can look forward. As more anglers join the fraternity, there will be increased pressure on many of our waters. Competition for a given population of fish will be greater and the catch per effort may even decline. Fresh-water habitat is being lost in many areas and frontiers are being pushed to their very limits.

At the same time, we might expect attitudes to change in relation to the number of fish. More emphasis will be placed on releasing fish and the angler who insists on displaying a stringer full of dead fish will be frowned upon. The fisherman of the future will be the person who can handle light tackle and come up with outstanding catches.

Tomorrow's angler will be much more sophisticated and his tackle will be better than anything we know now. The fishing-tackle industry has finally shaken the lethargy that has characterized it for years and realizes that it must move forward to survive. That means better equipment and innovations that will be fun to use as well as effective. Casting will be easier with better rods and reels that are engineered to perfection.

Science will help us. Much more work will be done with the effects of light on fish; the Cyalume lightsticks are only the beginning. Not only will new uses and applications be developed for these, but other types of light will become available. Sound is another area that begs for more research. We've toyed with it in the form of lures that make noise, but the true understanding of it has never been applied to commercial products. Look for breakthroughs in the area of near field displacement that affects the lateral lines of the fish we seek. More than one company has investigated the use of scents to appeal to the olfactory senses of fish. They, too, have only scratched the surface and there is more to come.

Keeping pace will be a problem, but a delightful one. For the boat fisherman, new navigational devices will help him to pinpoint the right spots and scanning sonar will help to find schools of fish or individual predators as they move underwater.

In spite of all these predicted advances, the contemplative aspects of the sport will remain. The angler who wants to cast a bass bug into the lily pads from a canoe will have room to do that and the trout fisherman will still have a chance to enjoy the outdoors and catch a few fish.

On the other side of the coin, we can expect much more regulation than we've seen in both fresh water and salt. Fisheries management has been underway in lakes and streams for a long time, but it is finally coming to salt water. There will be bag limits in salt water on more species than there are today and, hopefully, fish stocks will be managed for the benefit of our generation as well as future ones.

You can expect greater emphasis on salt-water fishing. If there is more detail than you anticipated in some of the chapters on marine angling, it is because I believe that more fresh-water anglers will turn to it in the years to come. Inland, transplants like the striped bass will bring new challenges to the diehard bass addict and perhaps our Great Lakes will see some new species.

It would be my guess that the fisherman of the future will travel more and that fishing in remote areas will become even more tempting because of better facilities. To my thinking, South America offers one of the last strongholds for the angler in both fresh water and salt. Many of the coastal sectors have yet to be developed for fishing and there are vast tracts inland that are yet to be reached on a consistent basis.

As you explore light-tackle fishing, don't let one glamour species cloud your perspective on other types of fish. If you work in a logical sequence and build your skills on a firm foundation, you will be ready to accept the new techniques and the new tackle that will be coming our way.

The most important thing facing us in the future is the preservation of angling habitat and the conservation of every species. That's a responsibility and a challenge that all of us must accept; without it, there can be no light-tackle or any other form of fishing.